Coming Out Christian in the Roman World

Coming Out Christian in the Roman World

*How the Followers of Jesus
Made a Place in Caesar's Empire*

DOUGLAS BOIN

BLOOMSBURY PRESS

NEW YORK · LONDON · NEW DELHI · SYDNEY

Bloomsbury Press
An imprint of Bloomsbury Publishing Plc

1385 Broadway	50 Bedford Square
New York	London
NY 10018	WC1B 3DP
USA	UK

www.bloomsbury.com

BLOOMSBURY and the Diana logo are trademarks of Bloomsbury Publishing Plc

First published 2015

© Douglas Boin 2015

ISBN: HB: 978-1-62040-317-4
PB: 978-1-62040-319-8
ePub: 978-1-62040-318-1

LIBRARY OF CONGRESS CATALOGING-IN-PUBLICATION DATA

Boin, Douglas.
Coming out Christian in the Roman world : how the followers of Jesus made
a place in Caesar's empire / Douglas Boin.—First U.S. Edition.
pages cm
Includes bibliographical references and index.
ISBN 978-1-62040-317-4 (hardback)
978-1-62040-319-8 (paperback) 978-1-62040-318-1 (ebook)
1. Christianity and culture—History—Early church, ca. 30-600. 2. Identification (Religion)
3. Christians—Rome. 4. Rome—Civilization—Christian influences. I. Title.
BR115.C8B545 2015
270.1—dc23
2014025356

2 4 6 8 10 9 7 5 3 1

Typeset by Hewer Text UK Ltd, Edinburgh
Printed and bound in the U.S.A. by Thomson-Shore Inc., Dexter, Michigan

To find out more about our authors and books visit www.bloomsburycom.
Here you will find extracts, author interviews, details of forthcoming
events and the option to sign up for our newsletters.

Bloomsbury books may be purchased for business or promotional use. For
information on bulk purchases please contact Macmillan Corporate and
Premium Sales Department at specialmarkets@macmillan.com.

I dedicate this book to my sister, Katie, and her wife, Anne;
to my nephew; to our mom, Joyce; and above all, to my partner,
Gardiner, as well as to his entire family.

I'm not always sure where we are, but at least here we can live on
the same page until the time comes to see one another again, soon.

Science, history, and art have something in common: they all depend on metaphor, on the recognition of patterns, on the realization that something is "like" something else.

—John Lewis Gaddis, *The Landscape of History: How Historians Map the Past*

Contents

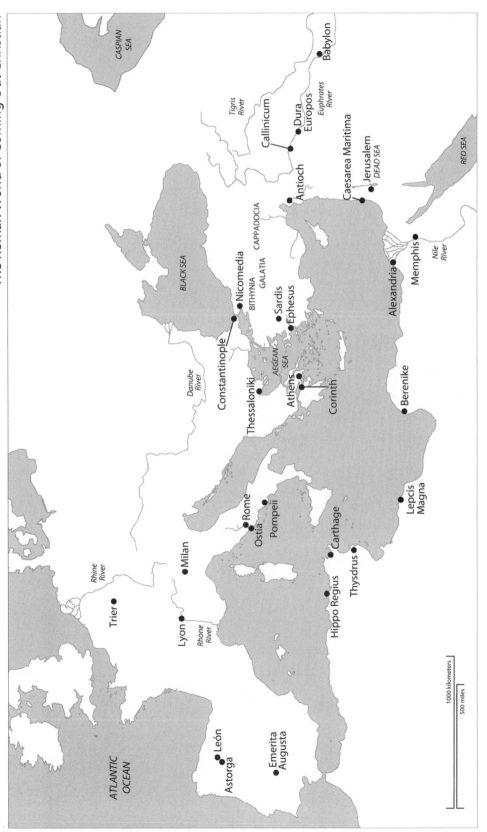

The Roman World of Coming Out Christian

"Who Am I to Judge?"

I have a confession to make. For a long time, I've been uncomfortable around early Christians.[1]

In school, I was brought up on the adventure tales of Homer. In my mind, I've struggled for honor on the battlefield with the greatest of the Greek warriors, Achilles, and I've fought for my own survival while cast away at sea, lonely and heartbroken for home, like Odysseus. I've listened to the thunderous voices of men in togas and tuned in to hear political shouting matches, in Latin, fought by some of Rome's most privileged senators. From the dusty, sun-kissed streets of the Forum to the jeweled dome of Rome, the Pantheon, I've always found the ancient world a pleasant escape. Lyric poetry, Athenian tragedy, Greek comedy, even Roman concrete: there's always been a surprise around every turn. Call me a conservative, but I don't think there was ever anything wrong with the ancient world. It was perfectly fine the way it was—before it changed. And I knew whom to blame.

Everyone knows that early Christians were a ragtag bunch, tent makers and philosophy teachers, daughters of wealthy Romans and sons of Roman governors. To me, they've always seemed like an impenetrable clique, obstinately different. Whether praying in their churches, greeting each other with their secret signs, or practicing their favorite sport, dodging wild animals, the pathological way they stuck together as a group made me uneasy. I had my Rome, full of impressive aqueducts, packed racetracks, and stately mansions. They had theirs, with tales of resurrection and rebirth, many of which had been written in rather childish Greek grammar. What could we possibly have in common?

Not that I have anything against early Christians. As a historian of the later Roman Empire, some of my best friends are early Christians, men like Augustine, whose late fourth century A.D. spiritual odyssey still offers guidance to those on their own Christian quest. Converting to Christianity was Augustine's choice, of course; but the way he has often forced his Christianity upon us, demanding that we see the empire on his terms, has always made me wonder: How had such a religiously diverse place like Rome become so spiritually bankrupt, so fast? Less than a hundred years before Augustine, Christians had won the right to practice their faith openly. It was and is a landmark in the history of political triumph. But at the time they did so—in A.D. 313—they made up no more than 5 to 10 percent of the Roman population.[2] The odds had clearly been stacked against them. How had they done it? Had they really "converted" everyone else to their side?

This question famously puzzled the great historian Edward Gibbon. In the late 1700s, Gibbon stood atop Rome's central prominence, the Capitoline Hill, and surveyed the sad ruins of the ancient city. There, perched above the fallen temples, law courts, and trading spaces, he ruminated on the events that had vanquished this once-great empire. Later, he recorded his thoughts in a multivolume book, *The History of the Decline and Fall of the Roman Empire*. Gibbon's opinions help us see the problem we're still wrestling with. In his book he pointed to "the inflexible, and, if we may use the expression, the intolerant zeal of the Christians" as a reason for their rapid success in ancient Rome.[3] To him, Christians succeeded in changing Rome because their beliefs were fundamentally incompatible with the world they lived in. Rome became Christian, in effect, because there was no other option.

Since Gibbon's time, many have picked up this banner and flown it proudly. Roman cities changed, according to one historian of early Christian architecture, because "Christianity was clearly incompatible with the old faith." One scholar has even attributed the rise of a Christian empire to "Christianity's latent and lymphoid lust for social dominance."[4] It's an argument intended to provoke.

Gibbon and those who follow him can marshal some pretty strong evidence to support it, too.[5]

Starting in A.D. 341, Christian emperors and Christian magistrates began to characterize other people's religions as foul and illicit. The Roman people who practiced animal sacrifices—a communal mainstay of civic life for centuries—were increasingly stigmatized as "criminals, madmen, and insane."[6] Laws similar to this one would continue to be issued through A.D. 435 (they are preserved in the Theodosian Code). Even when I read them in Latin, their intolerance still makes my stomach churn, and many times I've wondered if maybe—just maybe—Gibbon was right. Maybe intolerance had simply been hardwired into the mind of "the Christians," as Gibbon referred to them. Then again, I wondered, maybe we shouldn't be too quick to judge?

By training, I'm an archaeologist and an ancient historian. My love, my office, my playground, and my library is the city of Rome. It's an honor to have clocked so many hours working and living in one of Europe's largest capitals—nearly four million people in its current metropolitan area. I like this modern Rome: from the hipsters dressed in Autobot T-shirts in Pigneto to the market vendors from Bangladesh and China on the Esquiline, a hill that Romulus would hardly recognize today.[7] This modern Rome reminds me of a quieter one, the one whose streets I meander in my research: a Rome of working people and unfamiliar voices, men and women living just beneath the surface of history's more famous names and dates. As an archaeologist, my inclination is to see history from the ground up.

In many ways, we're all archaeologists now. We're drawn to human interest stories, too, the ones that peer behind the actions of the president, the prime minister, the queen. We understand that whether they're standing on their rooftops in a flood or they're huddled together on the Capitol lawn, other people's lives make up the tapestry of a nation. We understand that the history of our time can't be written in definite articles: the Americans, the Australians, the Chinese. So why, I wonder, have we chosen to treat the people of the past differently?

Gibbon is long dead, but bookshelves and shopping carts are still filled with studies of the Christians, the Romans, the early Christians in the eyes of the Romans. Even among those who reject the idea of "culture clash"—two cultures incapable of mixing, like oil and water—there remains a persistent belief that the Christians triumphed over Rome, well, because they had to. In this scenario, the men and women of Rome were suffering from an intense spiritual malaise until one day Christianity arrived. Soon, the simple people of this great world empire began converting from their unenlightened, errant ways, and a new era in history could finally begin. The "Pagan Rome" of the past became the "Christian Rome" of the early Middle Ages—one short layover at the Renaissance and a quick connection to the Enlightenment and our own day and age. History moves at quite a pace when painted with the broadest brush.

I prefer a trowel, a toothbrush, and a dental pick.[8] These are the tools that help archaeologists recover small, delicate artifacts. In history, they can also function as useful metaphors. They remind us to look for the subtle stories that haven't yet been told, the ones that bring nuance to the past. Besides, when it comes to what happened during the "Fall of Rome," there are many Romans—from the Isis worshippers at the harbor of Ostia to a remarkable group of Christian soldiers in North Africa who worshipped the emperor—who have been clamoring to speak for themselves. It's time we listened to all of them.

The many conflicts and persecutions that affect Jews, Christians, and Muslims today virtually demand that when we write about religion, we handle people's beliefs as if they were our own. The same holds true when we write about the past. It's easy to say but not so easily done. For starters, the sheer size of the Roman Empire sometimes seems to demand that we lump all the Romans together. At the dawn of their empire, around A.D. 14—reader beware; demographic numbers from ancient Rome are notoriously unreliable—the population of the Roman Empire tallied somewhere in the range of 44 to 60 million. Roman cities were located in every modern nation of the Mediterranean, the world's largest inland body of water. Roman territories dotted a coastline that measures more than half the circumference of the globe (see map).[9]

Throughout the empire, people worked as teachers, cooks, domestic servants, soldiers, and senators. Between them, social and economic divisions were clear, but they were not the gross chasms of today. The top 1.5 percent of Roman households held about a quarter of Rome's total wealth. Below them, another 10 percent of households held about the same amount.[10] The first group comprised the super-rich, at the bottom were the destitute and poor, but perhaps surprisingly to us, there are definite signs of people who lived in between, a kind of ancient "middle class." Whatever label we put on them, Romans have a range of stories to tell us. A significant number also had the means to do so. They left us their apartments, bequeathed us their kitchenware, and gave us their paintings.[11] Museums, auction houses, and entire countries have been dividing up these possessions for centuries (and like jealous siblings, they continue to argue over them, too).

For many years, I have been fortunate to walk through the warehouses of the Roman past and peer into many of those crates. What I've found in them are stories, stories that—perhaps not surprisingly—challenge many of the stereotypes we've harbored about Rome's early Christians. As it turns out, they aren't all alike after all.[12] Many of these men and women juggled their identities in highly creative ways. This book belongs to them.

It is the surprising story of two bishops in Spain who were members of their local Roman social club. It is the resilient tale of two Christian women in the palace, a mother and daughter, who participated in traditional affairs of state without fearing any repercussions. It is also the story of Christian soldiers in North Africa who dutifully took part in a festival for the Roman emperor when their regiment of Christians and non-Christians alike won recognition for their service. The Christians at the center of each of these moments come from periods that span four centuries of Roman history—and there are more—but men and women like them never stopped finding ways to be Christian and Roman at the same time. Even after A.D. 313, when Christians didn't have any legal reason to fear "coming out" anymore, many kept on doing two things at once. They visited the racetrack on festival days, when Rome's gods were honored. They went to the baths, where Rome's gods were honored, too. They lived hyphenated lives.

Many of these quieter Christians have been tucked away for years behind bigger names, labeled *martyrs*, but I think they have something important to tell us about the rise of Christianity. The Christian men and women who learned to juggle being both Christian and Roman played a role in raising the profile of their movement, too—not just their more opinionated peers. Our task is to look at the kaleidoscopic picture of their lives, from the lower end of the economic ladder all the way up to Christians in the imperial palace, from the first century A.D. to the moment of Christian triumph in 313 and beyond. That's what this book does. It tells a new history of the rise of Christianity in Rome, steering clear of any claim about the "intolerant zeal" of the Christians. I also steer clear of something else. The sociologist Rodney Stark once proposed that Christians triumphed in Rome through an effective campaign of Christian evangelism. The historian Robin Lane Fox flirted with a similar notion when, in his magisterial 1989 work *Pagans and Christians*, he talked about Christianity's innate superiority, "the faith's intrinsic appeal," as he called it.[13] My research has taken me in a completely different direction.

Through a process of fits and starts, Christians hit upon a powerful formula—of social organization, mobilization, resilience, and compromise—that led to new legal rights and greater social visibility. They achieved their political triumph without converting everyone else to their side. In short, this story is much more than a parochial tale of a few Christians trying to make a place for themselves in Caesar's empire. It is the history of nearly 60 million Romans—whose toppled columns too often serve as a shorthand for their civilization's cataclysmic fall—and how they proved to be much more ready and willing to change than we usually give them credit for.

CHAPTER 1

A Bewitching Sibyl

Rome, 63 B.C.

Many Italians are shackled with loans they can't repay, and the Senate has proven itself incapable of addressing the urgent debt crisis. A group of citizens is ready to force the government's hand. While a militia camps at Fiesole, in the hills of Florence, their allies in Rome plot to seize control of the capital. Their intent? To murder Rome's leading citizens. Purportedly, the mastermind of this antigovernment revolt was the senator Lucius Sergius Catilina—Catiline, as we know him. His operation did not end well. By year's end Catiline and his associates in Rome and Fiesole would be rounded up and executed—without a trial.

What does Catiline have to do with Christianity? On the surface, not much. Catiline and his gang were members of the Roman elite, seeking relief—better yet, demanding justice—for social ills that were gnawing at the finances of retired soldiers and many citizens. Theirs was a "civilized" world far from the dust and dirt of a donkey ride in Jerusalem. Ominous, foreboding clouds were rolling into Rome with Catiline's revolt, though. Some of his co-conspirators were motivated by more than real-world concerns. They were inspired by otherworldly ones. That's where Catiline's story dovetails with our own.

The man at the center of this growing mystery was Publius Cornelius Lentulus. Lentulus was a son of one of Rome's staunchest aristocratic families, the Cornelii; and although it may have shocked his ancestors to hear it, the good, toga-wearing Lentulus happened to subscribe to some fairly radical ideas about the legitimacy of the Roman government, including who should control it. This chilling information was revealed to the public after an emergency Senate meeting on December 3, 63 B.C.

By dawn, Catiline's plot to unleash havoc in Rome had been uncovered, and the arrested men, Lentulus among them, had been led before the Senate. Surrounded by their peers, the "conspirators" were asked to give their side of the story. Much of the evidence for their misconduct was circumstantial, but many fumbled through the proceedings and succeeded in incriminating themselves. Hours later, one of Rome's two chief executives, the ambitious Marcus Tullius Cicero—no one from his family had ever made it as high in the government as he—went before a crowd of nervous citizens to break the news of the foiled plot.[1]

The Forum was the center of Rome's civic life, but it wasn't all business. On any day of the week, children might be found playing games on the courthouse steps while they waited for their dads. Others might have come to the Forum as tourists—to see the site of Rome's eternal flame, for example, at the Temple of Vesta. A few more may have been on the prowl for a well-connected friend. As Cicero thundered in the Forum that day, all sense of routine would have been interrupted. As the crowd tuned in to what they heard coming from the speaker's platform, they may have grown increasingly anxious, too.

Catiline's network reached well beyond his camps in Tuscany, Cicero revealed. As he and the other senators had just learned, Catiline had tried to enlist the help of foreign mercenaries in his plan to topple Rome. (The Gauls, seeking to ingratiate themselves to Rome, had been the ones to alert the authorities.) Then, a bombshell: "Lentulus confirmed for us an important detail," Cicero said. "He said that believed he was the 'third Cornelius,' the one referred to in the prophecies of the Sibyl, the 'Cornelius' who has been spoken about by the priests."[2] What Cicero was implying was unmistakably dire, a threat to Rome's very way of life. The criminals were not just financially aggrieved. One of them, Lentulus, had been driven to act by his belief in prophecies recorded in Rome's most sacred books, the Sibylline Oracles. Cornelius Lentulus believed that he was the military leader who had been prophesied to bring destruction upon Rome that year, 63 B.C. The threat had been urgent; Cicero had acted.

Many Romans would have given their leader the benefit of the doubt, too. The oracles on which Lentulus was staking his claim were a collection of enigmatic poems, something akin to the nonsense we associate with Nostradamus. Roman tradition held that one of the last kings of the city, in the sixth century B.C., had purchased these cryptic documents from an anonymous seller who had acquired them from a renowned prophetess, the Sibyl of Cumae. From her cave on the Bay of Naples, at the seaside city of Cumae, the Sibyl enjoyed one of the ancient world's most direct connections to the divine. Only a handful of other cities throughout the Mediterranean—like Delphi in Greece or Erythrae in western Turkey—could boast such a treasure.[3] It was a rare opportunity indeed that her precious books had come on the market. The story of how Rome acquired these books was legend.

According to one version, the anonymous seller, a woman who may or may not have been the Sibyl, had approached Rome's last king and tried to hawk nine of the prophetic books to him. The king refused her outrageous asking price, so she burned three of them, hoping to pique his interest. When he stubbornly refused, she lit three more on fire. Finally, faced with a diminishing supply, the king could hold out no longer. He paid the original price and took the remaining books to the Capitoline Hill. There, in Rome's largest temple, the Temple of Jupiter the Best and Greatest, they were locked away, so that their difficult poetry could be deciphered, only when needed, by the proper oversight committee: Roman priests.[4]

These priests wielded enormous political influence because they were a branch of government. We tend to think of religion as something that belongs in its own separate section of the newspaper, next to horoscopes and sports. But to the people of Rome, there was no such black-and-white division. No Roman nor any early Christian would ever devise the intellectual tools needed to carve out a space between government and religion, or between church and state. Rome's priests were charged by the government to be vigilant, watchful for anything that might capsize the ship of state. Ancient Rome was a much stranger place than we sometimes care to admit.

Birds that flew in the wrong direction, sad statues that had begun to weep, bizarre goats that grew wool, and roosters that had suddenly decided to change sex: each of these disturbing events—Romans referred to them variously as prodigies, omens, portents, or even monsters—carried a secret message about Rome's future. Did the gods favor a piece of legislation or didn't they? Were the gods ready to march to the drumbeat of an impending war, or were they counseling restraint? Priests were duty-bound to interpret these signs, and everyone from the popular assemblies to the Roman Senate to the Republic's two chief executives, the consuls, hung on their evaluations. Naturally, it was a process susceptible to corruption. By the late Republic, many of Rome's officials were trying to micromanage this process.

In 59 B.C., less than a decade after Lentulus and Catiline were killed, one consul had proposed a program to redistribute land to veterans as a way to address Rome's nagging social problems. (That consul was Julius Caesar.) Caesar's colleague, who opposed the idea, claimed the gods would never support such progressive legislation and with the help of the priests tried to derail the policy. Caesar's partisans rallied to the cause. After a few well-timed threats, Caesar's co-consul was forced out of public sight for the rest of the term—trapped for the year in his home, where he was unable to lead the hunt for ill omens. Caesar's program passed.[5] This constitutional system, in which priests worked comfortably as politicians and vice versa, will seem abnormal to us, but it is the only world that Lentulus, Catiline, Caesar, and Cicero ever knew.

The Sibyl's oracles played an essential role in maintaining that system. Five hundred years after their monarchy had ended, Romans of Cicero's day were still trying to unravel her prophecies in times of national crisis: during periods of war, famine, or flood. Their cultural anxiety is wholly understandable. Read correctly, the Sibyl's musings pointed the government toward a course of action that had the backing of the gods themselves. No politician could afford to ignore the advice of such divine counsel. As Dionysius of Halicarnassus, a Greek observer of Roman customs, put it in the first century B.C.:

> There is no possession more hallowed to man or sacred to the gods which the Romans guard so carefully as they do the Sibylline Oracles. They consult them whenever the Senate demands—if, for example, factional strife has seized the city or if some great misfortune has befallen them in war or some wondrous signs and portents have been seen which are difficult to interpret (as often happens).[6]

These books maintained their venerable status throughout the early empire. The great poet of the *Aeneid*, Virgil, would warn his readers about the difficulty of deciphering Sibyl's visions and caution them about her filing system. The Sibyl, he explained, wrote her prophecies on leaves, then stacked them on the floor—a recipe for disaster. Whenever anyone opened the door to her cave, the leaves would spring into the air, then flutter back to earth, shuffled out of order. The implication? Her poetry could be made to say pretty much anything.

Sadly for scholars, almost every page of these poems has vanished. The first set of books was lost in a fire that destroyed the Temple of Jupiter. Later, the Senate commissioned a second set, and the Sibyl at Cumae, with the help of her colleagues abroad, obliged. This replacement set survived for some time—nearly five centuries—until, sometime right around A.D. 408, it, too, vanished. In fact, it was intentionally destroyed in a stunning bonfire meant to rid the government of its dependence on the accursed enigmas once and for all.

The Sibyls themselves were not erased from history, though. By the time their manic pronouncements went up in smoke in the early fifth century A.D., other prophecies—forged poems bearing their name— had begun circulating. Many of these cooked-up texts would captivate readers into the Middle Ages and Renaissance because they were thought to have "predicted" the triumph of Christianity over what we now call "paganism." Rome's prescient "women" were held in such high regard that five of them can still be seen, scribbling in their books, on the ceiling of the Sistine Chapel. Michelangelo Buonarroti painted the Sibyls there to assure us that even Rome's prophets had been smart enough to foresee a thoroughly Christian world. None of these women could have been very happy at being invited to the party on the pope's ceiling, for they never predicted any such thing. But let's not get ahead of the story.

What happened to Lentulus in 63 B.C. teaches us a lesson about the role of prophecy and belief in shaping history. What people believe really can and does make a difference in how they act. Sometimes, it can even make people do strange things. In 63 B.C., Lentulus was using the tattered fragment of a poem to bestow an air of inevitability on his military coup.

As he revealed in his Senate testimony, the "first Cornelius" had been Cornelius Cinna, a general in the early eighties B.C. The "second Cornelius" had been Cornelius Sulla, a dictator who had ruled later that same decade. Fast-forward twenty years, and there was Lentulus, boasting to be the "'third Cornelius,' the one to whom the rule of this city and the power to command it" were fated to come.[7] By December 63 B.C., that triumph had not only been delayed, it was permanently canceled, and Lentulus would soon be put to death by the very government he was trying to overthrow.

Things did not quite turn out the way he had envisioned.

It might seem natural for us to dismiss Lentulus' idiosyncratic interpretations of Roman prophecy as the calling card of a crazy man. But the job of a historian is not to judge the nature of people's beliefs, even when we disagree with them.[8] Beliefs are notoriously difficult to study, but that does not mean we should banish them from our histories. I am a firm proponent of the idea that we need to put people's beliefs under the microscope, dissect them, and scrutinize them to learn where they came from and how they shaped people's world views.

Not every historian would agree with this approach. For some, what people believe is inadmissible evidence. Because religion is a phenomenon apparently divorced from reality, religious motivation can't have a rightful place among the authoritative names, dates, facts, and figures that make up the "real" transcript of a time. Whether we're considering the causes of Catiline's failed revolt or the events that led to the "Fall of Rome," history has to be cross-examined with our eyes on real-world causes, not otherworldly ones.

Bryan Ward-Perkins, an Oxford archaeologist who has written extensively about life before and after the "Fall of Rome," has been a vocal advocate for this position. He articulated it forcefully in his 2005 study *The Fall of Rome and the End of Civilization*. "The new Late Antiquity," he explained, using a term scholars have given to the later Roman Empire, "is fascinated by the history of religion. As a secularist myself," he confessed, "I am bewildered by this development."[9] I employ a different method when writing about the past. My methods draw upon anthropological, sociological, and historical tools that were pioneered in the twentieth century and that continue to be refined today to aid the study of religion.

To begin, I follow the footsteps of the great historian R. G. Collingwood, who, in 1946, articulated some sage advice about the study of religion in his book *The Idea of History*:

If the reason why it is hard for a man to cross the mountains is because he is frightened of the devils in them, it is folly for the historian, preaching at him across a gulf of centuries, to say "This is sheer superstition. There are no devils at all. Face facts, and realize that there are no dangers in the mountains except rocks and water and snow, wolves perhaps, and bad men perhaps, but no devils."[10]

Collingwood's admonition is correct, in my mind. When people tell us why they acted as they did—for fear of demons, for example, or because they believe the world is about to end—we cannot afford to ignore their testimony. We may rationally disagree with it, but we cannot paper over it, however uncomfortable their views make us.

Other scholars have called for similar expressions of empathy and nuance in the study of religion.[11] "Historians must not confuse the passage of time with the accumulation of intelligence," John Lewis Gaddis has cautioned. In a succinct reflection on how historians go about their job, *The Landscape of History*, he observed, "Good historians take the past on its own terms first, and only then impose their own."[12] For me, Gaddis's approach is an essential part of my own method: Belief is and can be a powerful force in determining how an individual or group acts. We need to take account of it. But how?

Did Lentulus really think he was the "third Cornelius," or was his claim simply meant to galvanize support for Catiline's revolt? The question is moot, as are many others that relate to Christianity. Did the women who went to pay their respects at Jesus's tomb really see a resurrected man? Did one bishop of Carthage really believe that "the world [was] about to end"—in the third century A.D.? Did the emperor Constantine, a half century later, really see the sign of Jesus in the sky, compelling him to convert to Christianity?

Some would prefer we find scientific explanations for each of these episodes. Visions of the resurrection? A hallucination, some would claim. Constantine's conversion? Inspired by a natural phenomenon, "a solar halo," according to one researcher.[13] The bishop's claim that "the end of the world" was near? Well, there historians are usually flummoxed. How could anyone believe in the imminent Second Coming of the Messiah?

I'm not convinced these skeptical, even cynical, approaches are helpful. Our job is not to disqualify what people believed. It's to look for traces of what people believed. The anthropologist Clifford Geertz called these traces the "signs and symbols" of a culture's religious system.[14] (I will say more about the study of ancient "religion" later.) Our job will be to analyze this evidence for important patterns and to give it a larger context. That's how historians "map the past." It's teeming with colorful characters too.

It includes Romans who worshipped at the Temple of Isis at Pompeii, a Jewish community who petitioned officials in Roman Benghazi to hold their meetings in the amphitheater, and several enterprising Christians who undertook a home renovation project in Syria. These are the people whose stories we will encounter in our journey through the Roman world. Together, they will help us follow the winding path that Jesus's followers took to find their place in the empire. It's time we listened to all these people (especially the quieter ones).

CHAPTER 2

The Quieter Ones

A story about Christianity should begin with Jesus, but that's easier said than done. Every detail of Jesus's life comes to us as a puzzle piece from someone else's. Even the earliest documents about Jesus that we have—letters written by his Jewish follower Paul—date to the fifties A.D., two decades after Jesus was executed. The gospels, the narratives that offer some of the classic scenes in Jesus's life, arrive later. It's a frustrating game to play, trying to piece together a portrait of someone based on so much secondhand reporting, but we keep playing it. In an age that increasingly equates the number of one's "followers" with social status, perhaps it's only natural. Who wouldn't want to know more about an obscure first century man who's managed to accumulate 2.18 billion followers today?[1]

Here's what we think we know. Born in Nazareth, a carpenter's son, Jesus was a Jew who preached the imminent coming of God's kingdom, and he warned his followers to be ready. Predicting a time when the sun would grow dark, the moon would radiate no more light, and stars would fall from the sky (Mark 13:24–31), he is even thought to have told them, "Truly I tell you, this generation will not pass away until all these things have taken place" (Mark 13:30). The question is, were these Jesus's words, or were they the product of another person's pen—a script that Mark had given "Jesus" to read? Most biblical scholars do believe Jesus was a preacher with an urgent end-time message, but they also stress that he is more complex than a one-dimensional caricature.[2]

Jesus was unafraid to walk with lepers and prostitutes. He was also a teacher and a miracle worker. His voice alone was powerful enough to bring the dead back to life, and he was not afraid to lay his hands on people in need. One time, he is even said to have done so twice—that is, when his first attempt at healing didn't go as planned. "Can you see anything?" Jesus asked. "I can see people," the blind man said, "but they look like trees walking around." ("Then Jesus laid his hands on him again," Mark 8:22–26). Is this an ancient case of miracle malpractice? Probably not. Mark was finding a poetic way to describe the stages of uncertainty that had clouded the vision of many of Jesus's followers in the months, years, and decades after their teacher had been taken from them and executed.[3]

Why had Jesus been arrested? To answer that question, we have to interview a member of Rome's middle management. Pontius Pilate was prefect of the Roman province of Judaea from A.D. 26 to 36, and an inscription found in 1961 in the town of Caesarea Maritima, on the coast of modern Israel, helps us move him onstage for one of history's most dramatic acts (figure 1). The inscription from Caesarea informs us, in Latin, about Pilate's dedication of a temple in honor of the Roman emperor Tiberius. Tiberius took the reins of the state in A.D. 14 and held them steadily until A.D. 37. Two thousand years later, Pilate's temple for Tiberius is gone, but to see Pilate's own name in stone is to spy on the uneventful life of an ordinary administrator, one whose mandate included quashing civil unrest and executing petulant rabble-rousers.[4]

Based on everything we know about how Roman officials were expected to manage their territories, in fact, it is virtually certain that Pilate (and he alone) was responsible for executing Jesus. The canonical gospel writers, on the other hand, all of whom lived a generation or more after Pilate's death, found a slightly different role for him to play. All four writers neutered Pilate's authority by blaming "the Jews" for Jesus's death.[5] Each was trying to claim that their community was the true heir of Jewish tradition. Naturally, other Jews disagreed, but the oily finger pointing of the gospel writers did not go away. It is visible today as a long, insidious smear across centuries of Christian-Jewish relations.

Those first decades after Jesus's death were formational. Within twenty years, Jesus had become the subject of a popular oral tradition. The snippets of this tradition, which scholars have isolated based on clues in Paul, provide us with a transcript of what people believed during the first generation of the movement. According to one scholar's reconstruction, they believed

> that Jesus the Messiah [Christ] died, he was buried, he was raised on the third day, he appeared to Cephas and then, to the twelve; that he appeared to more than five hundred brethren all at the same time; and that he appeared to James and the apostles (1 Corinthians 15:3–7).[6]

Some aspects of this tradition will be readily recognizable, such as Jesus's death and resurrection. Some were quick to vanish. None of the gospel writers mention Jesus's miraculous appearance in front of five hundred people, for example. We stumble upon it today, fossilized in Paul's letter.

Jesus's followers themselves were never frozen in time, though. By the mid first century, they were growing, even maturing, as a community. As their first generation passed away, leaving behind many of their stories, other stories and storytellers stepped in to furnish a picture of Jesus that harmonized with their changing world. All four canonical gospels, attributed to the pens of Matthew, Mark, Luke, and John, come from this time. Specific moments in Jesus's life that were never colored in by earlier generations, such as the year of his birth or the circumstances under which his family sought asylum from Herod, now received new attention. Inns, mangers, flights into Egypt, all of these vivid details now suddenly appeared as part of the group's memory. They were elaborating on Jesus's life story as they understood it.

They didn't always agree with one another, either. Matthew placed Jesus's birth during the reign of Herod, the king of Judaea who died in 4 B.C. Luke placed Jesus's birth in another decade entirely: when "a decree went out from Caesar Augustus, ruler of the Roman world: that everyone in the empire should be registered for the census" (Luke 2:1). This census was much more modest than Luke implied. It was conducted in A.D. 6. only in the territory of Roman Syria by the governor of that province, Publius Sulpicius Quirinius. So was Jesus born four years "Before Christ" or ten years later? Biblical scholars prefer the former date, but they also insist—rightly—that the creativity of the two authors cannot be dismissed.

Seventy years after their teacher's execution, Jesus's followers, people who believed in his miracles, message, and resurrection, were not the curators of a stuffy tradition. Every one of them was wrestling with Jesus's memory while they struggled to find their own place in the Roman world. That's why it's so easy to get lost in the maze of contradictory statements they left behind. "Blessed are the poor," Jesus teaches in Luke's gospel (Luke 6:20). "Blessed are the poor in spirit," Jesus teaches in Matthew's (Matthew 5:3). So did Jesus preach to the poor, or didn't he? Whether they were debating the role of wealth in the early church or the matter of living in Rome, Jesus's followers were tied up in social contradictions from their earliest age.

Of course, amid so much social diversity, there's one thing that does unite this disparate band, one facet of their history that many people today confidently believe. It is the harrowing tale of how all of them endured relentless discrimination at the hands of their Roman neighbors. For in the decades and centuries after Jesus's death, or so we've been taught, Christians were persecuted everywhere and always throughout the Roman Empire. That, at least, is where our story usually begins.

The evidence seems deceptively simple. In the first century, the fanatical emperor Nero persecuted them for burning Rome. In the second and third centuries A.D., they lined up in Roman city squares throughout the empire to sign over their lives rather than worship empty gods. Early Christians themselves put a huge stock in their own tales of resilience and triumph. "The more you cut us down," a Christian named Tertullian wrote in the late second century A.D., "the more we grow. The blood of Christian martyrs is like a seed."[7]

Militant, self-assured, and possessing a flair for rhetoric, Tertullian has had a lasting effect on how we understand the struggle of Jesus's followers. The "martyr stories" he alludes to have been hailed as fundamental to the birth of the Church. Indeed, that's why most people still think that being a follower of Jesus was wholly incompatible with living in the Roman world.[8] The story Tertullian tells is also confrontational and aggressive, a battlefield divided between heroes and villains. Tertullian himself described it as a world of "angels and demons"—he makes reference to this inseparable, supernatural pair eight times in one text alone—to convince his community that they were locked in a cosmic war.[9] We'll talk about where Tertullian acquired his vision of warring "angels and demons" later.

For now, Tertullian's stark world view cannot limit the way we look at our evidence. Archaeology can provide some nuance. Tertullian lived in Carthage, North Africa. By the late second century A.D., Carthage was a highly metropolitan and dynamic city, host to a diverse mix of local elites as well as émigrés and expats from Italy, Rome, and the eastern Mediterranean. Archeological discoveries have revealed that for almost two hundred years, Carthage had been one of Rome's most important trading partners, supplying the capital with food, oil, and even ostriches and elephants for games. Because of the economic opportunities it provided, some locals even grew to see Carthage as a gateway to a better life. Within a few generations, families might see their son advance in a career that would carry him to the capital. Even those who chose to stay home benefited from the increased contact with Rome. Trade raised the quality of their life, and many took advantage of the change for a Roman education. By Tertullian's time, Carthage and a whole list of other cities throughout North Africa were teeming with these opportunities. The gods themselves—the defenders of civic life, the guardians of Roman prosperity, and the protectors of the emperor—ensured everyone's success. They brought Christians and non-Christians together, and the city flourished.[10] Their real-world dramas were probably much less frightful, too, than any battle between "angels and demons."

This sense of cooperation, the willing way in which a whole host of men and women embraced the Roman system and won their ticket to greater opportunity and success, was not new to Tertullian's time. By the early third century, it had been a characteristic of Mediterranean life for two hundred years. There were many North Africans who could testify to the lasting benefits of Rome.

Annobal Rufus would have been one of them. A native of North Africa, in the western region of Libya known as Tripolitania, he lived two centuries before Tertullian at a time when knowing how to strike a creative balance between "Rome" and "home" was the key to his success. Annobal Rufus excelled at juggling. He built a theater in his hometown of Lepcis Magna, east of modern Tripoli in Libya, and dedicated it to the emperor Augustus; he also advertised his own personal role in the project with a very public inscription.[11] That inscription still survives, set above a doorway to the theater in Lepcis Magna. Visually, it speaks to the dynamic, two-way process of exchange that fed the engine of Rome's growing empire.[12] Not only did it elevate Annobal in the eyes of Augustus by addressing him in Latin, it spoke to the people of Lepcis Magna in their language, too: neo-Punic. (The curvilinear forms of the local tongue, juxtaposed with the boxy Latin, form a highly visible contrast, in stone.) Together, Annobal's linguistic talents speak volumes about his ability to manage two things at once, navigating the worlds of North Africa and Rome. That's how many men like him would carve out a space for themselves in Rome's empire over the next two hundred years. Being Roman truly was a kaleidoscopic experience.[13] "Rome" was not a static idea. How have we come to let a man like Tertullian paint such a black-and-white picture of this time?

In history or theology books, Tertullian has a curious reputation. He's usually described as an apologist, a Christian who tried to "explain Christianity to outsiders and win converts to the new movement."[14] That's only partially true. Tertullian did passionately desire to win a greater social recognition for his group. He explained it this way:

> We worship one God, whom you see all around you, at whose thunder and lightening you quake and at whose favors you rejoice. (Indeed, you yourselves believe that there are other gods, too, all of whom we know are actually demons!) Still, it is a characteristic feature of human law—and, indeed, it is an expression of our innate ability to determine what we want—that each of us worships how we see fit.[15]

It's a progressive idea, that each of us be allowed to worship as we see fit. What this Roman from North Africa didn't quite master was the right rhetoric. Calling his neighbors "demon worshippers" at the same time that he pleaded with them to recognize the worship of the Christian God probably didn't win him many supporters. And when he claimed "The blood of Christian martyrs is like a seed!" there must have been many Carthaginians, including Christians, who must have taken stock of their nice houses and careers and disavowed any knowledge of him. We should not be misled into characterizing him as an early champion of "religious freedom," either, a concept foreign to antiquity.[16] Tertullian was doing nothing less than thumbing his nose at an entire well-established Roman way of life.

For Tertullian, only Christianity was "the true way of worshipping [*religio*] the true God."[17] The Latin word he was using may look harmlessly familiar to us, just like our word "religion." But the similarities are wholly superficial. These two words are different species, and it's essential that we not confuse them, especially if we want to appreciate the uphill battle that all Christians faced—not just Tertullian—in fighting for their right to worship openly.

The people of Rome, who cared deeply about their gods, wanted to ensure the gods looked favorably upon their empire. Roman writers used the word *religio* to refer to all the public worship practices and beliefs that served this goal. It was a grand concept that could include worshippers of major deities, such as Isis, Minerva, or Jupiter; but it was also flexible enough to encompass people's devotion to lesser ones. The god Chance (Fortuna), for example, was honored throughout Roman cities, as were the gods of an individual family at home or the deified notions of Victory and Peace, Hope and Faith, four virtues dear to the Roman state.[18] By the time of Tertullian, people's beliefs were as diverse as the 44 to 60 million residents of the empire. What brought everyone together was a level of social and civic commitment to Rome and to one another.

Who determined what was in Rome's best interest? Who decided what was "normal"? That unenviable task fell to the court of public opinion, unfortunately, where reason did not always reign. Any set of practices that was deemed "too peculiar" risked being seen as a *superstitio*, the root of our word "superstition." Many Romans of the second and third centuries A.D. described Christianity as a *superstitio* because they perceived that Christians were not being good citizens. Christians passionate about winning legal recognition for their beliefs had to find a way to confront this challenge, this civic stigma. They had to convince their friends and families that they were no less Roman than anyone else.

Tertullian was not wholly interested in that effort. He preferred to turn Rome's widely accepted world on its head. In his rhetoric, Rome's worship practices were the ones that were illegitimate. Romans were the ones who practiced a *superstitio*, not Christians. Only Christianity was "the true way of worshipping [*religio*] the true God."[19] In Rome's diverse society, many people would have been highly suspicious of this claim.[20] Christians who wanted to win the hearts and minds of their Roman friends and family had to find a way to meet them on terms that other

Romans found amenable. It may be surprising, but many of Jesus's followers did just that.

A whole host of Christians did live in the middle ground that Tertullian stigmatized. These followers of Jesus reached out to their Roman peers, made compromises in their daily life, and fought all the smaller, less metaphysical battles with their friends and neighbors that helped the movement grow. These individuals did not want to reject Rome. Rome was the only world there was, home to many different experiences; and they may have advanced Christianity's cause by leaps and bounds in ways we never talk about. The many Christians who employed those tactics deserve to have their story told. We've rarely sought them out. Why not?

For one thing, they're hard to find; people who try to fit in usually succeed in looking like everyone else. Second, our sources have painted such an evocative portrait of life inside early Christian communities that they've clouded our vision of what was happening on the outside. Many texts shed light on how bishops, deacons, and presbyters emerged as authority figures during the second and third centuries. This period, which witnessed the institutionalization of the Church, played an important role in helping the Christians organize, even grow, and cannot be quickly dismissed. Very likely, it helped convince the authorities that Christians were no different from other Greco-Roman social groups, all of which had their own peculiar hierarchies and social structures. The history of the institution's growth, however, cannot stand in for the history of everyone else.

Many men and women were not martyrs at all. Reluctant to antagonize their friends, unwilling to provoke the authorities, they didn't go out of their way to shove their Christianity in anyone else's face. These are men and women who lived at disparate times throughout Roman history, in places as far apart as Spain and Turkey; but they have all largely been written out of history by the voices of their peers. Contrary to what we've been taught—that their lives were irrelevant to the success of the Church—these men and women also played an important role in Christianity's struggle to come out of the closet. By virtue of their creative resilience, not their zealotry, they accomplished the most fundamental thing of all: they taught their Roman friends and neighbors to see Christians in a less threatening light.

And so we return to the place where the story usually begins: that Christians were persecuted, everywhere and always, in the Roman Empire. That's simply not true. For almost 250 years, Christians lived in a world where no one, not even the highest members of the government, cared what they believed as long as they made an effort to participate in the civic life of the empire. This idea may not seem to belong on the same bookshelf with so many well-known stories of lions and martyrs, blood and rabid "persecution," but there is not one shred of evidence to suggest that Christians were ever systematically persecuted for their beliefs until the second half of the third century A.D.[21] Tertullian may have felt persecuted, but there is no legal evidence to confirm any early Christian "persecution" until A.D. 253–60, a generation or more after Tertullian died. So why would so many people have thrown themselves to the lions if they weren't actually compelled to do so? How could we have gotten everything so wrong? Just who are these quieter Christians we've forgotten about?

One of the strangest details of early Christian history is that there weren't any early "Christians" for a while. No ancient writer uses the word "Christian" (meaning "follower of the Messiah"), derived from the Greek word *Christos*, until the end of the first century A.D. In fact, the word, which is first attested in the town of Antioch in Roman Syria, probably began its life as a slur.[22] We can glimpse the earliest history of Jesus's followers in the history of this one word. None of them wanted to have anything to do with it. For two generations after Jesus's death, there is no evidence that any of Jesus's followers, including Paul, a Jew, ever called themselves "Christians" or described their worship as "Christianity."

A word can get a new lease on life when members of the stigmatized group decide to appropriate it, though.[23] Fifty years after the death of Jesus, an anonymous letter writer was the first to address a community of Jesus's followers as "Christians" (1 Peter 4:16). It must have been a daring decision; he wasn't even confident enough to sign his own name to the document. An even stranger development was still to come. In the first decade of the second century, around A.D. 112–15, a version of the word "Christianity" (*Christianismos*, in Greek) appears for the first time in any ancient text. Contrary to what we might think, its invention didn't herald the arrival of a new religion.

The writer who coined it, Ignatius of Antioch, was articulating an urgent concern. Ignatius had heard that some followers of Jesus were meeting on the Jewish Sabbath, practicing circumcision, and still identifying as Jews. For Ignatius, there was only one way to be a follower of Jesus now; that meant being openly Christian (*Christianismos*), not identifying as Jewish. At the start of the second century A.D., three generations after Jesus's death, Jesus's followers very clearly had not worked out their identity issues. In short, being "Christian" in the Roman world was not an idea that was born with Jesus, nor even with Paul.[24] It began at the end of the first and the beginning of the second century A.D. when one segment of Jesus's followers, who felt increasingly comfortable with the negative term, began to apply it to themselves.

This act of appropriation is one of the earliest triumphs for Jesus's followers. For when individuals and groups consciously decide to embrace words that were once hurled against them, their act of reuse becomes a statement of empowerment, a way to triumph over the past. No group will ever speak with one voice, of course, as Ignatius of Antioch might reluctantly have admitted. But for Jesus's followers—drawn from both Jews and gentiles—this new word gave them a chance to do something they had been struggling to do for three generations. It gave them a shared sense of identity. Ignatius had been motivated by just that mission: "Having become disciples of Christ," he wrote, "let us learn to live by being openly Christian. For whoever is called by any other name than this does not belong to God."[25]

It's an essential development in the history of Christianity, but the fact that Ignatius had to argue his point at all suggests that many of Jesus's followers were not exactly ready to embrace the term, even in the early second century A.D. Why? The answer must be that reluctance and fear were still very real concerns. After all, a large part of the Roman world had never heard of these "Christians" before. Jews, yes, but who were these other people? The sudden appearance of a new group would soon give rise to social paranoia.

So it was that in A.D. 64, according to a later source, the emperor Nero blamed Rome's infamous but devastating fire on Jesus's followers. Did Nero harbor an open theological hatred for "Christians"? Not likely. It's more probable that rumors of this alien group had been lurking in the capital for years.[26] By Nero's time, these unfamiliar "Christians" must have seemed like a natural scapegoat for the catastrophe that had

devastated nearly two thirds of Rome. Characterizing Nero as xenopho-
bic may not redeem him in the eyes of many Christians today, but it
shouldn't condemn him, either. This—the very first age of "Christian
persecution," as it's often taught—had nothing to do with Rome's hatred
of Christianity. It was the result of one Roman emperor's regrettable fear
of outsiders.

In an age that was quick to blame strangers for anything that went
wrong, Jesus's followers could easily have become cells of disaffected
citizens, no different from Catiline's army. The evidence they left
behind shows us many of them consciously choosing a different path.
Many began brainstorming strategies that would win other Romans to
their side.

By the end of the first century A.D., Christian wives were being told to
obey their husbands, in language that reinforced Roman social expectations of gender (Colossians 3:18–4:1). Christian slaves were being told to
obey their masters, in language that reinforced—not undermined—the
Roman ubiquity of slavery (Ephesians 5:22–6:9). And all Christians were
now being told to "honor the emperor" (1 Peter 2:17), reinforcing Roman
expectations that everyone, including Jesus's followers, would unite
around shared civic values.[27] These pillars of family life—master and
slave, husband and wife, father and child—had been essential to many
parts of the Mediterranean world for centuries. One wise Greek,
Aristotle, had articulated their importance in the fourth century B.C.[28]
Romans valued them too. By mirroring the ideals that Greeks and
Romans held dear, Jesus's followers were showing that they, too, respected
what it meant to be a member of the Roman world. So they did as
Romans did. They placed a high importance on being good Roman
fathers, obedient wives, devoted children, and loyal slaves. These weren't
strategies that contaminated early "Christianity." They were built into the
movement from its start.

That said, at precisely the time that Jesus's followers were arguing over
whether to identify as "Christians" or keep identifying as a Jewish group,
authorities in one part of the empire—Bithynia, in northwest Turkey—
picked up some of their internal chatter. In A.D. 112, a problem involving
"Christians" was brought to the emperor, Trajan. It is the first time that
an alert about Jesus's followers had worked its way from the provinces to
the palace in Rome.

Trajan (r. 98–117) had received a letter from the governor of Bithynia, Pliny. Pliny had been approached by an unnamed informer who was horrified at the fact that there were people openly calling themselves "Christians" in his town.[29] This nervous source had alerted the governor. Dutiful manager that he was, Pliny listened and said he would look into it. Here's what he found:

These "Christians" were unmistakably queer (Pliny describes them as a *superstitio*). Indeed, many of them kept insisting, repeatedly and force-fully, that they were a "Christian." One, two, three times Pliny would ask, and many would profess the same answer, even when threatened with punishment. The puzzling thing for Pliny, though, was how normal so many of the other ones seemed. Members of the group swore oaths not to steal or to commit adultery; made sure to pay back their debts on time; even committed themselves never to act in a way that would be a breach of public trust (*fides*). Pliny, whose uncle had died in the volcanic eruption that had destroyed several Roman towns in the Bay of Naples in A.D. 79, could certainly identify with that. *Fides*, which means "reliabil-ity" or "accountability" in Latin, was a civic ideal so valued by Romans that they deified it. And as Pliny makes clear, many of the "Christians" he had encountered were Roman citizens—"out-of-their-mind crazy," he sneers, but citizens nonetheless. The one issue that kept nagging him was their legal status. What were the ramifications of being openly a "Christian" in the second century A.D.? Was the name alone grounds for punishment?[30] So he wrote to the palace.

Today, Trajan, born in Spain, is remembered as a successful general. The column commemorating his military victory near the Danube (in modern Romania) still stands proudly in the center of Rome, in Trajan's Forum, just down the street from the Colosseum. Tourists usually mill about it, staring up at the statue of Saint Peter that has been perched triumphantly on top, a potent piece of Renaissance propaganda meant to advertise Christianity's victory over the "pagan" past. Ancient Romans stared up at the top of the column, too, but for different reasons. Before it was dedicated by the Senate, in A.D. 113, the site had been dominated by a small mountain, a rocky spur of Rome's Quirinal Hill.

In the decades after Trajan's victory in Romania, construction work-ers and slaves had cleared away a portion of this hill—entirely removed it—to make way for Trajan's Forum. The column was erected, as its inscription states, to "show how high the hill was" that had been removed to make way for Trajan's new business center.[31] It was a powerful statement about the willpower of Rome and its people: Their empire did big things. It could even move mountains. Four years later, at Trajan's death, barbarians had been trampled, and cities were flourishing, from Britain to Bithynia to the border of the Euphrates. Trajan's ashes would soon be laid to rest inside his column. Successive emperors would forever be inaugurated with the blessing that they be "more fortunate than Augustus, better yet than Trajan."[32] Romans adored him.

Trajan is also famous today for having penned a rather measured response to Pliny: "Christians must not be hunted out," he told the governor. "But if they are brought to you and if they are so charged, then they should be punished." The advice from the top of the chain of command was unequivocal: Magistrates should not be wasting their time, or Rome's, poking around in the dark corners of the city. Pliny's job was to leave them alone. And no one, the emperor admonished, should ever be brought up on anonymous charges. "That sets the worst kind of precedent, and it's not appropriate for our day and age."[33] It was an enlightened answer, demonstrating the kind of sophisticated response to complex times that gave Trajan his justly earned reputation. Whether it did anything to lessen Pliny's anxiety, we can't say.

We also don't know whether it calmed any of Jesus's followers. Pliny and Trajan were outsiders, after all. Neither of them knew enough about the internal politics of the group, comprising both Jews and gentiles, to ask the kind of follow-up question we want to ask. Namely: How many of Jesus's followers still self-identified as Jewish, perhaps to avoid being hassled by the authorities? Just because one man, Ignatius of Antioch, had started a letter writing campaign to push all of Jesus's followers out of the closet—forcing them to come out as "Christian"—didn't mean that everyone else was ready to follow his lead.

Were all of Jesus's followers emotionally prepared to take such a hurtful, demeaning label, "Christian," and parade around town with it? No one at the time ever bothered to ask. That's why, even though Pliny's correspondence with Trajan about "Christians" is rightly a milestone in the annals of administrative history, it hardly helps us see the whole picture of what was happening in Rome. Jesus's followers were still wrestling with identity issues that neither Pliny nor Trajan had the willingness, or perhaps even the wherewithal, to understand. Both these perspectives—one from outside the group, one from within—are essential for measuring what was happening in cities throughout the empire.

At the turn of the second century, many of Jesus's followers were still stepping gingerly around their friends and family, notwithstanding the public pride of a few who had embraced their new label, "Christian." Why?

There were many moments throughout the year when people of the empire came together, in local cities and towns, to celebrate being Roman alongside each other. Whether one lived in Lepcis Magna or Corinth in Greece, these annual moments fostered a sense of belonging. These were the days on which Rome held the festivals for its gods, and they were like the civic glue of the Roman world.

These festivals functioned much like a contemporary civic calendar.[34] Today, for example, from Memorial Day to Labor Day, a sequence of holidays brings Americans together as a country. Not everyone celebrates them with the same vigor. Sometimes people even forget how they became embedded in our lives (President's Day? Presidents' Day?). Yet holidays like these make the rhythm of the year feel distinctly American, and anyone who has ever tried to celebrate them abroad—think about what it's like to have Thanksgiving in Rome—feels how much the abstract notion of time can shape our lives.

The sociologist Robert Bellah studied these ideas. What he found was that people often participated in their civic festivals for reasons that had very little to do with their "spiritual" needs. It's as if the festivals themselves were providing their own structure and meaning to people's lives—something akin to a "religion." Bellah called this concept a "civil religion."[35] Admittedly, Bellah was using this notion to write about twentieth century America. Consequently, he never had to wrestle with any of the vocabulary problems we've already encountered in our study of Rome (religio versus "religion," for example). That said, Bellah's ideas are worth mentioning here, if only as a useful tool for seeing Rome differently. A "civil religion," like the kind associated with Thanksgiving or Presidents' Day, exists apart from any one person's beliefs. And it has very little to do with buildings traditionally associated with worship, like churches, synagogues, or mosques. Instead, it fosters commitment to one another, even to the nation. That's why, in the States, Americans set aside times throughout our year for honoring veterans and for commemorating their struggle for independence. These values are so much a part of what it means to be an American that the time for celebrating them has become like a religion.

Romans did these things, too. They called it the practice of their *pietas*, the root of our word "piety." All throughout the year, cities and towns would celebrate festivals—some local, others more widely recognized—that would unite people in the shared experience of being a Roman. There was no formal profession of creed at any of these events and no written theology that Rome's priests imposed or enforced. The festivals were, by and large, open-ended civic commemorations, but they brought local communities together.

To celebrate the emperor's birthday, priests would sacrifice a bull. This ritual had a very specific set of protocols—for the priests. They had to prepare the animal for death: reciting prayers, pouring libations, burning incense. Afterward, more priests would inspect the animal's intestines for signs of ill omen. Everyone watched. No bystander was asked to pick up a knife to slice the animal's throat. No one was forced to pick over the entrails. In fact, the most important participatory moment came after the animal's death. That's when the civic banquet was held, a meal that brought everyone together for the well-being of Rome.

Some people did not want to participate in these festivals, and their reluctance to do so attracted attention. The Christian slave Blandina was allegedly killed in Lyon in A.D. 177 for refusing to take part. Hung up on a cross in her local arena, she was set out as food for the beasts. Less than thirty years later, two more women, Perpetua and her slave, Felicitas, were allegedly killed in Carthage for similar reasons. To many of Jesus's followers, these women were heroes. Evidence attests to their popularity; by the fourth century, the commemoration of Perpetua and Felicitas, who had died in North Africa, was included on a holiday calendar used in Rome.[36] In the Catholic Church, all three women are still revered. (Blandina's feast day is celebrated on June 2; Perpetua and Felicitas's, March 7.)

From Lyon to Carthage, it was Christians who chose to draw these lines in the sand, by standing apart, who were the ones that were summarily punished. Is it accurate, then, to say that all "the Christians" were systematically persecuted? Some felt persecuted, perhaps even justifiably so. But we shouldn't downplay the intensely personal and highly individual decisions that led Jesus's followers to act the way that they saw fit, given the circumstances. Many of them did choose to take part in Roman festivals.

During the third century A.D., at least two Christians in Spain did precisely what we have been told Christians did not do: they honored the emperor by taking part in a local sacrifice. One of these men was named Martial; the other, Basilides. Their stories are emblematic of all the people whose efforts at juggling we have lost, or willfully forgotten. Martial and Basilides lived and worked in Spain in Mérida (ancient Emerita Augusta), León, and Astorga. (Today, it's unclear exactly which man lived where, but what they did is more important than where they did it.)[37]

When the third century emperor Decius decreed that all Roman citizens should participate in an empire-wide festival, both men showed up. A document from the mid third century confirms their participation. Neither man gives us any indication that he felt any anxiety at doing so, however. Perhaps they found a way to tone down their identity to appear less threatening, and they played up their civic bona fides. They may even have quietly advanced the cause of their Christian brothers and sisters by doing so.

And why should they not have? At a festival, Romans rarely did any more than watch the death of the animal and share in the meal that followed. No Roman himself ever slaughtered the sacrificial beast. It was slaves in scrubs, tunics, who did that dirty work; emperors, magistrates, even ordinary citizens couldn't be expected to dirty their own togas (figure 2). When people of the Roman world attended a sacrifice, they made of it what they wanted to. They took part however they saw fit.[38] Why did Martial and Basilides feel comfortable enough to take part in a local festival while other Christians, like Blandina, Perpetua, and Felicitas, did not?

Martial is an intriguing case. He seems to have been a skilled juggler, able to embrace Roman culture without any qualms about sacrificing the essentials of his faith. We know, for example, that when he was not meeting with Christians, he participated in a local Roman social club with his son. This club held frequent banquets of its own. It also seems to have been a sort of funerary society. Members were in charge of providing a respectable burial for people who enrolled, many of whom did not have extended families or patrons—the kinds of wealthy people who were traditionally in charge of arranging a funeral.[39]

Groups like Martial's burial club existed all throughout the Roman world, drawing their members from all economic ranks. Many times, these members would come together to celebrate a banquet in honor of their club's patron deity, and the meal would strengthen their ties to one another and their community. For wealthier members, the meal might be an opportunity to preen before other citizens in the town. Men and women of means were especially important for Roman cities because their benefaction (in Latin, *beneficium*) helped pay for local upkeep.

Martial's personal contacts, by virtue of his membership in this club, must have been extraordinary. That alone would probably have made him, as a Christian, slightly less threatening to those in his social circle. Both he and Basilides, in fact, must have ranked among the most high-profile Christians in town. Neither had to fear the wrath of any ecclesiastical authority for being found out, either. Why? The two men were Christian bishops, and their flocks were located in the Spanish cities of Mérida, León, and Astorga. Should we be surprised? Paul had urged the community of Jesus's followers at Rome to be "subject to the ruling authorities" (Romans 13:1). Anonymous authors who had written in defense of Paul's message—to communities at Colossus and Ephesos in Asia Minor—did the same, as did the anonymous writer of the letter known as 1 Peter. All of these writers had been urging Jesus's followers to adopt strategies for civic engagement. Martial and Basilides were merely following the teachings of an earlier generation.

But criticism there was, launched by a fellow bishop who had a rather different view of what it meant to be a Christian. Cyprian was bishop of Carthage from A.D. 249 to 258, and he saw the acts of Martial and Basilides as an end-time abomination, literally. We know because he took to the mail and began an intense letter-writing campaign, thundering about the outrage to a group of fellow Christians. In his letter, Cyprian reveals how disheartening it was to hear that Martial and Basilides had been caught participating in a Roman festival, but everyone else should not lose heart:

> Don't let it get to you, dearest brothers, if you hear in the news that someone's slippery faith is making them waver or an inadequate fear of God is making someone hesitate or a peaceful harmony does not last. These things have all been predicted to happen at the end of the world. By the voice of the Lord and by

the witness of the apostles, it has been foreordained that, when the world is getting close to its end and the Antichrist is about to arrive, all good things will come to an end and evil, wicked things will be on the rise.[40]

Is this language a fair way to assess Basilides's and Martial's political choices? The same stark dualism of Tertullian's world view is here (in place of his "angels and demons," Cyprian adopts the terms "good and evil"), but there's more to the picture, too. There's an implication that Basilides's and Martial's participation in a Roman festival is a sign of the imminent end of the world, an act that will herald the arrival of a threatening beast (the "Antichrist"). Whether Cyprian really believed the world was about to end can be debated, but his choice of language is unequivocal. It leaves very little room for the gray areas of daily life in Roman Spain.

Cyprian was not done with painting in black and white. Later, he would coin a term to smear—with the broadest brush—any follower of Jesus who had ever gone to a Roman festival and "dared" to keep calling himself a "Christian." He called them "lapsed." In another text, he would inveigh against these enemies of the Church, men like Martial and Basilides, who had committed the double fault of being willing and able to juggle their lives as Christians and Romans:

> They think that what they're doing with their deceitful words is a form of peace. What they do is not peace but war! Anyone who is separated from the gospel is not joined to the Church, so why do they call this injury they have inflicted on us "an act of kindness" [*beneficium*]? Why do they use the term "piety" [*pietas*] to describe something that is impious?[41]

Like Tertullian before him, Cyprian was in the process of turning the Roman world on its head. Christians who tried to do good things for their Roman towns became traitors, and Christians who tried to participate in the civic life of their Roman cities became turncoats. The bishop of Carthage gained much by defining Christian identity in his terms. Very likely, he could have seen a rise in followers, people who, like him, thought that the third century was careening toward a precipitous end.

The urgency with which Cyprian took up the issue of how Christians lived in their Roman cities may have looked admirable to some. (It may also explain why he was esteemed as a founding member of the Church, an important bishop in the history of the hierarchy.) But it doesn't mean that every Christian in the third century A.D. shared his views or that he alone was responsible for the growth of the Church.[42] Other men like Martial and Basilides had now shown—to their friends, family, even to the local representatives of the emperor—that Christians could be just as Roman as everyone else. They were the ones building bridges.

Tragically, the second half of the third century and the first decade of the fourth did see the rise of a virulently aggressive period in Rome's relations with Jesus's followers. The first true attempt to hunt out and punish Christians for being Christians dates to this period (A.D. 253–60).[43] More punitive legislation, targeting "Christians," was about to enter the law codes, too.

During the reign of the emperor Diocletian (A.D. 303–12), Christians were forced to burn their books; their meeting spaces were confiscated and demolished. The legal rights of any Christian could also now be revoked if they were unwilling to take part in the civic festivals.[44] Most of Jesus's followers must have felt the personal and psychological sting of these laws, which specifically singled them out for attack. Some Christians saw them as confirmation of their irreconcilable spiritual war with the Roman Empire; what is astonishing is the fact that others saw it as a social struggle that could eventually be overcome. Valeria and Prisca were two such Christians.

Prisca was the emperor Diocletian's wife; Valeria was his daughter. Both were Christians, yet during the age of widespread Christian persecution, both honored Diocletian with sacrifice.[45] Were they closeted Christians, passing as something they were not? Not likely. To Valeria, the emperor was "Dad," and it is highly doubtful that she or her mother had been hiding their Christianity in a darkened corner of the imperial palace, surrounded as they were every day by a staff of nosy slaves and tutors, kitchen servants and bedroom attendants. When Diocletian asked the two women to sacrifice, they dutifully went through the motions. (Family dinners had probably become tense.)

Prisca and Valeria have not always been seen through such generous eyes. Our source for their story is Lactantius, a fourth century writer who understood his own Christian identity in ways that were radically different from theirs. Lactantius also understood his Christian history in ways that were radically different from those of earlier generations, as if somewhere between the first century A.D. and the fourth century, a thread of tradition had snapped.

In Paul's time, communities had spoken about Jesus's post-resurrection appearance to "Cephas and then, to the twelve." Lactantius believed there had been eleven apostles; the twelfth was added only after Jesus ascended to heaven. Lactantius also held a curious view of the emperor Nero. Nero, he claimed, was the first person who had ever "persecuted" Christians, even though we know that his xenophobia was to blame, not any "religious" motive.[46] These unique ways of understanding early Christian history colored Lactantius's vision of current events. "Diocletian compelled his wife and daughter to be polluted with a sacrifice!" he wrote.

From everything we now know about Roman sacrifice, we can say that Prisca and Valeria weren't compelled to do anything. Each of them could have opted for martyrdom if she'd wanted to. (Roman emperors didn't necessarily balk at the idea of executing a family member; Constantine himself would have his son murdered and may have planned the fire that killed his second wife.) Prisca and Valeria opted for sacrifice. Just like Basilides and Martial, both women may have weighed the pros and cons of committing such a public affront to the ruler of Rome—and decided that compliance was better in the long run. In the end, they went out of their way to act as Roman as possible, and Lactantius vilified them for it. Did this moment of compromise damage their Christian credentials, or did it benefit their cause?

When a Roman emperor could look up and see perfectly good Romans, who happened to be Christian, living in his own household, we should consider the possibility that Roman society had finally reached a tipping point. Laws and the legal status of "Christians" would have to change. And that's exactly what happened.

Within a decade, three emperors would try to put an end to Rome's untenable policies against Jesus's followers. The first attempt would be made in A.D. 311; it was quickly repealed. The next, in 313, would stick. The co-rulers of Rome at the time, Emperors Licinius and Constantine, decreed that the "Christians" would now receive full standing to worship without fearing legal reprisal. After such intense social conflict, this imperial "Edict of Milan," as it's often called, must have seemed like the only logical way to restore some sense of unity to the wider Roman world. A new chapter in Rome's history could begin (although the running debate over what it meant to be Roman and Christian would continue).

We will rejoin that drama later. Let us now meet a few more of Jesus's followers who, like Basilides, Martial, Valeria, and Prisca, lived on the margins of life in Rome but never quite felt hopelessly marginalized.

CHAPTER 3

The New Neighbors Who
Moved In Next Door

From Spain to Asia Minor to Jerusalem, by the third century A.D., Jesus's followers seem to be poking their heads up everywhere. It should be hard to miss them, but the fact of the matter is that we do. We can't find them—anywhere. Archaeologically speaking, it's as if they don't exist. They left us no depictions of the crucifix, the mark of so many Christians today, until the mid third century A.D. There are no indisputable scenes of Mary, the holy family, or even a simple nativity—star, sheep, shepherds—before the fourth century A.D.[1] During the most formative period of their group's history, Jesus's followers are entirely invisible. Why? Where is all their stuff?

The answer to these questions is not what we've usually been taught. Some believe that Jesus's followers were so lowly and downtrodden that none of them had the financial means to leave any sign of their faith on a ceramic cup or piece of cookware. Others believe they were so stricken with the theological fear of dabbling in graven images that they became artistically challenged.[2] Yet are there really no Christian statues or paintings or earrings or brooches because "Scripture"—which is to say, the second commandment of the Jewish Bible—resolutely forbade them to make such things? And did Jesus's followers really not have any access to wealth until the later empire? We need to go back to Jesus's time to consider what archaeology can (and cannot) tell us about this early age.

As it happens, while some of Jesus's followers were shouting about Rome as the whore of "Babylon," behaving in rather antisocial ways at Roman sacrifices, others were thoughtfully—and without any hint of drama—going on about their daily lives. If we excavate their stories carefully, we can even find many of them forging common ground with their non-Christian neighbors.

Paul is the first person to leave us any evidence for Jesus's followers. The letters he wrote to small, sometimes factionalized communities in Corinth, Thessaloniki, and Asia Minor were penned during the mid first century A.D. The earliest copy of them to survive, on papyrus, postdates his own life by two hundred years.[3] Today, they have been bound into a book and held to be divinely inspired. In the first century A.D., they arrived by mail, and not everyone was thrilled to get them.

Who was this pen pal to communities in Greece and Rome? Born and raised Jewish, in Tarsus, according to the writer of Acts (Acts 21:9), Paul is well known for being struck by God's voice, blinded by light, and thrown from his horse. The temperamental baroque master Caravaggio and countless other artists have seared this indelible moment of Paul's "conversion" into our cultural memory. Never mind that Paul neglected to mention any horse. It's the shock of the disruption, this forceful turning point in history—the time when Judaism and Christianity parted ways under their new leader to the gentiles, Paul—that has always been the most exciting part of the story. It makes for a nice painting, too, except that none of it happened that way.[4]

Paul set out on an uncertain journey. From Antioch and Jerusalem, where he worked as an itinerant preacher from the mid thirties to around A.D. 50, he would eventually follow a route along the west coast of Turkey across the Bosporus Strait. From there, along a major Roman highway, the Via Egnatia, he would begin another phase in his career: in Greece and around the Aegean Sea. By the year 50, he had arrived in Thessaloniki; by 51, Athens and Corinth. A few years later, he would make the three-day trip back to Asia Minor by boat, where he was imprisoned for a short time, before sailing for Rome. He is thought to have died in the capital, sometime around A.D. 60.[5] Paul's mission throughout this time was to spread Jesus's message "to the nations," that is, to the gentiles, non-Jews. He devoted nearly three decades of his life to it.

In hindsight, it can be difficult for us to see Paul on his own terms. Our rush to label him the first "Christian" is not historically helpful. Paul never identified as a "Christian," and he never used the word "Christianity" to describe what he was preaching. Indeed, he is a much more unfamiliar person than many would prefer him to be. Paul was a Jewish man who saw belief in Jesus's resurrection as an essential part of his Jewish identity and someone who understood his mission to "the nations," that is, the gentiles, as playing an equally important role in God's history.

Paul was not unique among his time in thinking of his identity in these terms. It is often said that under his leadership, "Christianity" and "Judaism" parted ways, like two roads diverging in the woods. There is no evidence that such a separation ever occurred this early, however, or that anyone involved in the Jesus movement during this phase (the Galatians, Romans, Corinthians, Thessalonians, or Paul) understood it in such a way. Jewish prophets—like Jeremiah and Isaiah, writers whose work Paul mentions—had long proclaimed a place for the gentiles in God's plan for salvation.[6] The history of the Jewish people themselves was a rich story of different, sometimes competing visions for what it meant to be Jewish. Paul, who believed that the resurrected Jesus was the Messiah, was taking up this call passionately, proselytizing about Jesus's resurrection by bringing it "to the nations" beyond Israel and Jerusalem. In doing so, he was also refashioning his own Jewish identity.

"You've no doubt heard about how I used to define being Jewish," Paul explained, candidly, to a gentile community in Galatia, in the central region of Asia Minor (Galatians 1:13). The Galatians were concerned about whether they had to be circumcised to be initiated into the group, just as Jews were circumcised. Paul's message was clear. Gentiles did not need to adopt this openly Jewish practice just to gain admittance. Paul himself was downplaying that aspect of his identity. What Paul hadn't given up, however, was his Jewish heritage and upbringing.

The people whom Paul met on the Aegean mission, largely non-Jewish, have even more intriguing stories. As it turns out, despite what Tertullian or Cyprian or Lactantius might have had us believe, the followers of Jesus we met in the last chapter weren't quite so unique after all in the daily compromises they made. There were people just like them in Paul's day, too. The messy residue of this early time, the decades following Jesus's death, still sticks to our fingers when we turn the pages of his letters.

One of Paul's letters allows us to see these people in their natural habitat: Corinth. Located on the isthmus between mainland Greece and the Peloponnesus, Corinth had been sacked by a Roman army in 146 B.C. A century later, during the age of Caesar, it became the site of a Roman colony. There, as in many towns throughout the Eastern Mediterranean, where Rome was on the rise, Romans and Greeks had come together in the late first century B.C. to forge a new, shared community. The idea was for everyone to benefit, in some way, from the expanding Roman peace.

For many citizens of Corinth, that meant finding ways to see and be seen at high-profile Roman events. The historic city center saw the construction of new Roman basilicas, where statues of the emperor were honored with a local cult (Roman basilicas were not "secular" spaces). Roman sacrifices were also a perfect occasion to participate in the new civic life of the city. After all, sacrifices were highly visible performances, usually, although not exclusively, enacted for the well-being of the local residents, for Rome, and for the Roman emperor.

Paul visited Corinth in the fifties and initiated one or two households into the Jesus movement. These groups would later identify themselves by the names of their patrons, such as Chloe and Stephanas (1 Corinthians 1:11; 1 Corinthians 16:17). Shortly afterward, Paul, the wandering preacher, would sail away, and Chloe's and Stephanas's groups would be left to their devices. What happened next? Initiates began to disagree about what it meant to be a member of the movement. We know because Chloe's people and Stephanas's people began to correspond with Paul.

Paul wrote three letters to the Corinthians, although only two survive, the latter two—inexplicably today called 1 and 2 Corinthians. What's important is not how many letters remain or what they're called. It's the evidence they contain. Like all of Paul's writings, his letters have been used to paint a quaint picture of a pure early church, a community of "real believers" whose humble lives were uncontaminated by the diseases of the "pagan" world and whose simple churches knew nothing of wealth and power.[7] A closer look at 1 Corinthians gives us a different picture.

Sources in Corinth have informed Paul that some members of the movement hadn't quite adopted Paul's preachings the way he had intended. Among Chloe's group and Stephanas's group, there were some, apparently, who saw no conflict between being an initiate and their ability to retain their high-profile roles as upstanding members of Corinth. Some were even taking part in local festivals and had been spotted attending banquets held during Roman sacrifices.[8]

We spy on these rule breakers today by peeking over Paul's shoulder as he picked up pen and papyrus. As Paul saw it, these men and women were reclining at "the table of demons."[9] Learning of their behavior through an informant and writing from Asia Minor, he drafted a letter telling them to cease and desist:

> If someone sees you, who have knowledge, reclining at a banquet
> in one of the sacred spaces dedicated to a statue [Paul calls it an
> idol] in a Greek or Roman sanctuary, won't the conscience of
> someone who is weak be emboldened to eat food that has been
> sacrificed to these idols, too?[10]

Reading this letter, one could think that the rules for what it meant to be Jesus's follower had always been crystal clear and that Paul was chastising the group for ignoring widely posted placards. Yet no such admonition against attending a Roman banquet had ever existed. Were the people of Corinth really breaking the rules? They were struggling to figure out their place in first century Corinth. Much later, of course, Paul's letter would be bundled together with others to form a collection called Scripture. For historians, it's better to put these words back in their lived context and imagine what it was like to find them when they arrived at the house.

When we do, we can see how life for Jesus's followers in Roman Corinth was a little more complicated than we have made it out to be. Followers of Jesus went to Roman sacrifices without any qualms about doing so—that is, until they checked their mail. This picture of the early group is not the one we usually take away from Paul's letters. We haven't even talked about the group's wealthier members.

In all of excavated Corinth, there are no traces of Jesus's followers. Where are Chloe's people and Stephanas's people? One explanation would go as follows: Jesus's followers never left any archaeological footprints behind because "the Bible" told them not to. Artistic images were "graven," and early Christians were too pious to transgress God's law. It's a comforting, Sunday-school idea, but it doesn't withstand historical scrutiny. To begin with, it shows a blithe disregard for Jewish history.

The first five books of the Hebrew Bible (the Pentateuch, or Torah: Genesis, Exodus, Leviticus, Numbers, and Deuteronomy) tell the foundational stories of the Jewish people, including the life of Moses. Moses, in one of the best-known episodes, leads the Jewish people out of Egypt. Camping in the Sinai Peninsula one night, he is called up to a nearby mountain where he receives a set of divine laws. These laws were "written [on tablets] with the finger of God" (Exodus 31:18, Deuteronomy 9:10).[11] They prohibited murder, stealing, adultery, lying, and taking the Lord's name in vain. They also promoted parental respect and apportioned the week so that one day of worship would be set aside to honor God. Above all, they asked the Jewish people to recognize no other god but God.

These precepts became guiding principles of Jewish custom. Hundreds more would be preserved alongside them. Some testify to the importance of Jewish charity (Deuteronomy 15:8). Others forbid tattoos (Leviticus 19:28). One asks that individuals put a mezuzah, or prayer scroll, on their doorpost (Deuteronomy 6:9). Another encourages the Jewish people to love their neighbors as they would love themselves (Leviticus 19:18). Together, these commandments set forth a shared vision for individual and communal behavior. Some are still devoutly followed to the letter; others, with a bit more creative negotiation.

The second commandment that was given to Moses deserves a careful look, for the injunction that the Jewish people "not make for [themselves] an idol" has often been understood as prohibiting the creation of all images (Deuteronomy 5:8), among both Jews and later Christians. In paintings, marble, limestone, glass, or any other medium, Jews, it was assumed, were barred from engaging in any creative endeavor that involved the making of images. Christians, who shared in Jesus's Jewish heritage, were believed to have inherited this same "anti-artistic" attitude. Hence, there are no identifiable Christian artifacts among those from Chloe's or Stephanas's communities in Corinth.

Archaeological discoveries of the past century have now helped us sweep aside this rather dusty view of Jewish culture. A site near Bethlehem, the Hellenistic city of Marisa, shows us why. Burial chambers in Marisa look just like elite Hellenistic tombs. The so-called Tomb of Philip in Vergina, Greece, for example, was colorfully painted with myths and landscape scenes. At Marisa, tombs were cut from the local bedrock in a similar style. In one, painted scenes of animals run along the tops of the walls. Many of these animals, including giraffes, were on display in a well-known zoo in Hellenistic Alexandria, in nearby Egypt.[12] The paintings at Marisa have been dated to the third through first centuries B.C. They reveal the extent to which Hellenistic art, as well as Hellenistic burial customs and Hellenistic culture, pervaded the eastern Mediterranean.

Jerusalem itself was not quarantined. Monumental tombs there tell a similar story. Many were decorated with pictures of anchors, ships, and shields. Several were built in popular architectural styles: with columns, capitals, and even Egyptian pyramid shapes. When it came to art and culture, the Jewish people were neither isolated from the common artistic language of their day nor were they allergic to it.[13] God's injunction to Moses—the second commandment of Jewish scripture—did not curb Jewish artistry. It cautioned Jews against worshipping their God in false ways. The second commandment encouraged Jews to be on the watch against idols, not images.[14] Archaeologists have pulled away the depressing pall that had been draped over aspects of Jewish life and culture.

With it, something else has come unmoored: an equally dim understanding of early Christians. For if the Jewish people had ample room for a vibrant artistic heritage, how did we ever come to believe that Christians harbored an innate artistic hostility of their own—especially if Jews who read and studied their own scriptural texts reached entirely opposite conclusions?[15] A fear of graven images doesn't explain why Jesus's followers are invisible in Corinth. To explain what was happening, we need to look elsewhere.

Perhaps Jesus's followers—Chloe's people, Stephanas's people—simply couldn't afford to leave anything behind? It's an ethically admirable assumption, that all of Jesus's followers were poor and disenfranchised, but it's not entirely accurate. Socioeconomic tensions were high among Jesus's followers in Corinth. Often, it was hard to get these people in the same room.

"When you come together [for your fellowship meal]," Paul says in 1 Corinthians, paraphrasing what he has heard from his local sources,

[I hear] it is not really to eat the Lord's supper. For when it comes time to eat, each of you goes ahead with your own meal and one goes hungry and another becomes drunk. Don't you have homes to eat and drink in? Or do you show contempt for the church of God and humiliate those who have nothing?[16]

Evidently, wealthier members of the group viewed this opportunity for fellowship, "the Lord's supper," as a regular Roman social event. They showed up to wine and dine, just as any Roman at a fancy dinner party would. And like any status-conscious Roman elite, they refused to associate with anyone who had been invited from Corinth's lower ranks. For the latter, who may really have counted among Corinth's destitute and poor, the meal was probably an important source of sustenance. The movement was supposed to act as a bridge between these groups, of course, but based on the evidence in Paul's letter, it appears that many of the more well-to-do couldn't quite "stomach" eating with people who were less well off.

These wealthier members can't be removed from the picture. Jesus's followers were dependent on them: Chloe in Corinth (1 Corinthians 1:11), Phoebe at Corinth's harbor city (Romans 16:1), Prisca and Aquilla (Romans 16:3–4), all of them hosted meetings in their homes.[17] These men and women need not have ranked among the richest 1 percent of their cities—a safe estimation would place them in the top quarter of the socioeconomic ladder—but the fact that they were able to offer rooms of their own for the group's needs does set them apart.[18] Not everyone associated with Jesus's movement belonged to a shiftless, penurious underclass.[19]

From the time of Jesus's death through the period of Paul, Jesus's followers, then, are invisible to us not because they lacked wealth but in spite of it. For who among their disparate group could risk standing up to rock the boat? All of them, especially the wealthier ones, chose what to reveal about themselves—to their friends, to their neighbors (and consequently, to us)—so as not to attract unwarranted suspicion about who they were. Not all of Jesus's followers were martyrs. Many of them lived in the closet, and that's why we can't find them.

For pilgrims living in a foreign land, as one anonymous Christian characterized this shaky, in-between existence, all hope for a normal daily existence was not lost. There were strategies for day-to-day survival. These "sojourners," as our canonical writer calls them (1 Peter 2:11), had to learn how to cultivate their street smarts.[20] Followers of Jesus had to find creative ways to integrate themselves into society, playing up the qualities they shared with their Roman peers, playing down the qualities that set them apart.

By the mid to late first century A.D., in fact, several strategies did begin to emerge, as we saw in the previous chapter. Christian women, slaves, and children were expected to obey the heads of their household, the Roman paterfamilias; and all households—slaves and masters—were expected to honor the imperial family. A large number of Jesus's followers took up this mission with vigor. They made the conscious decision to "tone down" their Christianity when in public. These were highly individual responses to difficult situations, and not everyone within the group agreed on the effectiveness, or the usefulness, of these strategies. By the late first century A.D., John of Patmos, the writer of the text known as Revelation, had launched a scorching, vituperative attack on the compromised morals of these "code-switching" Christians.

To John, Rome had been and always would be the whore of "Babylon" (Revelation 17–18), the harlot whose messy, cosmopolitan cities and thoroughly godless culture were a plague to Jesus's followers everywhere. To John, being Christian wasn't a matter of engaging in conversation or respecting Rome or even searching for common social ground. Christians were not "sojourners" in the Roman Empire; they were enlisted soldiers, waging a war inside the empire with truly cosmic dimensions.

According to John, the war had begun long ago. A powerful angel, Michael, had faced the "great dragon, the ancient serpent who is called the Devil and Satan, the deceiver of the whole known world" (Revelation 12:9). Michael had driven the snake deep into the ground, but it was forever threatening to return. John had seen it chasing after an unnamed woman and child. Now, it was even hunting down her children, the men and women "who kept the commandments of God, the ones who held to the testimony of Jesus" (Revelation 12:17). They were the "holy men and women, or saints," John calls them (Revelation 14:12). Everyone else— including followers of Jesus who found themselves on the wrong side of John's rhetoric—was pitching their tent with Satan.[21]

Based on disaffected voices like John's, it makes sense that we've seen early Christians as incapable of living in the world around them. John's

Revelation is a potent cocktail, garnished with menacing dragons and prickly rhetoric. Heavenly visions inspire the main character, the seer makes urgent pronouncements about the coming end-time, and battles between angels and demons provide the "supernatural backdrop" to current events.[22] As historians, what do we do with these strange, other-worldly motifs? One option is to ignore them, dismissing them as an embarrassment to rational thought. Others have proposed a more nuanced approach: that we appreciate how each person's palate for them will always differ. Some Christians who drank this potion may have learned to see Rome in less than flattering terms; they may even have been taught to think of themselves as soldiers in this cosmic drama. Others may have comforted themselves with John's poetic imagery, for highly imaginative tales like these can sometimes work like a soothing drug, offering hope for the future and a relief from present alienation. The message? One day things will get better.[23]

This world view is not unique to John's book of Revelation. Scholars have detected its traces in many other pieces of literature, many of which pre-date Christianity. These are some of its key signs: Writers dwell on a looming end-time, and there is usually the prospect of a cosmic catastrophe. History itself is conceived of as unfolding in discrete, clearly definable periods. The world is populated by angels and demons and is also assumed to be longing for God's salvation. There is a special need for God's kingdom to be made manifest, usually in the form of a king or leader who will come to tip the scales of the current "struggle" in favor of the righteous ones; and a final glorious victory awaits.[24] These eight characteristics, which were articulated by biblical scholar John J. Collins in a masterful study of scriptural and non-scriptural texts, help us talk about some of antiquity's most curious literary creations, like John's Revelation. All of them are signs of a writer's *apocalyptic world view*. We will stumble upon other manifestations of it shortly.

How did such an odd way of thinking about the world ever take root in the Roman world? For starters, it was highly adaptable. In the hands of one skilled writer, these ideas could give birth to inspiring supernatural visions, divorced from reality, a kind of writing scholars call "otherworldly apocalypses." In the hands of another, who looked to current events or recent history as his subject matter, they gave rise to a form of scathing political commentary. In these texts, writers "predicted" events that had already happened, and they used their prophetic "skills" to talk about the passing of one historical age and the prospect of better times ahead. Polarizing images, like dragons and beasts, were often meant to be taken as allusions to the audience's present day or the recent past. Scholars call these texts "historical apocalypses."[25]

John's vision of a woman seated on a beast that had seven heads fits the model of a historical apocalypse (Revelation 17:1–18). The beast, said John, had been labeled with a sign that read "Babylon the great, mother of whores, and of earth's abominations." Who was this woman? The beast's seven heads were meant to symbolize seven hills and seven kings, John told his readers (with a wink). Rome had been built on seven hills, and it had once been ruled by seven kings. John was comparing Rome to Babylon, the site where Jews had lived in captivity during the sixth century B.C.

Of course, when historical writings are removed from their historical setting, they can quickly take on a life of their own, transformed into vague, sensationalized predictions of impending doom. In this way, John's monsters and his vision of spiritual war—as well as his other frightening motifs, like the return of the emperor Nero (Revelation 13:3)—would roar back to life well beyond the time when he wrote them down. Many later Christians would come to believe they were carrying on this same battle.

While John was fulminating, Jesus's other followers were going about their daily routines. John of Patmos may have viewed their behavior as morally suspicious, but we know that many Christians were finding ways to do two things at once. One Christian, living in the second century A.D., explained it to his friend this way:

> People who call themselves "Christians" aren't any different from anyone else, either in where they come from or the language they speak or in their way of life. They don't separate themselves by living in their own cities; they don't talk some strange language; and they don't have an overly distinct way of life.[26]

Clearly, some Christians were committed to fitting in, but how did their talk play out in practice? Many of Jesus's followers navigated the ups and downs of the Roman world in two ways. Some passed as non-Christians, living their public lives in the closet. Others covered their Christianity, which is to say, they made choices to appear less threatening to their friends "in the know."[27] These Christians may have decorated their homes with lamps showing Jupiter, king of the gods, or they may have worn brooches with the emperor's image. These two strategies, *passing* and *covering*, which involved the delicate task of determining how much to reveal to their family and friends, helped Christians create a space for themselves. It seems to have worked. By the third century A.D., for example, several Christians were serving in the Roman army without complication.

In A.D. 212, some Christian soldiers, along with their non-Christian peers, were honored for their outstanding service. As a token of appreciation, the emperor bestowed on them a public honor, laurel crowns.[28] Some of the Christian soldiers accepted their recognition proudly and honorably. Today, we would know very little about their existence were it not for the radical decision of one of their peers—and for Tertullian, who got a hold of their "scandalous" story. Exactly one anonymous Christian soldier among the regiment felt he could not wear this crown. For him, laurel leaves were incompatible with his Christian identity. Waging war on the empire's behalf was one thing. The leaves of the laurel, which many Romans used to drape around statues of gods like Apollo, Jupiter, or Hercules, crossed the line. The soldier who voiced these opinions was soon arrested and imprisoned. His Christian army buddies must have looked at him with bewilderment, bemusement, and maybe even fear. They were either passing as non-Christians, which is to say, hiding in plain sight of their Roman peers, or they were wearing their crowns as cover, that is, blending in among a regiment of Romans who knew full well that they were Christians.

Tertullian, after he learned about their ability to do two things at once, expressed dissatisfaction. So much Christian compromising made him wonder whether it was proper for any Christian ever again to serve in the Roman army. For if Christians continued to enlist, he mused:

> So many details about one's military duty and Christian identity would have to be argued about at every turn just to be sure that nothing would be done against God while serving in the army which is also prohibited by God while outside the service. That or . . . the decision to be a soldier—including all the potential risks of exposure that came with it—would have to be endured on God's behalf, in the same way that the faith of a civilian

demanded [in Latin, the phrase is *fides pagana*]. For soldiers, like civilians, are not immune from criminal prosecution. And they are not granted immunity from having to be martyrs. A Christian can never be anything else than a Christian.[29]

For Tertullian, as for John of Patmos, being a Christian meant one and one thing only: standing up, putting oneself on the line, and coming out as proudly and as openly as possible, just like the soldier who refused the crown. Never mind that ever since the Roman centurion Cornelius had been called (Acts 10:1–33), many followers of Jesus had found a way to reconcile their beliefs and their military service. In Tertullian's mind, there was little room for these moments of conscience. No Christian was immune from martyrdom—solider or civilian. It was simply not possible for a follower of Jesus to do two, or be two, things at once. "No man can serve two masters," Tertullian taunted. Many Christians tuned him out.

Tertullian's vocabulary would prove long-lasting, though. The Latin word for a civilian—the English reader's eye will be drawn to its oddly familiar form—is *paganus*. I pause here to draw attention to it so that inquisitive readers can pick it up, like a clue. For words and their meanings can often change depending on who uses them and when. So it will be for this word, whose English cognate, "pagan," will come crashing into history during the fourth century A.D. like a rock thrown through glass. The entire Roman world of "pagans and Christians" that we have been taught about in our history books will be born from this one passage, but it is not the world we think we know. The internal dynamics of a group are always much messier than they seem from the outside.

While the soldiers of Tertullian's day were using laurel crowns to show how they could be Roman and Christian at the same time, other Christians throughout the empire were doing the same. That is to say, they were also forging a shared Christian identity by investing objects, signs, and symbols with a special meaning, for themselves.

By the late second century A.D., Clement, who lived in Alexandria, Egypt, had begun to brainstorm the sorts of designs he deemed acceptable for Christian rings or seals. Doves and fish and anchors were approved; so was the lyre. At first glance, this musical instrument may seem an odd design to associate with Christianity, but it may not have been so opaque in Clement's time. Clement tells us that it appeared on the ring of a famous sixth century B.C. Greek ruler, Polycrates.[30] Polycrates had been asked to forfeit the one thing he treasured most and to throw it into the sea; he chose his ring. Symbol of his authority, it was decorated with the image of a lyre-playing poet. About a week later, fishermen who were gutting their catch found it in a fish's belly and returned it. The king was suddenly stricken with terror; for he knew that anyone who enjoyed such fortune was bound to have his luck run out, sooner or later.[31]

Why did Clement like this story? Maybe it reminded him of Jonah, the man swallowed by a whale and spat out of its belly. Perhaps it sounded like the time when Jesus predicted the discovery of a coin in a fish's mouth. In that vignette, Peter asked Jesus whether they should pay the Jewish Temple tax. Jesus urged tax compliance; and then, with skillful showmanship, told Peter to cast a line and cut open his first catch. Et voilà, inside was a coin whose value matched the payment. Both these stories may have resonated with Clement and led him to appreciate the tale of Polycrates's ring. Then again, perhaps any image that told the tale of a ruler who voluntarily threw away his kingdom would have proved appealing.

Clement was eager for Christians of the late second century A.D. to renounce the finer things in life, and his writings invite us into a social space where many Christians of Alexandria were not entirely receptive to his message.[32] All around him were men and women who, "with an immoderate tongue," dared to apply the name of *agapē* (the name of the Christian fellowship meal) to "certain suppers redolent of fatty meat and fine sauces." This meat likely came from the city's sacrificial offerings, but where these Christians acquired it was the least of Clement's worries.

Many of the men and women he had his eyes on were dining in homes where extravagant plates of gold and silver were used at dinner and where a shared fellowship meal might lead to a memorable Roman night. In Clement's eye, these Christians were "insulting the meaning of the [Lord's] meal—with all their side dishes and fancy condiments, slandering its name, agapē, with all their drinks and luxury and signs of triviality."[33] A century and a half after Paul, few of the socioeconomic tensions within the movement had been resolved. There were still quite distinct ways of expressing one's Christian identity. Within a half century, however, this picture would begin to change.

*   *   *

Clement was not alone in wanting his community to build a common identity out of everyday objects. Many writers, as early as the second century A.D., recognized the sign of Jesus's death, a cross, in the mast of a ship.[34] It was not exactly a choice that was divinely inspired. Shipping and seafaring were the ubiquitous signs of trade, and new research is revealing just how interconnected Clement's world was.

Underwater archaeologists have now excavated shipwrecks, many of them far from the Mediterranean coast. These ships have often been found with their cargo intact: olive oil, salted fish sauce, and ceramics. The study of these remains, where they came from, and where they were headed has led to a fundamental reevaluation of the ancient economy. Risk taking and long-distance trade were much more prevalent than scholars used to assume.

Many captains, we now know, were not afraid of finding the shortest distance between two harbors. Fortified with the instrumentation for open sailing, they had the moxie to want to deliver their wares as quickly as possible. Receipts have been found in Egypt that record the days and months on which goods arrived or left, and many confirm that trade took place from November to March, the window of so-called unseasonable travel.[35] Year-round, merchants in harbor towns—from Ostia in Italy to Ephesos in Turkey—profited by participating in this network. These men and women were not in the ranks of the senatorial elite, but their labor attests to a vibrant "middle class."[36] Shipping was integral to their way of life, and it makes sense that many people, Christians and non-Christians alike, looked at their lives through the prism of the Mediterranean Sea. A mosaic from the floor of a third century A.D. house in Tunisia shows us how central it was (figure 3). The mosaic depicts one of the most popular seafaring tales of antiquity, the *Odyssey*.

In this scene, Odysseus sails with his crew past the island of the Sirens, mythical females whose enchanting songs invited sailors to their destruction. Odysseus is forewarned of the danger. Unwilling to forgo such a performance, he orders his crew to tie him to the mast. On the mosaic, Odysseus's arms are tied behind him, his feet are bound to the mast, and the hero and his crew sail safely by the Sirens. Odysseus looks as if he's been tied to a cross.[37] Could it actually be a copy of a lost Christian scene? No. There were no scenes of the crucifixion to copy—at least not in the Roman mainstream, not in the third century A.D.

To find the first depictions of Jesus's crucifixion, we have to leave the comforts of an expensive home in Roman Tunisia. In fact, we have to take a trip down a few of the seedier streets and alleyways of the Roman world. That's where we dig up some really interesting information about Jesus's followers.

Today, the crucifix is perhaps the one indisputable symbol of Christianity. The first two images to make an explicit reference to Jesus's execution in antiquity, however, appear two centuries after his death. One of these crucifixes comes to us on a gem with spells and incantations. The other has been scratched on a plaster wall. It may be natural for us to think the crucified Jesus was the unmistakable sign of his followers, but archaeology suggests caution.[38]

Crucifixion was a gruesome form of capital punishment. It took place along urban and suburban roads, and it gave authorities an opportunity to assert their power over mischievous, lowlife criminals. Romans who walked by them were taught to see the victims as the dregs of society. Victims themselves were pierced through their wrists and the sides of their ankles so that their flesh wouldn't slide off the wooden beam as they died. It must have been horrendous to see and a powerful deterrent. To be caught lingering near an execution risked being deemed guilty by association.

Making an image of the crucifixion brought similar risks. A general reluctance to be associated with the stigma of capital punishment may even explain why two of the earliest illustrations of Jesus's death come to us from outside mainstream society. One of these is a scene from Rome (figure 4). It shows a man with a donkey's head nailed to a cross. To the left of the victim is a second man, praying. A terse caption, scrawled in Greek, identifies the worshipper as "Alexamenos." Here is Alexamenos, the anonymous graffiti writer taunts, "worshipping his god."[39] The writer was using a sharp tool and sharper tongue to ridicule Alexamenos's devotion to this crucified, donkey-headed man. It has been dated to the early third century A.D.

By the third century, many Romans had heard rumors about Jesus's crucifixion. Roman historians writing a century earlier, Suetonius and Tacitus, had known about the troublesome events in Judaea during which Jesus was executed. Two centuries later, rumors had also begun to circulate that Christians worshipped the head of a donkey. "Public opinion, which is always right, would not be speaking such unmention-able things about Christians unless there were some truth to them," a Roman named Caecilius says, in a third century dialogue.⁴⁰ Where was such baseless gossip coming from?

As with any ill-informed speculation, the circumstances that led to the idea of Christian "donkey worship" are not easy to recover. Two centuries before the graffiti writer immortalized Alexamenos that way, however, one other minority group had fallen under similar suspicion. According to one report from the first century A.D., "Jews had erected the head of an ass" in the Jewish Temple in Jerusalem and "they worshipped it and deemed it worthy of great reverence."⁴¹ Third century Christians were being smeared with the same charge that had been hurled against first century Jews. What does that tell us? Three hundred years after Jesus's death, many Romans were still confused—maybe even willfully confused—about what distinguished a Christian from a Jew.⁴² From the outside, who could possibly tell the difference?

Around the time that Alexamenos found his Christianity under public assault, another artist was presenting a slightly different image of the crucified Jesus. This second artifact is roughly contemporary with the donkey-head graffito and is thought to have come from Roman Syria. A mottled green and red jasper gem, it depicts a crucified figure stripped of all his flesh, splayed on a cross like a skull-headed skeleton. The person responsible for the text has labeled him as "son, father, Jesus Christ." It is not exactly the most pious representation of Jesus's death.⁴³ Indeed, the writing on the reverse of the gem is a list of names. It is an extended prayer: to Badetophoth, the great Satrap Kmeph, and to Emmanuel.

No Roman would have dared utter the names of these deities at a civic event or festival for the imperial family. These are figures who have been conjured up from an underground world of hexes, curses, and spells. People who invoked these names and practices were trying to shift the balance of power in the universe. Their goal was to harness these forces against their enemies, like a business rival or a lover. A lead curse tablet from Rome, to be pierced with a nail during the climactic moment of hexing, provides a disturbing, if amusing, example of the retribution one hoped to achieve by practicing these dark arts. "[F]rom this hour, from this day, from this night," it reads, trample, crush, smash and consign to death Praeseticius, the bakery owner, son of Aselle, who lives in region nine of the city, where he can be seen going about his work. And hand him over to Pluto, lord of the dead. But if he snubs you, make sure that he suffer fevers, cold, and torments, so that the blood drains from his face and he break out in sweats, at midday, throughout the day, later in the day, and at night, from this hour, from this day.[44]

The curse continues in this vein, praying that the poor bakery owner be suffocated "in the public baths, in a private bath, wherever." The man or woman who paid for this hex was resentful and desperate. The archaeological record is filled with examples of curses like this one.

The authorities didn't look kindly on this behavior. Magic—ancient sources call it just that—could terrorize unsuspecting Romans, leaving people little or no means of protecting themselves. According to one late Roman writer, for example, some innkeepers in Italy were suspected of bewitching their guests with magic cheese, turning them into donkeys.[45] How were people supposed to protect themselves against this sort of witchcraft when all it took was the sip of a warm drink or a nibble from an appetizer with a hex on it to turn a weary traveler into a pack animal? Decent members of Roman society shouldn't have to abide magicians trying to transform people into animals against their will.[46] Magic threatened everyone's access to a fair deal, and so it was banned.

The magician who carved Jesus into an amulet shows us two Roman subcultures overlapping: the followers of Jesus and the practitioners of magic (figure 5). The magician himself must have heard something compelling about the power of a crucified Christ. Jesus's power was so strong, so similar to that of the great Badetophoth and Satrap Kmeph, that the names of all three figures could be put onto a single spell. It took quite a spark of inspiration to create this curious object. Two hundred years later, in the early fifth century A.D., Christians would appropriate it—transforming the crucifixion into a source of pride—just as their ancestors had done when they appropriated the slur of their name.

For Christians in one part of the empire, however, life was quickly changing by the mid third century. Archaeologists have helped us detect it. In the city of Dura Europos, located on the far eastern border of Syria, scholars working in the 1930s unearthed the earliest Christian building. The structure, which predates the legalization of Christianity by a half century, is an amazing discovery. Well before any of them had won their legal right to worship, some Christians had started to leave their mark on the world around them.

Dura Europos sits on the Euphrates River. One look at a map can make it seem perched on the edge of the empire. In some ways, it was. The Sasanian Empire, a dynasty of Persian rulers founded in A.D. 224, lay just across the river, through the marsh and beyond the lions. By A.D. 256, Sasanians had crossed the water, overcome the Roman army garrisoned there, and sacked the city.[47]

To see the Euphrates as a watery boundary between two empires is to miss its role as connector. A network of roads through the desert facilitated the transport of goods, as well as the movement of people and ideas, before Romans arrived. A gate in the city's western wall led to the merchant city of Palmyra on the way to Damascus or to points south, like Jerusalem. Travelers and traders arriving from the west would have spied Dura's walls as the welcome sign of a journey's end; and the Euphrates, like most waterways in the ancient world, was a vital conduit between north and south.

Dura Europos even included a Jewish and Christian population. Both communities lived down the street from each other. Today, scholars refer to this street as "Wall Street" because it originally lay along the inner circuit of the city's western walls. The wall's history is important. Here, in A.D. 256, Sasanian raiders attacked the city, and Dura's citizens and soldiers solidified their defenses. On the exterior of the city wall, they applied mud brick to protect it from battering rams. Along its inner face, they added a huge mound so that they could attack the Sasanians from above. In so doing, the people of Dura sealed their past and left us an important record that the sand and sun might have wiped out. For when Wall Street was excavated, archaeologists discovered the remains of a third century synagogue and a third century Christian meeting space beneath the earthen rampart. The latter is the earliest example of Christian architecture ever found.

Archaeologists have been able to reconstruct its history by studying a sequence of repairs and renovations.[48] In its first phase, around A.D. 232/233, the main floor of the building functioned as a house. It had a front door, a small foyer inside, and several rooms surrounding a courtyard. Stairs led to a second story. Many homes throughout Dura Europos follow this same layout.[49] There's nothing identifiably Christian about it, either. About a decade later, however, sometime around A.D. 241, the owner of the house undertook a series of renovations. At this time, the first-floor rooms were remodeled to create a more open floor plan (figure 6). In the house's southwestern corner, a wall that once divided two small rooms was knocked down to create a long narrow one. Here, a small platform was installed—to elevate a speaker or a reader above the din of the crowded hall. Inside the northwest part of the house, a basin was installed up against the wall of a narrow room with steps leading up into it for baptism. The scenes painted on the walls around the basin confirm that it was used in this way. Veiled women are seen processing toward the basin. Each carries a torch, used in ancient marriage ceremonies; and many early Christian traditions saw marriage as a cipher for baptism. It expressed the initiate's spiritual union with Christ, the Messiah.[50]

The area around the basin was also painted (figure 7). It depicts Adam and Eve in the Garden of Eden, as well as an image of man carrying a sheep or a ram on his shoulders. Although commonly interpreted as the "Good Shepherd," based on a passage in John's gospel (John 10:11–18), the same image is the subject of a Hebrew prayer that begins, "The Lord is my shepherd" (Psalm 23). In the repertoire of Greek art, this same image had also been popular since the sixth century B.C. The shepherd who tends his flock personified the quality of *philanthrōpia*, a ruler's love for humankind. One Greek writer, in the early second century A.D., praised the deeds of good rulers by evoking the image of a good shepherd. The image embodied the way a noble ruler "looks out for the health and well-being of those he leads."[51] Christians at Dura were representing ideas that other people valued, too.

The Dura Europos house is an extraordinary step for a group eager to come out of the shadows. Demolished walls and repurposed rooms may seem the natural "stuff" of our home improvement projects today, but as anyone who has undertaken something similar knows, remodeling takes time. Most important of all, it takes money. Christians here had found a homeowner wealthy enough and willing enough to provide a larger space for their meetings. The community was not only reaching outward to attract other members; they were also reaching upward to find people who could give them the space they needed.[52] Their conversations may have irked others within the group, but by the mid third century, some of Jesus's followers felt comfortable enough in their own neighborhoods and in their own living rooms that they felt they could risk making a little more noise. So they did. In Dura Europos, they renovated their home.

CHAPTER 4

A Safe Space—for Being Jewish

Just like Christians at Dura Europos, many communities won small victories without having to depend upon converting everyone to their side. The life of Marcus, son of Dama, born in Jerash in modern Jordan, can speak to the experiences of so many overlooked men and women who fought battles for acceptance every day in Rome. Marcus was a Syrian by birth who served in the Roman navy. He was stationed at Misenum, on the north shore of the Bay of Naples, one of two pre-eminent naval bases in ancient Italy—Ravenna, on the west coast, was the other. In A.D. 71, on account of a lifetime of service, the emperor Vespasian awarded him an honorable discharge. This decree was etched on a folded bronze plaque, the size of an iPad today, but it did more than vouch for Marcus' twenty-five years of service. It granted him Roman citizenship. That was something no one could put a price on.

Romans called this certificate a *diploma*, borrowing the word (meaning "folded") from the Greeks, and Dama's accomplishment was such a milestone that a copy of it was displayed outside the highest temple in Rome: the Temple of Jupiter the Best and Greatest (Jupiter Optimus Maximus) on the city's Capitoline Hill—where Edward Gibbon would go one day to wax nostalgic about the ruin of the empire. By Gibbon's day, that bronze monument was long gone, but in Dama's, it was a major presence. Dama's diploma, like many soldiers', was inscribed with a reference number, specifying the exact "tablet, column, and the row" where he could find his name etched in bronze, if he ever made a march up to the Capitol.[1] Climbing the hill in search of it—or in search of the name of a family member who had served in the past—must have been a point of pride for first-, second-, and third-generation Romans, who held their diplomas dear. It spoke to the process by which they had become more fully recognized members of society.

Diploma in hand, men like Marcus could then live out their days on their own terms. In an act of generosity, the emperor, we know, had even settled him and his naval comrades in the Italian town of Paestum. Some of his fellow enlistees left as soon as they were discharged. Some went home: to the Danube, to the Balkans. Others stayed and found work. Marcus was one of them. We know because archaeologists working in the nineteenth century found his diploma in the ruins of Pompeii, where he lost both it and his life in the natural disaster of A.D. 79.[2]

Whatever drew Marcus to the city that day or that year, we cannot say. What is clear is that he treated his diploma as something more than a sheet of bronze. Yes, it was something that had his name, a date, and his birthplace in Jordan. We read it for those details because, lacking any newspaper accounts about daily life in Rome, it satisfies our hunger for Rome's human interest stories. To Marcus, who knew full well what was scratched on its surface—it was his life, they were his memories, he had lived them, after all—the tablet was more akin to a badge of pride and security. It was something he kept close. A former soldier, he was also a man of foreign birth, living in a land where he might easily be profiled as a runaway slave. As archaeologist Steven Ellis sees it, Marcus' diploma might have helped him land a job or simply given him peace of mind while he traveled.

"Rome" may still be personified by the marble busts of senators like Cicero, upon whose every word Latin students hang today. But for every Marcus Tullius Cicero there was a Marcus son of Dama who hailed from a far different region of the Mediterranean. Both of these men were "Roman," but the diploma reminds us that many people—not just Jesus's followers—saw themselves as sojourners in the empire. And no one wants to feel like a stranger in their own home.

In that respect, Marcus was not alone. Another group took pride in their own bronze monument outside the Capitoline Temple of Jupiter. They were residents of Sardis (modern Sart), about sixty miles inland on the central west coast of Turkey, and they were a community of Jews. How had Jews living in Turkey come to win such a highly visible place in a Roman city? Had they converted everyone else to their Jewish faith?

The story of the Jewish experience in the Roman world is not usually told as one of political triumph. To understand why, we need to begin in Jerusalem. A city millennia old, Jerusalem today is less than an hour's drive from the coast. Driving that hill-country landscape has always been, for me, like making a mental journey into the past. The city is perched 2,600 feet (800 meters) above sea level. On the drive, the air can become cooler, if only for a moment, just as the limestone walls of the Old City come into view around a bend in the hills. Just then, depending on the time of day, the sun may even alight on the panels of a gilded dome, the Muslim holy shrine known as the Dome of the Rock, perched in the distance atop something like an urban tabletop, or plateau. Here is where the Jewish Temple once stood, before it was demolished by a Roman army, in A.D. 70 (figure 8).[3] In the nearly two thousand years since its destruction, that temple has never been rebuilt.

Capital city and contested space, a place of cooperation and a landscape riddled with the politics of all periods of history, Jerusalem can easily become an imagined place, as it does for those who live there as well as those who have never seen it. Advertisements and artifacts, organized tours and museums seduce those who are interested in its epic stories, or at least chapters of them. From visions of Jesus's death on the modern Via Dolorosa to tales of siege and defense, pulled from the Crusades, faith history has long shaped Christian and Muslim perceptions of the city.[4] Some of these accounts are more accurate than others. Beneath these accumulated traditions, however, are also the stories of the Jewish people who lived and worshipped here well before any tourist or Crusader arrived. This Jerusalem is not so easily visited, but what we find when we walk its streets is a rich, vibrant tradition that resists easy labels and descriptions—even in antiquity, even during times of crisis.

The period from A.D. 66 to 74 represents one of these moments of crisis. For that was when a Roman army erased the Second Temple from the landscape of Jerusalem.

No faith community can be socially, culturally, or even psychologically prepared for the decimation of its holiest site. By A.D. 70, the Jewish community had already suffered this trauma once. The names and dates of that earlier time, when the First Temple was destroyed, may seem to creep upon us like a fog—threatening to cloud our story in a flashback—but the past hides a crucial turning point.

In 586 B.C., an army led by King Nebuchadnezzar II of Babylon invaded Jerusalem and destroyed the Jewish Temple, capturing the Jewish people and forcing Jews to live as exiles in the Babylonian empire. During this time the temple and its platform would remain in disrepair, and they would continue to do so until the winds of political change blew through Babylon. Fifty years later, in 538 B.C., the ruler of the neighboring Persians conquered the king, freeing the Jews and allowing them to return home. Work on a Second Temple commenced thereafter, as did the production of stories to celebrate the return of Jewish life in the homeland. One writer would even hail the Persian liberator, Cyrus, as an "anointed one," or messiah, because he had freed the Jewish people from captivity (Isaiah 45:1).

In the centuries that followed, as work on the Second Temple proceeded—an effort that lasted from the end of the sixth century B.C. to the first century A.D.—other noises began to echo in the landscape around Jerusalem. The sound was quiet and muted at first; even as it traveled in the hills and the valleys, it must have been hard to hear over the din of construction. Later, it must have seemed like someone knocking at the door, and it wasn't going away, either. It was growing louder. It was the sound that accompanies the rumblings of a young empire.

People of the Mediterranean world had begun trading objects and ideas on a scale never seen before in antiquity. Since at least the eighth century B.C., Al Mina in Lebanon had functioned as one of the first Mediterranean trading posts, for Greeks and people of the Levant. Four hundred years later, that engine of cultural exchange was still chugging along when a twenty-two-year-old boy from Macedonia stood poised to give it an explosive jolt.[5] Over a period of a decade and a half, before his death in 323 B.C., Alexander would march from Macedonia to Persia to the area of modern Pakistan and India. Traces of his world emerge from the sand and dirt at almost every point where he and his army camped—from parts of jugs that once held wine made on Rhodes to fashionable dinnerware, the sort used in mainland Greece, that also shows up in buried settlements of Afghanistan.[6]

Archaeologists have excavated the remains of one settlement that dates to this time in the mountainous plains of northern Afghanistan, ancient Bactria. There, at the city of Ai Khanoum, Greek settlers built a palace for their ruler, a Greek theater where the plays of Sophocles were performed, and a bath complex where men would have exercised nude, according to long-established traditions associated with the Greek gymnasium. Acanthus leaves of the Corinthian order were part of the architectural vocabulary of the town, and Greek gods like Hercules, whose presence was discovered in the form of bronze statuettes, once protected the city and its people.[7]

Alexander did not stage-manage the march toward the Hellenistic world alone. The general and his successors played an important role in spreading Greek culture, but there were other people: colonists, for one, but also many locals who recognized new economic or social opportunities and found ways to take part in them.[8] By the time Alexander died, in 323 B.C., the roots of a shared world view were already taking root in the places he had conquered: Egypt, Asia Minor, even in the landmass between them. Alexander's successors—the Seleucid family in Asia Minor, the Ptolemy family in Egypt—were commissioned to live out his legacy.

Unfortunately, Alexander's memory was not strong enough to keep these two family dynasties, the Seleucids and the Ptolemies, united. In the third and second centuries B.C., each began to compete for a controlling interest in the regions where their influence overlapped. The territory of Coele-Syria, which occupies part of the land bridge between Asia Minor and Egypt—the place where Israel, the Palestinian territories, Lebanon, and Syria appear on the map today—became the epicenter of their struggle for Mediterranean supremacy.

For the people of Jerusalem, laboring along in their effort to rebuild the Second Jewish Temple, geopolitical change was the sound they heard rumbling outside their door. The world of Alexander, his successor, and everything they represented—Greek religious customs, like annual festivals for Hercules; Greek culture, like plays and performances; even increased trade between Persia, the Levant, and the Mediterranean, which slipped into daily life in the form of new dinnerware, kitchenware, and coins—was now showing up on their doorstep. The world of Hellenistic politics, culture, and foreign affairs was about to spill over into their backyard.

How does one draw a line around the scene of a spill? It's an unenviable task, trying to mop it up. Boundaries—religious boundaries, political boundaries, even spatial boundaries—are hard to find when people trade cultures and ideas so fluidly.[9]

According to one version of the events, here's what happened. In 169 B.C., the current heir of the Seleucid line, King Antiochus IV, lit a fuse. In Jerusalem the king began an aggressive campaign to annul Jewish law and tradition by forcibly transforming the city into a Hellenistic settlement. Jews, he decreed, would no longer be able to live by customs of their ancestors. Circumcision was outlawed. Like Greeks, Jews would now be forced to make sacrifices of animals they considered unclean, such as pigs. On the king's birthday, in 167 B.C., one of these unclean sacrifices took place at the site of the Second Temple, perhaps led by Antiochus IV himself. It was an ultimate act of Jewish sacrilege, a "desolating sacrilege," one Jewish writer called it.[10] Others rallied to resist. Mattathias led the charge.

Onetime priest of the Temple, father of sons known as the Maccabees, Mattathias had witnessed many Jews begin to offer sacrifices at the Temple, but when the king asked him, he refused—and spoke up. We hear his lament in the text known as 1 Maccabees:

> Alas, why was I born to see this,
> the ruin of my people, the ruin
>   of the holy city,
> and to live there when it was
>   given over to the enemy,
> the sanctuary given over to aliens?[11]

Mattathias's emotional words would prove a passionate rallying cry. Soon, he and his sons began a struggle to expel the Hellenistic rulers from the homeland. In 164 B.C., they triumphed. A new, undefiled altar would be erected at the Second Temple. On the twenty-fifth day of the Jewish month of Chislev, December 14, 164 B.C., the dedication of this new altar was celebrated with a festival lasting eight days. Jews had fought on both sides of this conflict—a detail of the spill we will return to a moment—but Mattathias's profound distress had been quelled and redeemed. Many mention him by name when they pray during the Jewish festival that commemorates the Maccabean victory: Hanukkah.[12]

Can verifiable history be wrung out of one text so neatly? If we go back to the scene and try to soak it up from a different angle, with the help of a second source, we find some continuities in the two stories, even some overlap. This text, called 2 Maccabees, also tells us of the Maccabean triumph, but in it we pick up something else: signs of a fierce shouting match. This political quarrel was taking place not between the Jews and the Greeks, however. Instead, it was raging among Jews.

The author of 2 Maccabees was eager to resolve an issue that was much more sweeping than the war against the political overreach of the tyrant Antiochus IV Epiphanes ("God-present").[13] The issue was how to define being Jewish in the increasingly Hellenistic world. This question was going to have more than one answer. By the mid second century B.C., Hellenistic culture—whether imposed by the king, welcomed by the populace, or some combination of the two—had become an identifiable presence in Jewish daily life. A Greek gym had been established in the shadow of the Second Temple, perhaps on Antiochus's orders; and Jewish residents visited it. Males were expected to exercise nude there, of course (a point which may have caused Jewish men a moment of self-consciousness), but the gymnasium was an institution, a place where men who valued Hellenistic culture forged a social bond. It was a place where they could discuss Greek plays, laws, and philosophical ideas. Some Jewish men valued the experience so much, they reversed their circumcisions.[14]

During the second century B.C., Jews had begun to embrace other Greek customs. The *ephebate*, a kind of Greek military academy and finishing school for adolescents who aspired to advancement in the civil service, was attracting enrollment in Jerusalem. New educational opportunities aside, some had also begun to dress in the Greek fashion, wearing trendy Greek hats. The Hellenistic king had also tried to unite residents of Coele-Syria by instituting sacrifices on his birthday—a regular and unsurprising part of the ruler cult associated with Hellenistic kings—and many Jews attended. Some may even have petitioned the king to establish a Greek city-state in Jerusalem, a city called Antioch-in-Jerusalem.[15]

One of the best-known Jewish men of this time was Jason, High Priest of the Temple, a fact which the now-anonymous author of 2 Maccabees was not happy about. The author relates the story of Jews who rose up to oppose Jason and to wrest the Temple away from him. For Jason was not just a puppet of King Antiochus IV, according to the author of 2 Maccabees; he was a collaborator, someone who was directly to blame for this disastrous period in Jewish history, one that saw "the pinnacle of the Jewish people acting too Greek" (in the Greek language, this idea is captured in one word: *Hellenismos*).[16] "Hellenism," as it is often unimaginatively rendered into English, was not a neutral idea, however. No Greek writer before 2 Maccabees had ever used it to refer to his own positive estimation of Greek culture. Herodotus himself, the father of Greek history, famous for extolling the spread of Greek culture, always used a different word ("Greekness") to praise it.

The writer of 2 Maccabees was taking sides in a Jewish cultural debate. His word choice—indeed, his word invention—alerts us to the ferocity of the conversation. Juggling Jewish and Hellenistic identities was out; only resistance to Hellenistic society would be the true hallmark of being Jewish. By the mid second century B.C., one wonders whether that was a tough sell. In Hellenistic Egypt, sometime between 246 and 222 B.C., Jews had constructed and dedicated a prayer hall at Schedia, near Alexandria. They had done so "on behalf of King Ptolemy III, Queen Berenike, his sister, wife, and their children."[17] Setting aside this place for reading and studying scripture while honoring the local king and queen, Jews were doing two things at once, even though they lived away from the Temple in Jerusalem. Papyrus fragments also confirm our picture of Jewish communities flourishing in Hellenistic Egypt. One fragment, dated 253 B.C., preserves parts of a letter from a man looking to acquire wool for a mattress. He has written to ask his friend to buy it from a local vendor named Pasis, whom he identifies as a Jew.[18] This description does not appear to be anything other than a casual observation about Pasis's identity.

Jews themselves served in the army of the Ptolemies, they worked as local policemen, and they were no less present to Egypt's rulers than they were in the lives of everyday residents of Hellenistic Egypt. One later writer tells us that Queen Cleopatra III (r. 142–101 B.C.) appointed two Jewish men as generals in her army.[19] Well before King Antiochus IV showed up on the doorstep of Jerusalem, many men and women had already learned how to be Greek and Jewish at the same time.

The author of 2 Maccabees, however, could not abide it. He had his own vision for what it meant to be Jewish; it meant never having to make a compromise. He was even able to articulate that idea quickly and succinctly in one word—in Greek, *Ioudaismos*. Or, as it's rather problematically often translated into English, "Judaism."[20] It is the earliest use of the word that any linguist has ever been able to find.

For us, Judaism will be a familiar sight, as recognizable as Christianity or Islam. Judaism today refers to the "religion" of the Jewish people, something separate and distinct from non-Jewish "religions." The Jewish author of 2 Maccabees didn't understand his term that way because he lived in a world "before 'religion.'" As the biblical scholar Brent Nongbri has shown, the writer's Hellenistic world was not unlike the world of Roman *religio*, a place where ancestral customs were constantly being defined, debated, and fought for.[21]

For the writer of 2 Maccabees, there were only specific Jewish people who illustrated what it really meant to be Jewish. One was a man named Eleazer, who preferred to die at the hands of Antiochus rather than eat the meat of the pig that had been sacrificed on the king's behalf. Another was named Razis, who in former times had never mingled with the gentiles. Now, he committed suicide when the king's forces came for him.[22] These men were "real Jews," the writer of 2 Maccabees argues, because they were martyrs who had heroically stood up to King Antiochus and suffered at his hands.[23] All other Jews who had their ideas about being Jewish—competing ideas—were excluded from "Judaism."[24] The terms of this shouting match, including the tendentious charge of what it meant to be caught acting too Greek, would eventually travel far in space and time, well beyond Antiochus IV and the Maccabees, well beyond the hills of Jerusalem, and well beyond the confines of any Jewish community.

In the aftermath of the successful war against Antiochus, the Maccabean family line would hold the Temple priesthood until the middle of the first century B.C. Then the winds of change would shift again. An army led by the general Pompey would seize Syria in 63 B.C., and the people of Jerusalem would watch a new imperial power rise, again in their backyard. Within decades, Rome had outsourced the rule of Jerusalem to a client king of the Senate's choosing. The august body in the capital chose a member of the local elite, Herod, to govern the region and make his own appointments to the high priesthood. Memory of Jewish independence was not lost. Soon, a debate over the nature of Jewish identity would begin again.

This time, it would be Roman rulers, not Hellenistic kings, who would be faced with a delicate task of having to balance their own interests in civic order with the puzzle of how to unite the many voices of the Jewish people. In the decades to come, one of Herod's sons, Archelaus, would prove particularly inept at this task. In A.D. 6, the Senate in Rome, unable to abide mismanagement, finally removed the client kingship from Herod's family. The province of Roman Judaea officially entered the register of Roman territories. Rome would administer it directly. Publius Sulpicius Quirinius immediately called a census (Luke 2:1).

Direct rule by Rome, including the obligation by administrators to raise taxes, provoked pockets of unrest, and by A.D. 66 an army would be called to the region—to enforce law and order in the empire's youngest territorial acquisition. Four years later, the Second Jewish Temple was smoldering, its stones pried loose and thrown down.[25] These limestone blocks still lie at the base of the Second Temple platform (figure 9). The Jewish Temple has never been rebuilt.

This dramatic military conflict can easily lead to facile assumptions that Jews were always and inherently incompatible of living, working, and worshipping in the world around them. Yet notwithstanding the polemical rhetoric of the writer of 2 Maccabees, many Jews had been living, working, and worshipping in cities throughout the Mediterranean since the time of the Ptolemies and Seleucids. Even in the Roman period, a period in which Jews suffered the devastating loss of their Second Temple, we still see them living hyphenated lives. In modern Benghazi, Libya (Roman Berenike), over a period of nearly six decades—from roughly 8 B.C. to A.D. 55, when tensions were beginning to flare in Jerusalem—Jews were negotiating a more visible space for themselves by working with the local elite.

Decimus Valerius Dionysius was at the fore of this campaign. Sometime between 8 and 6 B.C., he repaved the local amphitheater and plastered the walls to prep them for painting. These paintings are lost today, but the inscription that informs us about Decimus's involvement is colorful enough. A Roman living abroad, he hailed from a blue-blooded Roman family, the Valerii, and had been given a popular Hellenistic nickname, Dionysius, etymologically related to the Greek god of wine, Dionysus. Because of his generosity, he also garnered quite a following in Benghazi, and not just for repairing the amphitheater. Other constituencies benefited from the new stadium, too. They were a community of Jews. The Jews in Roman Benghazi were using the town's stadium (more likely, a room within it) as their "assembly space"—which is to say, in Greek, as their *synagogue*.

Valerius Decimus Dionysius had facilitated the Jewish community's access to public space. A generation later, perhaps around A.D. 24–25, Benghazi's Jewish community found themselves once again publicly honoring a member of the local government, Marcus Tittius. They declared their appreciation for Tittius by setting up another inscription in the amphitheater. Later still, in A.D. 55–56, they erected a third monument, commemorating everyone from Alexander to Zenodoros to Zosima, daughter of Terpolios, who had funded the latest round of repairs.[26]

Were all these people Jewish? Was Valerius Decimus Dionysius a Jew? In the eye-opening world of Roman Benghazi—a place where one of the most highly visible Roman buildings, or at least some portion of it, worked a double shift over the course of a half century—we shouldn't be surprised to find lots of people who resist easy labels.

The Jews at Sardis, who were proud of having a bronze decree displayed on Rome's Capitoline Hill, now seem less like an anomaly than they may have first appeared.

Around 49 B.C., they wrote to the Roman magistrate, Lucius Antonius, to inform him that the community had enjoyed several long-standing rights during the Hellenistic age, specifically, the right to legal assembly and the right to have their own worship space, "a place they called their own."[27] During the Seleucid period, the kings had previously granted these rights; but with the recent change in management—Rome controlled Asia Minor now—they needed to be renegotiated. The Jewish community drafted a petition. Lucius granted it. Was there anything threatening about the Jewish people or about Jewish worship practices that would disqualify them from participating in the civic fabric of the town?

To Lucius, the answer was no. In his reply, he refers to "Jewish citizens of Sardis." Other manuscripts suggest that he referred to them as "Jewish citizens of Rome." Whatever their precise legal status, Jewish residents of Sardis, just like Jewish residents of Benghazi, had made a place for themselves in Caesar's empire. Centuries later, they would construct a synagogue in much the same spirit: by retrofitting it into a hall in one of the city's largest public bath complexes.[28] If "coming out Jewish" in the

Hellenistic and Roman world called for a delicate balance of individual and group self-awareness, matched with a passionate community activism, the Jewish community in Sardis had done just that. Over the course of nearly six centuries, from the Hellenistic kings to the later Roman Empire, they'd won "a place they called their own" through a process of political engagement.[29]

Other Jewish communities would do the same. One lived at the harbor of Rome, Ostia, and one individual there seems to have helped raise the social profile of the group. Mindius Faustus left behind a bilingual dedication, in both Latin and Greek, that helps us chart the group's rising fortunes. In the late second or perhaps early third century A.D., Mindius dedicated "an ark for the sacred [Hebrew] scriptures." This "ark" must have been like a wall niche or perhaps slightly larger, like a cupboard or cabinet.[30] Unfortunately, archaeologists—and I am one of a team who has worked at the Ostia synagogue—have never found any trace of this shrine. The Torah shrine currently visible at the synagogue is a grand affair, but it was installed in the early fifth century A.D. It probably functioned for a century or more, speaking to the longevity of the Jewish experience outside Rome on the cusp of the Middle Ages.

Mindius Faustus brings us back to third century A.D., though. He donated his ark "for the well-being of the emperors" and etched this Latin phrase at the top of his announcement. The ark's dedication was written in Greek. Mindius' use of these two languages—Greek for his Jewish audience; Latin, the language of friends, neighbors, and Roman authorities—speaks to his own hybrid identity. Dedications made "for the well-being of the emperors" are as ubiquitous in the Roman world as *E pluribus unum* on American coins.[31] Just as Annobal Rufus of Lepcis Magna had celebrated the construction of a new theater in neo-Punic and Latin, Mindius Faustus of Ostia was celebrating the construction of a new Jewish Torah shrine by speaking to two groups at once.

Was Mindius abandoning his Jewish faith? No, he was borrowing a page from a playbook developed centuries before when Jewish residents of cities like Sardis negotiated with local Roman officials for "a place to call their own." Even as the window for rebuilding the Jewish Temple in Jerusalem was shutting, in a Mediterranean world where all Jews would live as sojourners until 1948, many Jewish communities were hitting upon innovative ways to keep their traditions. At Ostia, Benghazi, and

Sardis, they were engaging their non-Jewish neighbors in constructive dialogue.

Alexandria at Egypt, A.D. 38

Groups are rarely monolithic, however, and in a world governed by Rome, many local factors could influence the quality of life for Jewish groups throughout the Mediterranean: an agreeable magistrate, a receptive town council, a heightened level of community activism. A sour combination of any of the above could also lead to toxic local flare-ups.

In Alexandria—a fiercely Hellenistic city that always prided itself on being located at the doorstep of Egypt, not in it—riots erupted in A.D. 38, and members of the local Jewish community were the target of aggressive and focused anger. Jews had long been a healthy segment of Alexandria's population. Alexandria itself holds the distinction of being one of the only ancient Mediterranean cities known to have had specifically Jewish neighborhoods—not because Jews were segregated there but because they demographically dominated parts of the town.[32]

Here, in this Hellenistic capital, among a mélange of local Egyptians, Hellenized Alexandrians, and Greek expats, Jews, too, had been negotiating their rights and worship privileges since the time of the Ptolemies. The result was a sometimes uneven but tightly bound social fabric, a place where the Hellenistic elite and non-elite lived side by side amid the local population. As can often happen during moments of prosperity, the privileges of residing in the Ptolemies' crown jewel trickled down to many. With the defeat of the last Ptolemy, Cleopatra, however, the government changed. Egypt was annexed to Rome and designated a special province of the emperor. Administrators from Italy poured into the town. The new rulers and their tax policy were about to upset the status quo.

Rome granted a tax exemption to Hellenistic elites. Local non-elites were not so lucky. Speaking in a disorganized voice, they merited no exemption. Two separate but equal categories were born—Hellenistic residents and local residents, both of whom lived in the same city. The division seems to have compounded problems for the city's Jews. Their community comprised both lower-class and middle-class locals, as well as those who moved among the elite.[33] Within a half century, tensions would flare.

In A.D. 38, the ruling Roman magistrate, apparently at the instigation of three locals, revoked the rights that the city's Jewish community had previously negotiated.³⁴ In the aftermath of this decision, synagogues were torched, and Jewish shops and households were destroyed and pillaged. The memory of these Alexandrian riots has been seared in literature as one of history's first "pogroms."³⁵

What ultimately went so wrong? Some see an early illustration of "anti-Semitism," which is to say, racial prejudice. Others see a social fear and hatred of Jewish neighbors, a kind of Judeophobia, divorced from race. Still others point to the brewing sense of economic injustice that must have stoked the tensions between the elite Hellenistic residents of Alexandria and the non-elite locals. Since Alexandria's Jewish community crossed these lines, they would have found themselves at the center of the debate.³⁶ The picture is still not entirely clear.

As word reached Rome, however, the emperor Claudius (r. A.D. 41–54), new to the throne, intervened. The fact that the emperor had chosen to weigh in on the events—we have a copy of his letter to the people of Alexandria—shows the magnitude of the situation.³⁷ All residents of Alexandria, Claudius decreed, should aim for a life of goodwill and brotherhood with one other. For that, he appealed to a greater good, a sense of common decency. In particular, he appealed to the concept of *philanthrōpia*, goodwill toward one's fellow human beings and citizens. Two centuries before Christians would depict that same civic ideal at Dura Europos, in the guise of the "Good Shepherd," Rome's emperor was encouraging Jews and Greeks in Alexandria to unite behind it. It was a diplomatic way to repair a fractured and fracturing civic bond. Claudius's desire to promote civic harmony was noble and would have played to the best in all parties.

Unfortunately, others were not as generous. Where Claudius looked at Jews and saw conversation partners, the more narrow-minded and opinionated would always see the opposite, people who harbored a visceral hatred of fellow human beings (*misanthrōpia*). Many Egyptian and Greek writers, for example, turned the Exodus story on its head, suggesting that Moses had been forced to leave Egypt because Jews were incapable of living among foreigners. The chance recovery of a letter from Egypt, dated to the early or mid first century B.C., also shines light on the dim and hostile alleyways of ancient Judeophobia. In it, a man expresses concern for the upcoming travel of his friend, a Jewish man named

Ptolemy. We don't know Ptolemy's destination, but his friend, Herakles, did feel the need to remind him to be careful: "You know they really loathe Jews there."[38] How pervasive was this prejudice? We cannot say.

For me, the most poignant aspect of this personal letter is the way it takes us back to a specific time and place. For just like Marcus, son of Dama, a man from Syria whose life we lived through his diploma, here is someone else in the Roman world who saw himself as an outsider. Here is someone who, through no fault of his own, was forced to ride a slightly bumpier road around town than his friends and neighbors. In antiquity, we can't overlook the psychological anxiety that could often come by having to leave one's "safe space" behind.

Fear and hostility, however, never prevented the Jewish people from becoming more visible participants in Mediterranean daily life. Cities like Sardis, Benghazi, and Ostia and places like Rome, North Africa, and Spain confidently testify to that. Political and military events may have profoundly shaped Jewish life—the destruction of the Second Temple in A.D. 70 forever altered it—but the Jewish experience lived on, in all its rich social diversity.[39] Some of these experiences were spurred on by a devout, even righteous sense of mission. Efforts to take back Jerusalem from the Romans gained momentum in the early second century, for example. In A.D. 115–117, while Pliny and Trajan were corresponding about the vexing question of "Christians" in Asia Minor, Jewish revolts were flaring up locally throughout Egypt, North Africa, and Mesopotamia. It was an anxious time to be a Jewish rebel.

One Jewish writer saw his struggle as the final war that would lead to the triumph of the Jewish people.[40] The fall of Rome was near! He had "proof," too. Rewinding the reels of Roman history—and pausing conspiratorially at several frames—he showed his audience how a divine hand had been guiding their revolt. Events that he had foreseen taking place during the reign of a man "whose name has the first letter of the alphabet" [A, for Augustus] had already been fulfilled:

> Memphis!
> Memphis will be turned upside down on account of the
>   wickedness of its rulers
> and of a woman who has never known slavery in her life,
>   who will fall upon a wave.

And that man [Augustus] will set up laws for people and put
   everything under his command.
But after a long time, he will hand over power to another
who will have "300" for his first initial [*T*, in Greek, for
   Tiberius],
just like the name of a beloved river [the Tiber, in Rome],
   and he will rule over Persia
and Babylon![41]

Of course, it's easy for anyone to predict the outcome of events that have
already happened, and that's what this Jewish poet was doing. Writing
during Trajan's time but setting his visions in the past, he was "predicting" that the emperor Augustus would capture Egypt—symbolized by its
old capital, Memphis. And he was "predicting" that the emperor Tiberius
would one day triumph over Mesopotamia—symbolized by Babylon.
Why these places? Egypt and Mesopotamia just happened to be sites of
Jewish conflict in the poet's day. "Memphis" and "Babylon" were code
words, places where the heavy hand of Rome's empire was bearing down,
threatening the Jewish way of life—or so the poet would like us to believe.
Conditions had become so grave, the poet was claiming, that even that
monstrous emperor who had begun the war in Judaea was poised to
return: that "terrible serpent bringing grievous war," "the ruler whose
mark was fifty" [*N*, for Nero].[42]

It's a strange one, this poem. In it, the poet sees history as unfolding in
a sequence of very clearly defined events. These, he believes, will lead to
the overthrow of Roman oppression and give rise to a ruler who will
bring salvation to the Jewish people.[43] If the poet's themes sound strangely
familiar, they should. We have walked back into a field of literature we've
encountered before. The poet is espousing three elements of an apocalyptic world view.

These kinds of texts are never easy to interpret. To begin, for Jews
living in Egypt, North Africa, and Mesopotamia in the early second
century A.D., this poem might actually have sent some comforting
messages. To some, the poet was telling them to weather the storm, to be
resolute during this time of social strife. Things really would get better,
soon. Others, of course, might have heard a slightly different note. The
poet's nervousness might have stoked their fear—fear of a future "even
worse" than the present.[44] The only remedy was resistance to Rome. Their

struggle had been centuries in the making; but God, through the help of his prophet, had foreseen its outcome all along. Victory was guaranteed. Their struggle would not end in vain. The Roman Empire would fall!

Things did not turn out exactly as the poet had planned.

The Jewish revolts of Trajan's time were quashed. Two decades later, in A.D. 132–135, leaders organized yet another military campaign to take back Jerusalem; but it, too, would gather momentum and fail. By then, Rome's tolerance for this provincial unrest may have been wearing thin. As punishment, the emperor Hadrian expelled all Jews from Jerusalem. Already bereft of their Temple, they would now be physically cut off from the sight of its majestic platform. In the centuries that followed, the Temple platform itself would forever remain barren, perched atop the Roman city like an urban prairie. We are still living out the effects of this moment in second century Roman history.

Jerusalem would be rebranded a Roman colony, Colonia Aelia Capitolina, part of the emperor's campaign to inject new Roman life into the city. The new name was based on the emperor Hadrian's family name, Aelius. It also combined Hadrian's family history with an homage to Rome's cult of Jupiter Optimus Maximus on the Capitoline Hill. At this point, even the name of the province would be erased. No longer Judaea, it would henceforth be called Palestina.[45] Rome had triumphed over the hills of Jerusalem. In this stunning Jewish defeat, however, there would still be quieter moments of triumph.

After A.D. 135, as all prospect for worship in Jerusalem receded, the mental space where the Temple once stood would come gradually to be filled with something else—a question, one that may have sounded strangely familiar to many Jews who were steeped in history and tradition. The question was, how would the Jewish community define being Jewish as residents of the Roman world? The answers would come from every direction.

By the early third century A.D., rabbis had begun to preserve and pass down their interpretations of Jewish scripture, as they were applied to life without a Temple.[46] Almost contemporarily, we find many of the first Jewish worship spaces outside the Jewish homeland beginning to appear in the archaeological record. We've already visited the street where one of these buildings was erected. It's Wall Street, and the synagogue is at Dura Europos. There, slightly up the road from the first house we already visited, is yet another window onto the past.

Over the course of a half century, starting in the late second century A.D., the owners and their construction crew began to build a larger meeting space for the Jewish community. Fragments of a Hebrew liturgical prayer, on parchment, have been discovered on the site. Devotional graffiti, in multiple languages, were scratched on its doorjambs, following common local custom.[47] By the time the final renovations took place, sometime around A.D. 244/245–256, not one but two neighboring homes had been renovated, converting the property into a synagogue.[48] The back room of one home was transformed into a large open hall. They installed a niche for the Jewish scripture, the Torah, in the western wall of this room. From Dura, it is the direction facing Jerusalem.

Colorful pictures covered every wall in this renovated home: Moses being discovered in the Nile, the time when the Red Sea swallowed up the pharaoh's army. In other panels, depictions of the Ark of the Covenant, Samuel anointing King David, and—on the face of the Torah niche—an image of the seven-branched lamp stand that had once been kept in the Temple: the menorah. The Roman army had stolen the menorah during their sack of Jerusalem. In Dura, it had been painted on the synagogue wall as a memory of a time that no longer existed. Mentally, it must have helped many people tend the still-fresh wounds of this painful time. Depictions of the menorah become widespread throughout the Roman world, starting in the third century A.D. Just like the Jewish community in Sardis, however, the Jewish community at Dura Europos had found "a place to call their own" without converting the entire town.[49] They had done so by conversing with their neighbors and tearing down walls.

CHAPTER 5

What Goes On Behind Closed Doors

One more group deserves its time on stage before Constantine enters. This group lived on the margins, too, battling stereotypes and triumphing over random acts of discrimination. They were followers of the goddess Isis, a deity first worshipped in ancient Egypt for three thousand years, before they came to Rome. Sources are filled with horror stories—tales of omens and portents—alleged to have trailed behind the worshippers of Isis wherever they went. On one occasion, in 59–58 B.C., Isis worshippers were spotted in Rome at the same time that someone reported seeing an owl. An accursed, ill-omened beast—never an auspicious sign—the owl tarnished the whole group. It turned them into outcasts and cast doubt on the legitimacy of their worship. A decade later, another owl was sighted. In first century B.C. Rome, there was no end to these inauspicious signs. An Isis anxiety began to spread.

Someone said that he had seen a statue sweat—for three days straight. It was a fitting symbol of the nervousness of Romans who were afraid of "outsiders." The hysteria metastasized. After an earthquake interrupted the regular rhythms of daily life, some began to wonder whether it was a sign. Had the gods turned against Rome? A swarm of angry bees had also recently been seen attacking a beloved statue of Hercules. Was there a connection? In even more disturbing news, a bakery had been flooded with blood.[1] It was as if Rome was under siege.

The problem, of course, was not the sudden outbreak of bees, or earthquakes, or sweating statues.

Romans had never seen Isis worshippers before.

Today, Isis is a poster child for Egypt. Her name summons images of obelisks and hieroglyphics, the papyrus reeds of the Nile and the lure of a land where time was once measured in dynasties. Many museums display seated granite statues of her nursing her divine son. These may look familiar to us, thanks in part to their resonance with another iconic image. Isis's role as "Mother of a God" had been popular for a more than a millennium—well before anyone thought of depicting Mary, mother of Jesus, the same way.[2]

Isis took on a robust new dimension during the age of the Ptolemies. The Ptolemies had come to Egypt as outsiders, and in Isis they saw an image beloved by locals and the ideal goddess who could bring people together in Hellenistic Alexandria and Egypt alike. In the early third century B.C., Ptolemy I popularized Isis worship alongside that of a Greek god, Serapis. This divine union blended elements of the Ptolemies' Macedonian world, where Serapis was thought of as the king of Olympus, Zeus, with features of the land they now controlled. "Serapis" itself is a contracted name based on those of two popular Egyptian deities, Osiris and Apis. With Serapis and Isis, the Ptolemies articulated their vision for a harmonious world throughout Egypt.[3] Should we call Isis, the offspring of their initiative, Egyptian? Perhaps, in the same way we call Chinese take-out containers Chinese. (They were invented in Chicago.)[4]

In the years to come, Isis and Serapis would remain wildly popular in Egypt. In an increasingly integrated Mediterranean, their adherents soon sprouted up in other cities, too, places visited by Ptolemy I, touched by his kingdom and its ideology, even cities far removed from either.[5]

In Italy, worshippers may have been attracted to the Isis and Serapis cults as early as the second century B.C. Over time, these marginal communities expanded, drawing their ranks from Hellenized Egyptians living in Italy, as well as other Greeks and Romans, women and men, freeborn citizens and slaves alike. There is no evidence to sustain the assumption that these two "foreign deities" appealed exclusively to a lower-class, humble following.

By the first century B.C., however, many of Isis's worshippers had begun to attract the kind of attention no one wants. In 59–58 B.C., according to one later source, a group of worshippers had been banned from approaching Rome's Capitoline Hill. In a spectacular government crackdown, the Senate had even decided to remove their altars from the site.[6] The Senate's decision may be the first act of discrimination against them, but it would not be the last. Less than a decade later, in 50 B.C., the Senate—led by one grandstanding politician—announced again that Isis's followers would not be welcome in Rome. Lucius Aemilius Paulus led the conservative charge, sending a crew of workmen to dismantle a popular Isis shrine. When they dallied, Lucius put aside his toga. Then, "he grabbed an ax and hacked at the doorposts of the temple."[7] For Lucius, it must have seemed like the fastest way to humiliate the Isis worshippers and capitalize, politically, on the stigma associated with them.

The Roman people had ideas of their own. When Isis's altars on the Capitoline were overthrown in 59–58 B.C., a group of concerned citizens—their names are unknown to us—fought to have them restored. They won. Even Lucius's behavior looks, in hindsight, like an act of political desperation. As soon the workmen that day assembled for duty, they walked off the job when they saw which shrine they had been ordered to dismantle. "None of them," we learn from our sources, "dared to lay a hand on [Isis's] temple."[8] Lucius Aemelius Paulus was leading from behind. Other people were driving social change in Rome.

How had that happened? Had Isis's worshippers converted everyone else?

The social triumph of the Isis worshippers was not inevitable. Discrimination against them would continue for quite some time. Less than a generation after Lucius tried to take an ax to their shrine, the "Egyptian rites," as the Senate referred to them, were prohibited again.

In 28 B.C., the Senate decreed that followers of Isis could not worship anywhere in the sacred center of Rome, the *pomerium*.[9] This area was demarcated by several inscribed boundary stones and by the invisible line connecting them that snaked through the streets of the city. The pomerium wasn't exactly coterminous with the city walls. Rome's Campus Martius—once the training ground for the army but now increasingly gentrified with a new voting hall, a theater, and baths—was excluded from the pomerium. But it wasn't a small piece of real estate, either. Seven years later, in 21 B.C., even the Senate's policy of containment had to be adjusted. Isis's worshippers were pushed out further, beyond Rome's first mile marker.[10] The man behind these policies is one of Rome's best-known figures, Octavian Augustus.

Augustus was the heir of Julius Caesar, avenger of his murder. In 27 B.C., the Senate bestowed on him the name "Augustus" for ending nearly a half century of civil war. This word, practically untranslatable, drew its meaning from concepts like *augment* and *authority*, as well as *august*. "Augustus," having increased the fortunes of the Roman state, was being recognized for his accomplishments. Over the next four decades, until his death in A.D. 14, Augustus would oversee the restoration and flourishing of Rome's people, its power, its ideas. During this dynamic age, many of the mechanisms of government remained in the hands of the Senate and the people, just as they had for centuries.

Augustus's style of transformational leadership, rooted in a sense of "courage, clemency, justice, and devotion to the gods, to his family, and to Rome," as he himself phrased it, shaped Rome in new ways. Latin poets such as Virgil, Horace, Propertius, and Ovid ruminated on this "Golden Age." Simple terra-cotta or brick-and-mortar temples that had crumbled or chipped, Augustus and others now rebuilt in marble. Augustus was strengthening all of Rome, as it were, with a set of new and stable foundations.[11] The marquee names on these urban landmarks were Olympian gods whose temples had presided over Rome for centuries.

Jupiter, Juno, and Minerva had been given one of Rome's greatest architectural wonders. Completed in the late sixth century B.C., their temple was built of local volcanic rock, wooden beams, and terra-cotta tiles. According to legend, the kings who had once ruled Rome had planned and paid for it. Scions of the Republican age had taken care of it and repaired it.[12] For many years, it held Rome's Sibylline books. Lightning would strike this temple in 9 B.C. and again in A.D. 56, and it would burn down and be rebuilt many times after. Natural disasters, however, would never deter the Roman people from investing money and meaning in their city's most important religious site. Even the memory of its foundation would remain a powerful talking point about Rome's "global" exceptionalism. According to a legend circulating at the start of the fifth century A.D., builders had chanced upon a human head while digging the temple's foundation. What else could such a sign have meant but that Rome had been destined to be the ruler, or "head," of the world?[13]

Today, only the foundations of Jupiter, Juno, and Minerva's temple remain, but Romans once revered it. Inside, priests cared for its statues. Outside, they sacrificed animals at its altar. Victorious generals even deposited their spoils in its coffers, for in a world without banks, temples functioned as vaults. For all Romans who gathered in its shadow—nearly everyone; the Capitoline Hill commands a dramatic view—this one building shaped their identity as a city. Augustus must have been proud of having repaired this one temple.

Others Romans were proud of Augustus, too. In neighborhoods throughout the capital, people began dedicating shrines outside local businesses and in the streets outside their apartments to honor Augustus and his family. Such altars had long been a feature of urban life. Traditionally, they were erected to honor the Lares, protectors of the crossroads. Every household worshipped a set of similar gods, including the figure of the family's Genius, a deity who was responsible for protecting the head of the house. In Augustan Rome, altars to the Lares of Augustus and his family's Genius were now set up on street corners everywhere. These monuments served a bit as neighborhood flags, waved by local communities who wanted to find their own place in the changing times.

Under Augustus, everything felt renewed—almost as if Rome had been reborn. The excitement was palpable through the year. Rome's calendar, as we have already seen, was structured around specific holidays, and throughout the year, festivals and celebrations would electrify the city. Rome's birthday, the Parilia, was one of these days. It was celebrated every year on April 21 and gives us a good picture of Augustus's Rome.

The events of the day went something like this. A farmer began with a dash of spring cleaning, scrubbing out his animal pens. Then, he would deck his freshly scrubbed halls with boughs of festive branches. Next, he lit a fire, so that the smoke could purify his sheep for the upcoming year, and he prayed for another year of good fortune. To conclude the rites, he would sprinkle himself in dew and leap across the fire. It will all seem very primitive to us, but it was strange to many Romans, too. How had such simple farming ceremony—sheep, bonfires, animal pens, and dew—ever come to be linked with the birthday party of Augustus's now-thriving empire? No one could say.

One Augustan poet, Ovid, was puzzled enough to investigate. In his research, he found no fewer than seven explanations as to why Romans were still celebrating the birthday ritual as they did. These included spec-ulations about the holiness of water and fire, but they also involved some highly imaginative ideas about what had really taken place on April 21, 753 B.C., the day the city was thought to have been founded.[14] Which explanations did the Romans believe? It's impossible to say. On April 21, there's still fire in Rome, although now it's launched above the city and clouds everything in smoke. Questions about the origins of the Parilia do the same. Ovid didn't know where the birthday rituals came from. Many Romans didn't know, either. Yet each year, many people were (and still are) emotionally invested in the rituals associated with that day.[15] By the mid second century A.D., the Parilia would come to be known as the Romaia, the Festival of the City of Rome. Old-world Rome was out. The city had a birthday celebration that was more appropriate for a Mediterranean empire.[16] Rome's festivals were capable of changing, just like its people.[17]

Now the "mysteries" really do begin to look strange. Why did Romans join them, even Augustus? (For that is exactly what happened.) In 27 B.C., only a year after banning the "Egyptian mysteries" from Rome, Augustus set sail for Greece to be initiated into the "mysteries" of Demeter. What did Augustus hope to get in Greece that he couldn't get at home, and why was he banning some mysteries in Rome while partici-pating in others abroad?

To find out, we need to go to Eleusis, too. Located in the plain of Attica, fourteen miles northwest from Athens, Eleusis sits on a bay facing the Aegean Sea. There, performances of the "mysteries" ran, year after year, for nearly eight centuries. Over a series of eight days at the end of September and beginning of October, Greeks and, later, Romans flocked to the city to take part in the rites. People would trek to Eleusis until the end of the fourth century A.D.[18]

The synopsis of what happened at Eleusis is probably familiar to anyone who has ever picked up a dog-eared paperback of classical myths. It is the tale of Demeter and Persephone.[19] Persephone was playing in the fields one day when Hades, Zeus's brother, abducted her, taking her away to his underground lair to make her his wife. Upon hearing the news, Demeter, disguising her appearance, went to Eleusis to grieve. In the form of an old woman, she worked as an au pair. She kept house, made beds, and taught locals how to manage their chores. One high-class family in particular took her in, and she was even asked to raise their boy and to see that no harm came to him. This she did—the way any god would. She took the baby at night and plunged him into a fire to make him immortal.

Of course, birth mothers have their own ideas about child rearing. When the boy's mom caught the nurse kindling her child one night, she rushed in. Demeter could barely contain her rage. Throwing off her disguise, she cursed the family: "You, by your own thoughtlessness, have harmed your son irreparably," she told them. "I would have made your beloved son deathless and ageless for all his days and would have granted him an honor that could never perish." Then Demeter issued a set of demands. "Let all the people of this city [Eleusis] build me a great temple and an altar down below. I will instruct you in my mysteries, so that ever after you perform them in a holy way and soothe my mind."[20] The mysteries at Eleusis had been founded.

Demeter was not done. She cursed the earth. Food shortages and starvation sent towns into panic. The other Olympian gods wondered how to respond. All Demeter wanted was her daughter, Persephone, back. The lot fell to Zeus to find a solution. Sources confirmed that Persephone was alive. Hades agreed to allow his bride to rejoin the world above. Soon, mother and daughter would be reunited at Eleusis, although Persephone, who had enjoyed a meal while with Hades, would consequently be required to spend a portion of the year at her husband's side. Demeter eventually agreed to lift the food embargo. Trees and flowers bloomed. The goddess then appeared and revealed her "holy mysteries" to the leaders of Eleusis. "Happy are those," an ancient Greek poet tells us, "who dwell on this earth who have seen these things [these mysteries]. But whoever is uninitiated in them and who takes no part in them will not share in anything similar, even after they're dead, down in the realm of darkness."[21] So ends one of Western literature's most iconic myths, written down around the seventh century B.C.

What could any of it have possibly meant to a Roman emperor like Augustus?

To answer that question, we need to go backstage. The sanctuary of Demeter at Eleusis is situated against a low hillside, nestled above the town's bay. There, inside a sacred precinct was a building called the Telesterion. The Telesterion was not a temple, with a cult statue inside, but an audience hall, the site of the mysteries. Many of its walls are still visible today. Its first phase, which dates to the sixth century B.C., may have looked something like a small warehouse loft. One hundred years later, the Telesterion was rebuilt on a grander scale.

Every September, a new group of people arrived from Athens to be initiated into the mysteries. The interior of the Telesterion by this point was forested with columns, and it was able to accommodate upwards of three thousand people. Inside, people would stand, or sit, on a tiered row of steps that lined its walls and look out into the recesses of the chamber. Lit by windows along the ceiling by day, by night it must have been a cavernous hall, where lamps and torches flickered.[22] What an atmospheric place in which to receive the mysteries: the "sacred things" that the goddess had revealed, things which it was forbidden "to transgress, to inquire about, or to share with other people, for a great reverential awe keeps any sound of them in check."[23] What happened on the other side of the Telesterion's doors?

Even in antiquity, inquiring minds wanted to know. Just as the Internet is flooded with rumors about the beliefs and practices of minority groups ("Do Mormons really get their own planet when they die?"), the Greek and Roman world was awash with speculation about what went on at Eleusis. One person had heard, from a friend of a friend, that after the initiates entered the hall, a priest would open a sacred box and slowly remove a "sheaf of wheat," a symbol of the earth's fertility. From this grain would shine forth "the great and powerful light which comes from the One who lacks any distinguishing characteristics."[24] Another commenter rattled off a rather dubious inventory of the items he thought were inside the box:

> Are there not cakes of sesame seed and pyramidal cakes and truffle cakes and round cakes with decoration all over them and lumps of salt and a snake, the symbol of Thracian Dionysus? And aren't there also pomegranates, fig branches, fennel stalks, and ivy, and more large cakes and poppy seeds? . . . Not to mention, the unspeakable token of the goddess Themis, some marjoram, a lamp, a sword, and a "woman's comb"—by which, of course, I mean to say, in a more pleasant and more "mysterious" way, a model of the female genitalia?[25]

The grab bag nature of the list, including the odd sex item, is enough to make Augustus's visit to Eleusis seem downright bizarre. Then again, that was probably the goal. The people describing the contents of the mystery box at Eleusis were Christian bishops, and the flippancy with which they purport to give away the secret of the show—seven hundred years after opening night—tells us quite a bit about what they thought of the initiation rites. They were threatened by them. For them, what happened on the inside, whatever it was, had to be made to look and sound absurd.

Their comments also suggest that "the secret of the mysteries" might not be the most important thing we're looking for. After all, were the gods of Eleusis really so different from what Augustus knew back home? Demeter and her daughter were Olympians, and much of the "mysteries" took place in public. People from Athens and all over the Greek world could attend; they could watch the parade to the sanctuary; above all, many of them knew when to put it on their calendar. These rituals gradually became identified with vibrant Greek communities. By the end of the fifth century B.C., for example, Athenians celebrated the festival of their own healing god, Aesclepius, during the exciting lead-up to the Eleusinian mysteries. The festival at Eleusis itself would not have been possible without the generosity of the Eumolpidae, the local family of priests who sponsored it.[26]

Eleusis may not have been as "mysterious" as some people thought it was. The organizers of the festival had been bringing people together for centuries. Drawing upon the story of mother's loss and her joyful reunion, the priests had choreographed a physical and emotional journey that replicated Demeter's own loss and reunion with Persephone. As participants departed for Eleusis, they ventured into darkness, leaving the comfortable world of Athens behind. As they crossed into the hall of the Telesterion, initiates would hear the mythical story of a family torn apart. Then, along with that year's class of three thousand, they would celebrate the journey they had all taken together. By the fifth century B.C., the mysteries were providing three thousand people a year with something they never knew they wanted. Eleusis was making them into a more tightly knit community.[27] Initiates left one world (by "dying") and joined another (by "rising"). Did they emerge with a new "spiritual" outlook? Maybe. As the anthropologist Victor Turner pointed out decades ago in *The Ritual Process*, his classic study of these themes, initiation rites are man-made. Even when they follow a pattern of "dying" and "rising," people don't necessarily emerge from them any more spiritual than when they started. Turner's research helps unlock the mystery of why Augustus went to Eleusis.

Cultural ambassador, consensus builder, Augustus understood the benefit of building communities, too. He knew how important it was to get people on board with his shared vision. What could have been more natural, as the curtain was rising on a new era of Roman peace, than for the first man of Rome to go to Eleusis, to forge a bond between old-world Greece and the center of the new empire? This wasn't magic; it was statecraft. The Roman people may have had their own vibrant traditions—their neighborhood shrines, their family Lares, a cult of Jupiter on the Capitoline, the city's Parilia—but by Augustus's time, what it meant to be Roman was getting a little bigger. There was even a space for local communities in Greece.

How would the Isis worshippers find their place in Augustus's empire? Their meeting spaces were being swept outside the city while Augustus was going to Eleusis. Isis worshippers must have been indignant at the hypocrisy. Many would probably have torn out their hair in frustration, too—had it not been for the fact that male initiates into the Isis cult were required to shave their heads. A small price to pay for admittance, but it also happened to distinguish them from almost every other worshipper in Rome. Alas, perhaps it really is no "mystery" why so many Romans blamed them for everything from earthquakes to owls.[28] They looked different.

In one comic novel written in the second century A.D., Apuleius's *Metamorphoses*, we get a glimpse of how Isis's bald-headed worshippers would always remain a source of Roman laughter and derision. At the opening of the story, a narrator named Lucius has been touring Roman Greece, making friends, sharing adventures, when their conversation turns to "the whispered murmurs of magic."One friend heard that a local innkeeper had put a hex on her partner and transformed him into a beaver. Another suspects that the innkeeper where Lucius is staying also is a witch.[29]

Lucius, his intrigue piqued, decides to investigate. One night, by stealth, he spies the innkeeper rubbing herself with a potion. She changes herself into an owl right before his eyes! Impatient to learn the trick, Lucius asks one of the servants to steal him some of the ointment so that he can replicate the transformation. The slave brings the wrong potion, however, and when Lucius puts it on, he is turned into a donkey. For the remainder of the novel, he's shunned by his own living horses, stolen by highway robbers, even pawned off to a life of hard labor in a bakery, where he is forced to turn millstones, day after day, until Isis intervenes.

Coming to Lucius in his sleep, Isis reveals the antidote that will change him back: rose petals. Then, she inspires him to seek out one of her priests as soon as he can and to undergo initiation into her mysteries. Lucius follows all the instructions. First, he must fast, and then make a vow of celibacy (something that no Roman priest ever had to pledge). Next, he has to buy an entirely new set of clothes, fancy Egyptian linen robes (men traditionally wore a business suit of wool togas or, for relaxation, a casual tunic). Then, Lucius had to agree to spend several nights with Isis in her local sanctuary, away from his family and friends. Finally came the moment of ritual depilation, the moment when Lucius, as an Isis initiate, would have to say goodbye to his hair. To Latin readers of Apuleius's novel, all of the details were so oddly "un-Roman," but that's what made it so funny. We can see traces of something profound.

Lucius's initiation follows the blueprint of Eleusis. He is separated from the world. He undergoes initiation rites that introduce him into a new community. Even the Isis myth—the goddess brings her brother, Serapis, back from the dead—contains the motifs of "dying" and "rising." In some ways, there was nothing about the Isis cult that was structurally different from the cult at Eleusis. So why were Isis worshippers being targeted by the Roman government? It wasn't because of their bald heads; hair grew back (for some).[30] One answer is that they lacked what the people of Eleusis had been enjoying for centuries: well-placed allies and financial support.

Isis worshippers were certainly daring. Less than a century after the cult arrived in Italy, her worshippers were meeting on Rome's Capitoline Hill. Conservatives may have winced, watching this band of bald-headed misfits conduct their circus on Jupiter's doorstep, but what location could have been more appropriate for a group trying to put Romans at ease? Isis worshippers were reaching out, engaging their neighbors, worshipping their goddess in the most public place possible: right outside the Temple of Jupiter the Best and Greatest. We see this same pattern of outreach elsewhere. In two cities south of Rome, Herculaneum and Pompeii—both of which were buried in A.D. 79—acceptance was already a fact of life well before the volcano erupted.

One homeowner in Herculaneum commissioned a painting that depicted an Isis ritual (figure 10). On it, a chorus of bald-headed worshippers, draped in the same white linen garments that Lucius was required to buy, gathers on the steps of an Isis temple. The group is singing and playing music. In the foreground, a bald priest, or attendant, conducts a sacrifice on a small altar. An Egyptian temple looms in the background. Egyptian sphinxes watch from the other side. And at the center is another priest, holding a golden vessel. He is framed neatly before the temple's open door and shows the mysterious object to the initiates. The painting depicts what is essentially a stage set. From the foliage to the ibises, everything in it evokes a land far from the Bay of Naples.

Was the homeowner an Isis worshipper? There's no reason to assume he was. In fact, evidence from nearby Pompeii suggests that many people were welcoming Isis worshippers into their community without becoming initiates during this time. Pompeii had a very prominent Isis sanctuary.[31] In A.D. 62, an earthquake leveled it and many other parts of the town. Less than two decades later, in August A.D. 79, an ash storm would descend upon the city, preserving it. When archaeologists later unearthed the Isis sanctuary, they found statues of Bacchus and Venus, as well as paintings with Egyptian motifs—scenes of the dog-headed Egyptian god Anubis, for example, and of Isis holding her obnoxious rattle, the *sistrum*, which worshippers loudly brandished during their rituals. They also found several inscriptions inside the sanctuary.

One was a public notice from a person who had repaired the temple after the earthquake. "Numerius Popidius Celsinus, the son of Numerius," it said, "used his own money to restore the Temple of Isis from its foundations, which had collapsed due to the earthquake." Numerius was later awarded a free position in the local government "on account of his generosity." The fact is all the more noteworthy because Numerius, we learn from this inscription, was only six years old.[32] Why was a six-year-old—with his entire political future ahead of him—throwing his career away by putting his name on an Isis temple? Obviously, Numerius didn't fund the restoration project. His parents did; but their decision tells us something important. Even for members of their generation, the stigma of being an Isis worshipper had started to lift. They knew that by putting their son's name on the Isis temple, they would cause him to reap the rewards. They were right. Times were changing—in Pompeii.

How had that happened? Archaeology gives us a few leads. One key piece of evidence is the statue of Venus that was found in the Isis sanctuary. Venus was a goddess dear to the Roman people—mother of Aeneas, the legendary founder of Rome. Caesar's family had called upon her as their divine protector. Augustus prayed to her in that role, too. Caesar and Augustus did not have a monopoly on Venus' support, though. In the late first century B.C., the Roman general Sulla had prayed to Venus for help in an important battle. It was a fight for control of Pompeii, a conflict that that scarred the town (pockmarks of artillery fire are still observable in the city walls). In the end, Sulla triumphed, and he celebrated by renaming the town to honor his family and the watchful goddess who had helped him capture it. Forever after, the city of Pompeii would be called "the colony founded by Lucius Cornelius Sulla with the divine guidance of Venus."[33]

For Isis worshippers, putting a statue of Venus inside their sanctuary was no simple act of interior decorating. Venus was put there to shake hands with other residents of the town. She was being enlisted as an ambassador, a diplomat, just like her counterpart, the "Good Shepherd" at Dura Europos. Her message? Even Isis worshippers were concerned for the civic well-being of Pompeii.

Social change must have been proceeding at a breakneck pace by the second century. Even Lucius, the protagonist of Apuleius's novel, confirms it. As he hastens to the Isis sanctuary for his initiation, the priests begin to pray for the health of "the great Roman emperor and for the Senate in Rome, the equestrian order, and all the Roman people, and for all the sailors and ships which are governed under the rule of our empire." The Isis festival itself that day had begun with a procession to the shore, where a ship was launched into the sea, celebrating the symbolic return of spring weather. The story is fiction, but the details are real. In the early second century A.D., coins from Alexandria show the Roman emperor with depictions of Isis on the reverse ("tails"). On one, Isis is shown watching over the empire as the protectress of sailors and shipping (figure 11). Just as Rome's birthday, the Parilia, had become a holiday fixture, now Isis would join the march of Roman time.[34]

By the third century A.D., Isis and her festivals had become more visible still. A painting of the "Isis ship" festival was found at Rome's harbor town, Ostia. It may have come from a home. Scenes of Isis also appear on a richly decorated mosaic floor from a home in El Djem (ancient Thysdrus), Tunisia. The larger mosaic to which it once belonged depicted the months of the year and the four seasons. Each panel is labeled. Workers stomp on grapes during the September harvest. Clothes are tossed aside and hilarious role reversals ensue in the panel for December, the time of the topsy-turvy Saturnalia. The panel for the month of November is even more arresting (figure 12). Two linen-clad men are joined by a third, who hides his face behind the dog-headed mask of the Egyptian god Anubis.[35] For the Roman family who lived in this Tunisian home, it was as if the entire month of November consisted of one long celebration of Isis.

Between El Djem, Ostia, Alexandria, and Greece, the stigma that Isis worshippers once carried was fading. That's probably why, by A.D. 375–378, three Christian emperors demonstrated their own support for a local Isis community. Sometime during this four-year window, the emperors announced the restoration of an Isis temple at Rome's old harbor town of Ostia. They "ordered the temple to be restored," as the Latin dedication tells us.[36] Had followers of Jesus converted to Isis worship? If so, were they required to shave their heads? The questions are meant to be facetious. By the later empire, very few Romans were giving two hoots about owls anymore. Isis worshippers had triumphed.

CHAPTER 6

At the Threshold of the Palace

From the details we've collected, across cities and centuries, we can now discern a pattern. In Ephesos in Asia Minor, Jews won a worship space to call their own by petitioning their local Roman magistrates for it, not by unilaterally withdrawing from civic dialogue. In Italy, Isis's worshippers pledged their allegiance to Pompeii by appointing Venus, patron goddess of the colony, to act as their local ambassador. And on the banks of the Euphrates in Roman Syria, Christians depicted a shepherd caring for his sheep, the image of goodwill, or *philanthrōpia*, in their baptistry. Their choice of this popular image, in their own church, reminded them to show concern for their neighbors. Each of these groups was finding a greater visibility in its town, but in none of these instances was the group's success dependent on someone else's conversion. It was dependent on conversation.

We have come full circle, back to A.D. 313, moments away from hearing that the emperors had granted Jesus's followers the right to worship openly. Christians, a disenfranchised minority, were about to celebrate their indisputable political accomplishment. We should not escort the non-Christians of Rome off stage so fast, however. At the turn of the fourth century A.D., they comprised almost 90 percent of the empire.

To some, that's an inconvenient number, but it's an essential benchmark for us. Jesus's followers did not win their legal rights because the majority of their neighbors were hungering for an alternative to their way of life. Their sacrifices, their temple celebrations, and their urban festivals were not dying, defunct, or even in need of "revival"—not in the early fourth century, the mid fourth century, or even the late fourth century, as archaeological evidence has now made clear.[1] Romans would be restoring their temples, sacrificing their animals, burning incense at their statues and altars, and worshipping the gods at the theater, at the racetrack, and at their baths well into the late fourth century, as we will see. Indeed, the ways they worshipped their gods—the very conservative social fabric of their empire—would prove more resilient than we usually give them credit for.

These weren't people suffering from a deep, aching spiritual malaise. Rome's Isis worshippers have taught us that people could join "mystery cults" for reasons that had very little to do with spiritual needs. They, like the initiates of other "mystery cults," were often looking for a community. That's one reason the emperor Augustus went to the Greek city of Eleusis.

Three hundred years later, what Romans valued, what they believed, even how they worshipped—what Romans described as their *religio*—was never fixed or immutable. It was flexible and open to change. That's why what it meant to be a Roman was always getting bigger. And that's why, at the dawn of the fourth century, the Roman people show no symptoms of a terminal spiritual "illness." Some scholars have claimed that Romans needed Christianity, that it offered them "a revitalization movement that arose in response to the misery, chaos, fear, and brutality of [ancient city] life."[2] The fact is that Romans didn't need Christianity at all. The majority of them were doing just fine.

Without a doubt, the age of Constantine is one of Rome's defining moments. Jesus's followers had not only found their way from Judaea into a smattering of Roman cities. They had taken up residence in the palace on the throne. By century's end, one brand of Christianity would be enrolled in the law codes as the only official *religio* of the empire, and every act of Roman sacrifice—in public and at home—would be summarily outlawed.

How did an empire of sixty million people change so quickly, given that nearly 90 percent of them were non-Christian a century before? Had all of them finally converted to Christianity? Or was it that Edward

Gibbon was right all along and the Christians were now poised to unleash their "intolerant zeal" on a naïve, unsuspecting empire?

The time has come to look up from the dirt and dust. For the story that we built from the ground up five chapters ago is about to take us to the top of the Roman government. There, we will rejoin the debate already in progress about what it meant to be a follower of Jesus in Rome. Enter Constantine, Rome's first Christian emperor.

Rome, A.D. 312

It is night in Italy. Constantine and his army are encamped north of Rome, perhaps having pitched their tents somewhere near Malborghetto, in Latium, where an old farmhouse today preserves the shape of an arch erected as a Roman victory monument. Was it Constantine's? The picture is no clearer now than it was in October A.D. 312. That day, no one could say which way the winds of war would blow, and war was upon the Roman Empire.

The embers of the fires must have been dying as the general's weary troops sought rest. The past few weeks, they had marched across the Alps and across northern Italy. The years before Constantine came into power, the middle to late third century A.D., had also been bumpy, roiled with political and military troubles; but Rome had weathered the storm. These had been trying times for the government. Emperors were being killed on the battlefield—one of them died at Fallujah, Iraq—fighting a rising superpower, a reborn Persian Empire. Rome's new geopolitical neighbor would be ruled by a family called Sasanians, and under their leadership the word "Iran" would be chiseled into history for the first time. For Romans, the rise of the Sasanians would prove a steady source of diplomatic and military engagement for the next three hundred years. There would also be moments of quieter conversation.

The mystery cult of the god Mithras is thought to have come from Persia although Romans had likely invented these origins to give the cult an exotic cachet. Initiates of Mithras would find their place in Caesar's empire, too. In Rome, we can detect a healthy pulse among their communities throughout the fourth and early fifth century A.D.[3] Even during times of significant political challenge, not everything about "Persia" was culturally threatening.

Traditionally, however, this period in history, prior to Constantine's ascent, shoulders a substantial part of the explanation for why Christianity triumphed in the fourth century. Admittedly, rampant turnover in the palace, calculated at one new emperor every two years, does not look good on paper. What new research has shown is that this period of turbulence was limited to Rome's upper atmosphere.

In cities throughout the Mediterranean, taxes continued to be collected. Town councils continued to deliberate about local concerns. Buildings, including temples and shrines, continued to be repaired and, in some cases, entirely built anew. The third century bishop of Carthage, Cyprian, may have framed this time in apocalyptic terms ("These things have all been predicted to happen at the end of the world!"); but the world actually never came to an end. By the early fourth century, Rome's government had rebounded, and the mundane reality of life in many Roman cities went on through at least the sixth century A.D.[4]

A reorganized constitution helped. In A.D. 284, Diocletian established a framework to ensure more institutional continuity in the event of crisis. Two men, each with the title Augustus, would work with two junior partners, each with the title Caesar, to ensure the steady management of the state, geographically. This creative exercise in power sharing between the eastern and western halves of the Mediterranean would remain in effect until A.D. 324, when the son of an imperial bodyguard, fresh off the defeat of his eastern co-ruler, put an end to it. For the first time in nearly forty years, the Roman Empire would be under the management of a single ruler: Constantine. At Malborghetto, however, those battles were still to come. In A.D. 312, Constantine's eyes were focused on Rome.

Born in the Balkans, acclaimed Augustus at York, in England, by A.D. 312, Constantine was eager to acquire a larger swath of political territory. That fall, he marshaled his army. Together, they crossed the Alps, descended through Turin, and blazed through Verona.[5] Their destination? Rome. Their mission? To topple its ruler, Constantine's brother-in-law, Maxentius. Constantine and his army would celebrate a resounding triumph, inspiring many to wonder how it could have happened.

According to a later source, the Christian writer Lactantius, a tutor in Constantine's palace, the emperor's victory had been inspired by a miraculous vision. Lactantius tells us what happened that night inside the general's tent—and what followed: "Constantine was moved in his sleep to put the heavenly sign of God on his soldiers' shields and then to go into battle. And so he did as he was ordered. The next morning, turning a letter X on its side, with its top bent around, he branded CHRIST [the Messiah] on all the shields. Equipped with this sign, the army took up their weapons."[6]

Maxentius marshaled an impressive defense. He did everything he could, in fact—followed every governmental recommendation—to stop Constantine's attack on the city, even consulting the Sibyl's prophecies. What had she and her priests foreseen? "An enemy of Rome would die that day."[7] At the now famous battle of the Milvian Bridge, it was Maxentius who drowned in the Tiber. Constantine seized the city. The next morning, the man whose army had elevated him to junior emperor in York, England, now controlled Roman Spain, Gaul, Italy, and parts of North Africa. Constantine had stumbled onto a territorial fortune, matched only by his rivals in the eastern empire.

One year later, A.D. 313. The co-ruler of Rome and his partner in the east, Licinius, would meet at Milan to settle a pressing social question: the status of Rome's Christians. It was not the first time that Roman emperors had chosen to confront this perennially thorny issue. Just two years earlier, April 30, A.D. 311, Christians who had awoken in the city of Nicomedia (modern Izmit, Turkey) had heard from their emperor that they were now able to practice their faith legally. No longer branded followers of an illegal set of worship practices, Christians had finally won the hard-earned triumph they had been fighting for.

With one swift decision, the emperor had rolled back almost a decade of legalized discrimination. In the words of this edict, Christians were now permitted "to be openly Christian [*Christiani*] again."[8] It was a dramatic reversal for the empire's Christian community, but Constantine had nothing to do it. It was the lesser-known ruler, Galerius, married to a rather savvy diplomat, Valeria—Diocletian's daughter—who had been the first to wake up to the changing times, perhaps because he was comfortable waking up next to a Christian. The jubilation would not last long. Galerius's edict of toleration, from April 30, A.D. 311, would quickly be repealed after the emperor's death. Christians and their supporters must have been justly disillusioned, rocked with so much political uncertainty. They were getting close. They were so close to carving out their own space in the world they lived in.

Then, A.D. 313. Constantine's victory, followed by his meeting at Milan. The joint rulers of the Roman world resolved once and for all to end the policies that had been dividing one Roman from another. The co-emperors' statement was made available for immediate release, announced to cities of the eastern Roman Empire from the imperial palace at Nicomedia (hence its rather erroneous name, the "Edict of Milan").

Christians and their allies were probably holding their breath as members of the government read it aloud in the town's forum, in the law courts, and in the markets:

> When we, Constantine and Licinius, were fortunate enough to convene in Milan and began to take under consideration everything that pertains to the public good and to its security, among the many things that we felt would be beneficial for the people by and large was that certain matters must first and foremost be set in order, matters which preserved the respect for divinity.
>
> Consequently, we gave to Christians and to all people a free ability to follow the worship practices [religio] that each one wished, so that whatever divinity there is in the heavenly seat above may be appeased and made favorable to us and to everyone who has been put under our rule.
>
> Indeed, in accordance with sound and most virtuous reasoning, we believed that this course of action should be enacted so that the opportunity would not be denied to anyone at all—whether he wished to dedicate himself to the worship practice of Christians or whether he wished to dedicate himself to another kind of worship practice [religio] which he judges perfectly appropriate for himself.
>
> Either way, the result is intended to be the same: that the highest divinity, whose proper worship [religio] we pursue with our free minds, may preserve his accustomed favor and goodwill for all.[9]

The law was unequivocal: Christians were not to be harassed any further—a remarkable protection for a group that comprised no more than 10 percent of the population at the time—but the emperors' concern was larger than one minority group. Their task was managing the well-being of the entire empire, not just one part of it.

As Constantine and Licinius explained, "When you see what we have granted to Christians, you are going to understand that the ability to practice one's own way of worshipping (*religio*) openly and freely has been granted to others, too, for the peaceful well-being of our time, so that each person may have a free opportunity to worship whatever god he has chosen."[10] What it meant to be Roman had just gotten a little bit bigger, as it had been doing for centuries.

What really happened to Constantine on his march to Rome? How much weight should those events bear in explaining the political victory of Rome's Christian community? Galerius's edict, from A.D. 311, frustrates any easy attempt to connect Constantine's conversion to the new legal rights for Christians, as does Licinius's own participation in the conference at Milan. (Like Galerius, Licinius worshipped Rome's traditional gods.) Christianity's gains hadn't been predicated upon everyone's conversion, regardless of what Emperor Constantine saw, or thought he saw, before the battle against Maxentius.

But what did the emperor see? Even in the early fourth century A.D., the history of what happened at the bridge, of these seminal events, was the combined product of the emperor's memory and the memory of everyone who had heard him speak about them.[11] Lactantius narrated the scene one way. Many years later, Eusebius would sit down with the emperor to listen as the aging general told war stories about how he came to power, and the story would change.

The two men, bishop and emperor, had first met in A.D. 325, on the Asiatic side of Istanbul, at the ancient city of Nicaea. By then, more than a decade had gone by since Constantine's victory in Rome, but more had changed than just the seasons. In A.D. 325 Constantine had taken complete control of the empire.[12] The emperor and the bishop would forge their friendship shortly after this period of consolidation. The project of promoting the emperor's legacy had begun.

Over next fourteen years, until Eusebius's own death in A.D. 339, the bishop would write and revise four versions of what happened that day at the Milvian Bridge almost two and half decades earlier.[13] Eusebius says that he laid eyes on the military standard under which Constantine's army had fought. Just like Lactantius, he, too, relates its backstory. The emperor, Eusebius says, remembered calling out in prayer that day, asking for help in the pending battle. While he was praying, a marvelous sign appeared. About noon, Eusebius says, "when the day was declining into evening, the emperor said that he saw in one part of the sky the trophy of a cross of light above the sun, and along with it had come a text message: BY THIS, YOU ARE GOING TO CONQUER. Not knowing what to make of the vision, Constantine had gone to bed, puzzled. In his sleep, everything was illuminated.

A second vision—this time, of the one called the Messiah, Christ— appeared with the same sign and explained its meaning. If Constantine put this symbol on his soldiers' shields, it would protect his army in battle. When the emperor awoke, he immediately resolved "to worship no other God than the one who had appeared to him." By mid morning, Constantine had a new symbol; the first two Greek letters of CHRIST, X and P (chi and rho) were to be fashioned atop the army's standards. The soldiers had a new banner, and Maxentius had a meeting with the Tiber.[14]

What do we make of these reports? Treat them with skepticism, cynicism, or credence? Could Constantine's vision have been politically calculated? What had he really seen in the sky? Might Rome's first Christian emperor have not fully converted to Christianity in A.D. 312? We should tread carefully here. From Chloe's people to Martial and Basilides to the home renovators at Dura Europos, Jesus's followers had been seeing their world in shades of gray for three hundred years. Even at the start of the fourth century, there was more than one way to be a "Christian." Now, that included the Roman emperor.

Constantine must have fascinated the Roman people. An emperor who was openly Christian, he was a living sign that, at least for this one minority group in Rome, things could and did get better. Constantine certainly fascinated his biographer. "Serving as an ambassador for the Messiah of God with all outspokenness," Eusebius of Caesarea tells us, "Constantine persevered in all things. If any one accused him of being a 'Christian,' he did not take that name as a mark of shame but spoke about it solemnly and openly." The emperor, Eusebius reports, was a man who "prided himself" on his Christianity.

Constantine must have struck quite a pose. The same Greek verb, "to pride oneself" (*enabrunomai*), had been used to describe men like Julius Caesar who made risky fashion choices, such as wearing loose-fitting clothes. Caesar prided himself on his look, but he was also derided as too effeminate by his conservative peers.[15] Three centuries later, if language is any key, Constantine was acting with similar audacity. He had taken the stigma associated with the word "Christian" and had wrapped himself in it, proudly. Many Christians, maybe even their allies, must have been overjoyed at the emperor's self-confidence.

Christian visibility soon increased everywhere—from the hill country of Jerusalem, where a church was built to commemorate the site of Jesus's death to the Balkans, Greece, and North Africa. The early fourth century was also a time of church councils, at Arles and Nicaea, meetings that were attended by opinionated bishops who wrestled with theological ideas.[16] No wonder many still want to characterize this time as one of Christian cultural triumph as well. Seen from the inside of the movement, it really does begin to look as if the scales of the Roman world had begun to tip toward Christianity's favor with this one man's rise to the top.

But did it? The answer is most definitely not.

The worship of Rome's gods continued: at temples, at the baths, in the streets, and at the racetrack. Beastly, bloody, but wildly entertaining gladiator games and animal hunts remained popular entertainment in the Colosseum and elsewhere. There were a few structural changes to Roman society. Bishops had now earned the right to adjudicate legal disputes, much the same way that members of the Jewish community had been granted a similar privilege; but overall, the Roman world was not suddenly divided into opposing camps. Christians and non-Christians did not begin to live their lives on the squares of a chessboard. Cities remained diverse, dynamic places. Many people in them saw the Constantine they wanted to see.[17]

In A.D. 310, one poet lauded Constantine's military might by attributing it to Apollo. Urban planners in the empire's new, second capital, Constantinople, would erect a statue of Apollo as the sun god atop a victory column in the city's new forum. Romans elsewhere would develop their own artistic vocabulary to portray their ruler. A delicately carved stone cameo, an expensive piece of jewelry, presents us with a portrait of Constantine shown wearing a lion skin on his head.[18] In the fourth century, this exquisite gem must have been one of its owner's most valuable possessions, pinned on for special occasions. Anyone who complimented it would have spied Rome's first Christian ruler looking back at them in the guise of Hercules, just as everyone in Constantinople saw Apollo, in the guise of the sun god, looking down at them from the center of the forum.

The emperor's public image in Rome, too, suggests that the fourth century did not witness any radical break with centuries of tradition. Among the many spaces open for business in the capital was the soaring vaulted hall known as the New Basilica. A stroll from the Colosseum, the New Basilica has bequeathed us a template for our lofty urban train stations and grand museum spaces. In antiquity, it's where judges officiated and where magistrates met with concerned citizens. In the fourth century, everyone who entered it was greeted by a colossal marble statue of the emperor. Seated at one end was Constantine in the guise of the god Jupiter, king of Olympus, the Best and the Greatest (figure 13). Rome's rulers had been fancying themselves in this role for three centuries. Rome's first Christian emperor was still speaking the same language.[19]

Even the Roman Senate, that quaint institution of the Republican past, seemed confused—or couldn't bring itself to say what everyone else already knew. In A.D. 315, they had commissioned an arch to celebrate Constantine's ten years as a ruler (and to celebrate his recent victory over Maxentius). For the message inscribed across the top, they settled upon the vaguest Latin possible. Stonemasons were told to ascribe the emperor's success to "the inspiration of a divinity." Looking up at the Latin as tourists still do today, scholars have long scratched their heads and wondered, "Which divinity?" Seventeen hundred years later, the masons who chiseled the news are dead; their work orders have vanished; and the Arch of Constantine—one of the most famous monuments in the Eternal City—still won't talk.[20]

Constantine as Apollo, Hercules, and Jupiter, a triumphant ruler "inspired by a divinity": how do we reconcile so many apparently conflicting images of a Roman emperor who, we are told, was unabashedly "proud" of coming out a Christian? Airbrush these many pictures into a composite, or try to think some of them away? One thing's for sure: it's not as if Constantine was trying to pass as something he was not. During his reign he met with bishops, and cities saw a building boom in Christian architecture. Many new churches would be paid for out of the emperor's purse—at Rome's Vatican Hill, for example, and in the suburbs of the city. What it meant to be a Christian was still very visibly under construction at the start of the fourth century, but many Romans did know the obvious about their emperor. Constantine had come out Christian, even if there were a few who were grumbling about it.[21]

What was about to happen in later Rome, the wholesale proscription of an earlier way of life, has been tackled from various angles. One historian thinks that by the end of the fourth century A.D., it was "perhaps inevitable" that Christians would try (and succeed) to restrict the worship practices of non-Christians.[22] The implication, of course, is that Jesus's followers couldn't help but be the radically intolerant worshippers they inherently were. History is not the story of what's "inevitable," though. These were downright confusing times for Jesus's followers. We must not fail to appreciate that.

In A.D. 312, Constantine had accomplished what many of them had likely never thought possible. Christianity had found its way to the most intimate chambers in Caesar's palace. But whose Christianity? After three hundred years of family quarreling, to whom did this patchwork quilt of obedient soldiers, quiet home remodelers, and fervent martyrs belong?

Did it belong to the memory of Chloe's people, the men and women of Corinth who had feasted at banquets but had been chastised by mail for doing so? Would bishops in third century Spain have a voice in the matter even though one of them, Martial, had flirted with the apocalypse by holding a chair in a local Roman social club? And what about the Christian daughter of the emperor Diocletian? Would there be any room for the memory of people like her? Valeria's Christianity had hardly caused a scandal in the palace—even when her dad asked her to take part in affairs of Roman state—until someone leaked the information and tried to use it against her (Valeria would later be executed when her husband, Galerius, died). For Jesus's followers who cared even moderately about their group's cohesiveness, the social chasms that existed among them must have seemed daunting, if not downright impossible, to bridge.

And so we come full circle to rejoin a debate three hundred years in the making. The conversations that Jesus's followers had been having for centuries—"What does it mean to be a Christian in the Roman world?"—were now about to be fought, awkwardly at times, in plain view of their friends and neighbors.

Without a doubt, the age of Constantine was a far different time than the second century empire of Trajan or the early third century world of Septimius Severus. In A.D. 212, all freeborn residents of Roman cities had been granted citizenship, transforming the empire into a larger political entity than it ever had been before. In this geographically diverse world, many people would find their own way of being Roman: speaking two languages, creatively mixing local and Roman customs. In the largely Greek-speaking cities of the empire, for example—places like the Balkans, Greece, Syria, Egypt, and Turkey—many Romans began to explore, adopt, and adapt Greek literature and philosophy. By the fourth century A.D., many of these Roman citizens were justly proud of their own Hellenistic heritage.

Followers of Jesus navigated this changing world, too. Many did so deftly. We know because, just like Chloe's people in the time of Paul, they earned the scorn of their uncompromising peers. "Being openly Christian is not about 'acting like a Greek,'" the bishop Eusebius of Caesarea would insist, in the years after A.D. 313.[23] For Eusebius, the threat to his community must have seemed grave. As Christians in the Eastern Empire had begun to live more openly in their cities, many were doing so in ways that downplayed their differences and played up their connection to the local culture. For Eusebius, such behavior was unacceptable. In his mind, people who called themselves Christians were not supposed to look or act like something they were not.

By the end of the fourth century, other churchmen in the Eastern Roman Empire, such as John Chrysostom in Antioch and Bishop Athanasius in Egypt, can be heard speaking to their communities in these same terms. At Antioch on the Orontes River, a resplendent imperial city of the late fourth century A.D., men and women dined in grand houses amid exquisite mosaics that must have been the pride of the workmen who laid them.

One priest, John Chrysostom, had his vision for what it meant to be Christian in such a thoroughly Greek and Roman environment. "'If a man sees you, who have a knowledge' of how to worship God, passing the whole day in unprofitable and hurtful associations, won't the conscience of a weak man be emboldened to pursue these acts even more earnestly?" If the chastisement sounds vaguely familiar to us, it should. Chrysostom, writing in the late fourth century A.D., was playing a cover version of Paul's letter to the Corinthians (1 Corinthians 8:10).

In the mid first century, Paul had been warning people in Corinth not to participate in their civic dinners. Four centuries later, Chrysostom was warning his community not to flock to Antioch's racetrack and root for their favorite horses, or go to the theater and applaud their favorite actors. Any Christian who did so risked engaging in what Paul had called "unprofitable and hurtful associations." The solution? No games, no races, no theater; Christians should not be caught acting like Greeks.[24] John Chrysostom was fighting the same cultural war that Eusebius had been, a generation earlier.

Being caught acting like a Greek was not the only existential threat that fourth century Christians faced, however. Three hundred years after Jesus's Jewish ministry, none of his followers could quite agree yet on how to understand their own Jewish heritage.[25] In Eusebius's day, some were holding the "Lord's Supper" on the Jewish Sabbath, Saturday. Many leaders were still circumcising their initiates, not baptizing them, as Paul had recommended.

Eusebius would point his pen at these people, too. "Being openly Christian is not about 'acting Jewish,'" he would lament to his Christian readers.[26] If that warning also sounds familiar, it should. Eusebius was singing the same tune Ignatius of Antioch had in the early second century A.D. Back then, Ignatius had coined the idea of being openly Christian (*Christianismos*) so that Jesus's followers would stop identifying as Jewish. Two hundred years later, Christians of Eusebius's day were still coming to their own conclusions about what that meant.[27]

These were not heady theological debates. Within a generation after Eusebius's death, the force of Roman law was being summoned to address these perceived problems. If someone found a "Jew" who was previously a "Christian," an edict of A.D. 357 decreed, that person's property would be confiscated by the Roman state. By A.D. 388, Jews and Christians were forbidden to marry. The issue of Jesus's Jewishness was one that had not been resolved by his later followers.[28]

To put it bluntly, Christians had walked straight into fourth century Rome lugging some fairly significant cultural baggage. Both of Eusebius's anxieties—that Christians not *act like Greeks* and that they not *seem too Jewish*—would fester throughout the rest of the century. Soon, these unresolved identity issues would begin to cause massive headaches for everyone else, not just for the empire's Jewish community. Very few Romans would have seen this explosion coming, but then again, why should they have? Why should the curious struggle of one minority group in Rome to find their place in Caesar's empire ever have been an urgent concern to them? By the end of the century, one of the least studied eruptions in Roman history was about to disrupt the lives of everyone in the empire: Christians, non-Christians, and Jews alike.

By A.D. 337, Constantine would be dead, interred alongside tombs for the holy apostles. As the roughly 90 percent of non-Christian Rome went about its usual routine—gods, temples, sacrifice—those who had been looking for guidance about being Christian would face a daunting task. They would have almost twenty-five years of the emperor's public life, policy pronouncements, and personal experiences to pore over. It was a sizeable but confusing legacy. Less than a decade before his death, in A.D. 325, the emperor had given one of his final answers to the idea of what it meant to be a "Christian." It was also one of the strangest.

This period marks a crucial time in Roman history. Only a year earlier, in A.D. 324, Constantine had raised an army against his co-ruler Licinius and summarily defeated him. For the first time in a generation, Rome was now reunited under one ruler.

Then, sometime after his defeat of Licinius, Constantine set to work planning a new palace for the empire's second capital to be named after himself, Constantinople. The city's formal dedication would not be celebrated until six years later—in A.D. 324, there was still much to be done to build it—but at least Constantine did not have to start from the ground up. A Roman settlement, replete with temples, a forum, even a racetrack, had been situated here, at the tip of the Golden Horn since the late second century A.D. By the time Constantine was finished investing in it, the city would have its own senate; and its residents would receive a free grain allowance, a quality-of-life perk that was held only by residents of Rome. The empire, in effect, would now have two capitals, not just one. There, amidst the temples, forum spaces, new churches, walls, fountains, houses, and harbors—all the things that distinguished a fourth century Roman city—Constantine would leave an important clue about his Christianity. It was displayed above the door of the imperial palace.[29]

Eusebius stood at the threshold of the palace and described what he saw. Above the door was the familiar logo of CHRIST, the chi-rho, placed like a talisman above Constantine's head. Below it was Licinius. Licinius wasn't shown as a flesh-and-blood Roman sporting a conservative toga or military cuirass, however. "The hated enemy and savage beast," Eusebius says, the one who had "besieged the God's Church through godless tyranny and brought it into the abyss [was depicted there] as a snake." What was the reason for depicting a Roman emperor with such artistic license? Eusebius explained: "Passages in books that belong to God's prophets have talked about this man [the enemy who would besiege God's Church] as a dragon and a crooked snake." Constantine himself would use the same imagery in a letter sent to bishops after A.D. 324. Licinius, he wrote to them, had been the embodiment of evil: the snake, the serpent.[30]

In Istanbul today, there is nothing left of Constantine's palace—not even the door. Yet the image Eusebius saw, which Constantine references in his own correspondence, does survive. It appears on a series of coins issued at roughly the same time (figure 14). One side ("heads") shows Constantine. The other ("tails") show a military standard, topped by the chi-rho, piercing a writhing snake beneath it. The coin's legend celebrates, in Latin, the dawn of a new period of "Public Hope."[31] From the palace door to coins in people's purses, Rome's first Christian emperor had started talking about his victory over Licinius, a fellow Roman, by drawing upon imagery and language expressing an apocalyptic world view.

Why?

The defeat of the end-time beast, the battle of good versus evil, and visions of a spiritual, metaphysical conflict did have a long history. Among Jesus's followers, they had provided something in short supply once: hope. During the first, second, and third centuries A.D., when few could worship openly, images like these reassured them that things would get better. (We remember that one way people may have interpreted John's phantasmagorical Revelation was to read it as an uplifting message. Visions of victory may have inspired hope in times of crisis, real or perceived.) Their journey to hope had taken slightly longer than expected, of course. But by A.D. 313, Jesus's followers had reached the promised land. No longer "sojourners" in someone else's empire, they were fully recognized good neighbors. They were also Roman citizens whose worship practices benefited the state.

By all reasonable accounts, the political rhetoric of the "evil serpent" as a cipher for Rome should have been stamped with an expiration date—A.D. 313—the year when that hope had finally become a reality. In A.D. 325, however, little more than a decade after their political triumph, Constantine was drawing upon polarizing images he had dug up from a bygone era, talking about his recent military conquest as if it had been a victory in a spiritual war. That same year, he would deliver one of the oddest speeches in Roman political history.

The Easter holiday was twenty-four to forty-eight hours away. Nearby, at Nicaea, bishops would soon begin debating the relationship between Jesus and God. (A creed that some Christians still recite today is one of the best-known products of their deliberation.) Constantine was about to reflect on the role that divine providence had played in leading Rome to a new Golden Age. A copy of the emperor's remarks has, almost miraculously, survived. No scholar today doubts its authenticity. One historian has even described it as a kind of "stump speech."[32] It is a thrilling text to read, a kind of behind-the-scenes political document so rarely found in the archives of ancient history.

The Christian God was guiding his "holy ones," Constantine said. It was the very term John of Patmos had used to describe the angelic army of believers in Revelation. John himself had adapted the imagery from the Jewish book of Daniel—with one significant change. In Daniel, the "holy ones" referred to heavenly beings, otherworldly protectors, angels who fought demons.[33] John had transformed the term and applied it to human beings who saw themselves as waging a battle on earth.

Constantine developed this theme in his speech. The emperor, a man who had come to power after seeing visions in the sky, was now convinced that everything around him had taken place according to God's plan: the people around him, "they have witnessed the battles," he said. "They have seen the [recent] war, when God's providence granted victory to his people [over Licinius]. They have seen God coming to aid our prayers."[34] Licinius's resounding defeat had made everything clear, to him.

How could the emperor be so certain? Constantine was about to take his audience on a grand tour, unwinding the spools of time and pausing to show them "proof" of God's intervention. First, Virgil, the closest Rome ever came to having a poet laureate, whose golden verses were memorized by schoolchildren even in Augustine's day. Virgil had foreseen the birth of the Messiah, or so the emperor was now proclaiming in his speech. Never mind that Virgil died in 19 B.C. and that the poet from Verona had been writing four decades before Jesus was born.[35]

Next, Daniel. Daniel was a Jewish prophet who had survived a night in a Babylonian lions' den, where he had seen a vision of Jesus the Messiah, too, Constantine declared. Never mind that this chronology, too, was off. Jews had been forced to live in Babylon as captives after the destruction their First Temple, in 586 B.C. After their liberation, many Jewish writers would return to that period to tell unsung stories about their outspoken heroes and resistors. One of these resisters was Daniel. Punished by the king, left to be devoured by lions, Daniel had survived because he had been protected by God's hand. Later, he wrote about several visions that provided comfort to him and were passed down to fellow Jews.

These visions are recounted in the Book of Daniel, narrated in his name, included in the Jewish Bible. In it, horned beasts threaten the existence of God's people, and the end-time is fast approaching. Of course, even Roman writers were able to suspect what biblical scholars today state with confidence: the book was edited during the tumultuous cultural world of the Hellenistic kings, the writer Porphyry said in the early fourth century A.D.[36] The beast was a reference to Antiochus IV Epiphanes, the Hellenistic ruler whose policies contributed, directly or indirectly, to the Maccabean revolt. Daniel's visions have come down to us as a piece of political rhetoric, a "historical apocalypse" meant to offer hope for a Jewish community who may have felt deep pangs of disaffection during the second century B.C.[37]

Constantine was a great admirer of Daniel's resolve. Thrown amid lions, Daniel had survived, the emperor said, because of his "immaculate piety toward the true God." That's why, on the morning after his incarceration, his enemies were amazed to discover him alive! When they peered inside the cave, they could see Daniel standing there "with his hands upraised, praising Jesus the Messiah."[38] Never mind that Jesus does not appear in the version of the story read by Jews.

Constantine would later place statues of Daniel and the lions at fountains in Constantinople. It was a curious choice. Eusebius had urged

Christians not to seem so Jewish, but both bishop and now emperor were vocal that Jewish prophets—Daniel, Moses, Abraham, and others—had "predicted" Jesus's coming.

The emperor had even more to say about the topic of Jewish-Christian relations. "No one," Constantine went on, "would ever have been more blessed than this people"—here he was referring to the Jewish people—"had they not willingly cut off their souls from the Holy Spirit."[39] In a letter, Constantine would make this point even more explicit. Jews, he wrote, were guilty of "killing the Lord."[40] It's an astonishing accusation. For the first time in the annals of Roman history, the midlevel functionary who executed Jesus, Pontius Pilate, was being issued an imperial pardon. At a distance of three centuries, Constantine was fully absolving him for any liability in connection with Jesus's death.[41] Roman authorities hadn't killed Jesus. In Constantine's mind, Jews had.

And then, the emperor started talking about the "Sibyls," the inspired women who have haunted our story since 63 B.C. Even these homegrown Mediterranean prophets, Constantine said, had recognized the inevitability of a Christian future. In one of their poems, the Sibyls had delivered a secret message to him.

The clue had been written as an acrostic: "Jesus the Messiah [Christ] was the Son of God, the Lord and Savior."[42] Constantine then assured his audience about the poem's authenticity. It was not just some document conveniently cooked up to support his argument. Cicero, he said, that respected Republican statesman who had quashed Catiline's revolt, had actually seen it. (Fact check: Cicero never laid eyes on it.) In his well-read Latin treatise *On Divination*, which includes a discussion of the Sibylline prophecies, Cicero does allude to acrostics—each line in a prophecy might begin with a letter that spelled out a secret word or theme—but the man whose head and hands were cut off in 43 B.C. for having executed Catiline without a trial never gets around to mentioning "Jesus."[43]

Constantine believed that Rome's Sibyls had predicted Christianity's success. But had they? The answer is definitively no. Constantine's "Sibyl" was not a prophet. Like all the so-called Sibylline Oracles we possess today—handed down to us in a sixth century A.D. manuscript—"she" was a fraud; and "her" text was a Christian forgery.[44]

Constantine was not alone in his zeal for these righteous prophecies. Many individuals, both Christians and Jews, had been circulating false

"Sibylline Oracles" for centuries and citing them as if they had the force of scriptural authority. A hundred years earlier, Clement, bishop of Alexandria at Egypt—he who railed against the use of fancy pots and sauces at the "Lord's supper"—cited one so-called Sibylline Oracle in this way. Alexandria was spiritually depraved, Clement thundered. The city was doomed; its destruction was near. The historic Temple of Serapis, the architectural and cultural wonder of their resplendent Hellenistic seaside town, was going to be sacked and burned. How did he know? A "Sibyl" had told him: "And you, Serapis, who are set upon so many glistening-white stones, you will lie in ruin in thrice-unhappy Egypt," Clement claimed "she" said.[45]

By the fourth century A.D., others were still putting their faith in poems like these. Lactantius would quote them. Tutor to Constantine's son, he may have been reading them and sharing them while working in the palace.[46] Emperor Constantine was now citing these texts as if they were divine pronouncements, too. He was using them to articulate a new vision for Rome, even relying upon ones that had not originally been written by or for Christians. "'Memphis' and 'Babylon' have received a just reward for their wayward worship," he told the audience in his speech. "[These cities have been] left desolated and uninhabited, together with their gods."[47] If these words look familiar, they should, too. An anonymous Jewish rebel in Egypt had "predicted" the imminent destruction of "Memphis" and "Babylon" at the start of the second century A.D.[48]

Two centuries later, that obscure Jewish "prophet" had found a distinguished following.[49] His frenzied words were now being attributed to a "Sibyl." (That is where we find the fragments of his poetry today, in a text that scholars have named the *Fifth Sibylline Oracle*.) Constantine was quoting it—one more Christian appropriation of Jewish history—to talk about his recent triumph over Licinius.[50]

Virgil, Daniel, Rome's Sibyls—everywhere Constantine looked, in A.D. 325, he was convinced by the predestination of a Christian empire. It must have been an extraordinary speech to hear. Did anyone ever question his interpretations? We don't know. Some of his statements probably did raise a few eyebrows. To say that "Memphis" and "Babylon" had been punished was to imply that an evil, godless empire had been toppled. Constantine, the leader of sixty million Romans, was claiming to have seen the "fall" of Rome. Meanwhile, outside the room—from the

Forum of Constantinople, crowned by Apollo, to the Forum of Rome, lorded over by Jupiter—no such thing had actually happened. If people were looking to the emperor to figure out what it meant to be a Christian, by A.D. 325, many of them must have been downright confused by the kind of Christian the emperor had become.

In Constantine's rich public life, which spanned almost a quarter century, where was the real Christianity Christians were supposed to use as a model for their own? It always seemed to be shifting, changing. Did it come from after the Milvian Bridge, when the emperor showed no signs of a dualistic world view? Or did it come from after Licinius's defeat, A.D. 325, when the emperor's Christianity was increasingly being fed on the poetry of "Sibyls," the visions of Daniel, and revelations of John? The first set of documents was falsely represented to be something it was not: a government sanctioned prophecy. The second belonged to the Jewish people. As for the third, Christians in Constantine's day hadn't decided whether to keep it or throw it out. Revelation wasn't even an accepted part of the Christian canon yet. It would remain an outlier, too, until later in the fourth century.[51]

Indeed, Revelation had become a toxic text. In the mid third century A.D., one bishop in Egypt had become so convinced of its literal truth, he thought that God's kingdom would reign for a millennium and that it would happen on earth, soon. A fellow bishop tried to disabuse him of that timetable, but whether this friendly intervention swayed his colleague is unclear. Still, by Constantine's day, the tide may have been turning against John's visions, as Christians began to muse whether it was right to classify them as a "revelation." That word seemed entirely inappropriate for a story that was, on first reading, so maddeningly incomprehensible.[52]

By A.D. 337 then, the year Constantine died, many of Jesus's followers must have thought of themselves a bit like the blind man in Mark's gospel. They could see things now—a world full of Romans—but everything around them still looked cloudy. Many of them couldn't even agree on the composition of their own Bible. With the "Edict of Milan," Jesus's followers had merely passed from one stage of uncertainty to another.

As for the Roman world, what did it look like from the outside? How much did Constantine's conversion change society for everyone else? The answer is, very little. Few Romans lived their lives as if they were waging a metaphysical war. Even fewer were anxious about the return of someone else's Messiah. Christians may have won their place in the empire, but Rome wasn't hastening toward a fiery end because of any social change.[53] Life in the Roman world was never a zero-sum game—unless, that is, someone had been taught to see it that way.

CHAPTER 7

"Soldiers" in God's Heavenly Army

Constantine's successors took up his imperial vision with élan. They completed his unfinished projects and planned bold statements of their own. Roman metropolises—in Antioch, Alexandria, Constantinople— drew sailors, businessmen, and in some cases now, even pilgrims, as people crossed the Mediterranean easily and efficiently to trade wine, oil, or grain or to visit churches. (The Church of the Holy Sepulcher, in the shadow of the barren Jewish Temple Platform, drew a fair number to Jerusalem.)

Elsewhere, emperors were undertaking daring feats of engineering. An obelisk from Egypt, which had been destined for Rome but had been stuck in the harbor at Alexandria for decades, was finally put on a barge big enough to transport it. When it arrived in the capital, in A.D. 357, Constantine's son, Constantius II (r. A.D. 337–361), had it triumphantly marched into the city through the Ostian Gate, Rome's symbolic departure and arrival point for Egypt, where a pyramid had been erected in the first century B.C. The obelisk was placed in the center of the Circus Maximus. The message was inescapable. The Rome of Trajan, which had once moved a small mountain in the second century A.D., was still doing big things two hundred years later.[1]

This was not an empire showing any outward signs of stress. There may have been the occasional logistical problem. If wine or food wasn't delivered on time, there could be riots, and Rome's politicians did not always rise to the moment the way we might expect a government official to do. When, in A.D. 354, forecasters predicted famine, politicians implemented emergency measures and expelled all foreigners from the city.[2] It may not have been the most enlightened policy, but it's understandable. The borders of the fourth century empire were more permeable than its cities. At the Euphrates, there were Sasanian Persians. At the Danube, a collection of tribes ("Goths"). In Africa and elsewhere, more people who didn't look or act like Romans—"barbarians," they were called, diagnosed with a "savageness madness" (*rabies*, in Latin) and always threatening "ceaseless slaughter and pillaging."[3]

Many fourth century Romans didn't know what to do with these people other than stereotype them. The Huns of the Central Asian steppe, north of the Black Sea? They didn't season their food, dressed the same way at home as abroad, and wore one set of clothes until it fell apart. They were so ugly, Ammianus Marcellinus said, you could mistake them for a two-legged animal, like one of the monsters you might see sculpted into a Roman bridge. (They also never got down from their horses.) As for the Persians, they slouched and—something entirely incomprehensible to a Roman of more refined ways—they had no set dinnertime.[4]

Foreigners in Rome may not have led an easy life, but the fact that they were there tells us something. Every corner of the world, Ammianus says, looked upon the city as the Mediterranean's "mistress and queen." The city of Rome was not a stale, whitewashed capital in the fourth century A.D. It was colored with diversity and with many people's memories. Even in the decades after Constantine, visitors could stand in the old Roman Forum—at the new speaker's platform—and imagine the ghost of Cicero harping on the Roman virtues of yore.

Constantine's son, Constantius II, who visited Rome in A.D. 357, gazed upon the famous Temple of Jupiter on the Capitoline Hill. He saw the Pantheon lording over the Campus Martius like the mayor of its own city. Some baths in Rome, people said at the time, were as large as provinces. In the center of it all? A solid mass of white stone, travertine, "whose highest point can scarcely be seen with the human eye," said Ammianus. Today, much of its exterior has been stripped—the building is a skeleton of its former self—but the Colosseum still takes us to a different time, usually to the early or high Roman Empire. There's no reason it can't take us to the fourth century, too. Even then, Rome was still perceived to be "an eternal city."[5]

This—the age of Constantine's successors—would be a crucial time for Jesus's followers. It's the time when the world of "pagans and Christians" would be born; but it's not the world we've been taught to think it was.

Many people believe that the word "paganism" was invented to describe—indeed, to slander—the beliefs of non-Christians. Pick up any history book, and there's probably some version of the following story. "Believers in Jupiter, Minerva, and Mars did not think of themselves as 'pagans,'" we are told, in one recent study of the first century B.C. poet Lucretius. "The word, which appeared in the late fourth century, is etymologically related to the word 'peasant.' It is an insult, then, a sign that the laughter at rustic ignorance had decisively reversed direction."[6] Even at the time, 2011, these were fairly uncontested views.

Decades earlier, the great historian of the early church Henry Chadwick had once famously remarked: "The pagans [of Rome] did not know they were pagans until the Christians told them they were."[7] A generation of church historians, theologians, ancient historians, and archaeologists were brought up to see the Roman world in these terms. According to this view, as the empire's Christians proselytized more vigorously in the years after Constantine, they derided men and women who resisted Christianity's "superior" message. Soon, Christians were mocking even the most cultured and urbane Roman senators for being too "rustic," if they didn't convert fast enough. The debate between "pagans and Christians" had begun, product of a frustrated evangelism and sign of a growing clash of faiths.

Today, the tide has turned. Many historians have become so uncomfortable with notions of "religious conflict," they have eliminated any reference to "pagans and Christians" in their writings. In the classroom, students now learn about the rich shades of gray that separated Rome's "pagans" from its Christians. In still other cases, it's become fashionable to make these two religions, as we call them, plural—"paganisms" and "Christianities"—in order to dispel any notion of two monolithic clashing cultures. (In the academy, adding an s signifies complexity.) The need for nuance is undeniable here, but when people start hurling slurs at one other, historians are obligated to talk about that phenomenon, not bury their heads to it.

The fact of the matter is, Christian sources are embarrassingly full of derogatory remarks about "pagans" in the decades after Constantine. Why? Were "the Christians" suddenly incapable of living peacefully alongside their non-Christian friends, family, and neighbors? My research has led me to a new way of understanding this crucial period in Roman history. The word "pagan," as fourth century Christians used it, had nothing to do with non-Christians.

We can speak confidently about this point thanks to one man who lived in the mid fourth century: Marius Victorinus.

Victorinus might just be the most famous Christian no one's ever heard of. Born and raised in North Africa, as Constantine was coming to power, by the 350s, Victorinus had become a preeminent teacher in Rome. Wealthy families paid him to educate their children. Later, he would be awarded a senator's status—literally, put on a pedestal. By A.D. 354, a statue had been erected for him in one of Rome's most majestic spaces, the Forum of Trajan.[8] The emperor Constantius II, who stood in the Forum in A.D. 357 and was overwhelmed by its architectural grandeur—its column with one of Rome's best lookout platforms, Trajan's equestrian statue, all of it surrounded by rich yellow and purple-veined marble—walked right by Victorinus's statue without saying anything about him, as far as we know. But why should he have? Victorinus lived a thoroughly traditional life.

Ambition had brought him, perhaps at a young, idealistic age, to the center of the Western Roman Empire. There, he had devoted himself to teaching and to the gods, whose worship was an inescapable part of civic life—even in the mid fourth century. According to one later writer, Victorinus was even known during that stage of his life to have associated with followers of that "barking dog-headed Egyptian god, Anubis."[9] What our later source means to say, of course, is that Victorinus had worshipped Isis—even if our late fourth century Christian commentator can't quite bring himself to say her name. Four centuries after a grandstanding politician had misread popular opinion and tried to dismantle an Isis shrine, some Romans (such as Augustine of Hippo) were still more comfortable talking about Isis's worshippers in tired, worn-out stereotypes. But we should not be too hard on the bishop of Hippo. Augustine wasn't interested in describing, for us, the complexities of life in fourth century Rome. He was interested in narrating what happened to Victorinus later. For with one stunning, jaw-dropping announcement, sometime in the early to mid fourth century, Rome's preeminent teacher, Victorinus, would come out Christian.

Even after A.D. 313, even after the emperor himself (and his family) had come out as Christian, Victorinus's experience cannot have been an easy one. To begin, Victorinus had a very thin support system. After he began to feel more comfortable embracing his Christian identity, he shared the news with a close friend, Simplicianus. Victorinus had caught the latter one day as he was going to church, and out of earshot of the passing crowds, Victorinus told him, "You know that I'm secretly a Christian, right?"

Simplicianus, already a baptized Christian himself, apparently did not appreciate the emotional angst that had accompanied his friend's confession. If Victorinus really was a Christian, Simplicianus said—and here one imagines him speaking in a slightly catty, taunting tone—"Then how come I don't see you in church?"[10] Victorinus was quick to parry, "Do the walls of a church building really make someone a Christian?"[11] Each time they saw each other in the street, the two men would continue this joust, until one day Victorinus relented.

No longer nervous or shy, he asked Simplicianus to lead him into the church:

> And so, the time for the profession of faith had come, a moment which, in Rome—for those who are about to arrive in your grace, God—usually happens as follows. After one has committed the appropriate words to memory, the profession is then made from a higher platform so that the entire community of the faithful can see. The priests, however, asked Victorinus if he wanted to do it in a more private fashion [secretius], as was standard practice for anyone who seemed to be hesitant because of nervousness.[12]

Victorinus decided to walk straight up to the platform. As he did, everyone recognized who it was. "They uttered his name with a joyful murmur. For who, let's be honest [says Augustine] didn't recognize Victorinus?" Reading Augustine's *Confessions*, our source for this story, it's natural to cheer along. It's harder to appreciate Victorinus's hesitation. Augustine understood it. "Victorinus," he says, "was afraid of offending his friends." In mid fourth century Rome, friends and social networks were still important.[13]

Victorinus's friends—Isis worshippers, Mithras worshippers, Jupiter worshippers—were not dinosaurs. Their calendar was packed with festivals for their gods. One of these calendars, from A.D. 354, has been extensively studied. It tells us the dates for many of the Isis celebrations held throughout the year. (It is also the first document we have that places Jesus's birth on the date known as December 25). Gods who did not have their own dates on the Roman calendar—Mithras, for instance— were still present throughout Rome, too.[14] In many cities throughout the empire, even animal sacrifice, associated with gods such as Jupiter, had not vanished.

In A.D. 398, Valerius Publicola wondered, was it right for a Christian to buy firewood that had been sourced from sacred groves? What about wine and olive oil? If, at some point during their manufacture, some by-product of them had been set aside for use in a sacrifice to Roman gods, would it still be all right for a Christian to purchase them? And what about the prospect of visiting the local butcher?

> If a Christian goes to buy meat at the city market and has it in his mind to buy something specifically that did not come from a Roman sacrifice, what happens when he sees something that could be all right but then he starts to have second thoughts about whether it did or did not come from a sacrifice? If he finally decides that it didn't [come from a sacrifice], is he doing something wrong if he eats it? . . . And what if someone should intentionally mislead a Christian by saying that the meat did come from a sacrifice but afterward goes back to tell that Christian, "Just kidding!"—if at that point the Christian is confident that he really has been lied to, is it all right for him to eat it or to sell it (and maybe even enjoy the profit from the sale)?[15]

Very little had changed since the time of Cyprian in some respects. Back in the third century, the smell of animal sacrifices in Carthage had assaulted the bishop's delicate senses. He had lamented how Christians "ran to the forum of their own accord" in order to take part in the city's festivals. Later, after sniffing their clothes, he had even confessed how much it pained him to see them "returning from the altars of the Devil to the house of the Lord . . . with hands filthy, reeking of smoke."[16]

A century and a half later, we still find some of Jesus's followers, Valerius Publicola prime among them, in their town's forum fretting about Roman sacrifice. Even at the dawn of the fifth century, sacrifice—whether to Jupiter, Hercules, Minerva, or any number of gods in the festival lineup—was a defining part of urban life, for many. Valerius himself couldn't avoid it.

Nor could Marius Victorinus's friends, or, by extension, Marius Victorinus. As an accomplished public intellectual, he took his first steps toward the Christian community in Rome cautiously, shakily, and with hesitation. Why? There is no need for us to assume that Christians had suddenly soared demographically. The sociologist Rodney Stark, for example, once estimated their numbers at nearly 50 percent of the empire—slightly in excess of that, actually (52.9 percent)—by the mid fourth century A.D.[17] Yet Christianity's political triumph under Constantine had not set off a controlled implosion that toppled everyone else's traditions. The emperors had carved out a space for Christians within the empire, inviting them to participate in it. Many Christians were accepting that invitation gladly, eager to build on the momentum of having "one of their own" in the palace. They began to build public worship spaces of their own.

Many Christians modeled these spaces on the form of well-known Roman buildings—basilicas—places where Romans worshipped their gods, too.[18] Constantine constructed one of the most famous, the Lateran basilica in Rome. During the course of the fourth century, other basilicas would soon appear, such as those dedicated to Peter, who was thought to have been martyred at the Vatican, or to Paul, whose basilica still stands on the Ostian Way. Around Rome, Christians were making a strong public statement about their willingness to participate in the well-being of the empire.[19] Now, two famous martyrs were being enlisted as ambassadors for the movement. People who worshipped Peter and Paul in their Roman basilicas did so for the good of Rome.

What hadn't gone away was the stigma of being a "Christian."[20] We can see this stigma in Victorinus's honest question, "Do the walls of a church building really make someone a Christian?" If Christians could find their own way to the faith, as Victorinus had, why should they be required to come out in front of everyone else? Why couldn't they just be Christian at home? Many Christians of Victorinus's day were doing just that, building churches on their estates and installing chapels in their houses. Many were lavishly decorated with frescoes or mosaics of saints and martyrs. Archaeologists can spot them easily. In all likelihood, Victorinus was intimately familiar with them, too. These properties were the source of his most dedicated clientele, the children of rich parents.

As Simplicianus had delicately phrased it, however, if people in the mid fourth century wanted to call themselves "Christians," meeting in people's houses was no longer good enough. Jesus's followers, who had been meeting quietly and unobtrusively in private homes for three hundred years, had decided to undertake a radical renovation of their public image. The new message was, Everybody out! Christians who met in people's homes were now increasingly stigmatized by their own Christian peers, much the same way that the Christian bishop Eusebius had mocked his own Christians peers because they were acting too Greek.[21]

But what if a Christian didn't really feel comfortable being "out"? Marius Victorinus's experience shows us just how difficult it continued to be for Jesus's followers in the mid fourth century A.D. That's also precisely the moment when something happened that would change both Victorinus and the Roman world irrevocably.

Around the mid fourth century, Victorinus began to leave behind a paper trail in which he denounced other Christians for refusing to enlist as "soldiers" in God's heavenly Christian army.[22] These followers of Jesus were now being condemned for what Victorinus called *civilianism*. Or, as we probably recognize it, using its more proper Latin form, *paganism*. The unassuming man who had famously asked "Do walls really make someone a Christian?" had taken up the urgent task of policing his own Christian peers using military imagery and notions of spiritual war. The words "pagan" and "paganism" had come crashing into history.

In this heated conversation that was about to erupt between Christians in the Western Roman Empire, some Christians were being charged with acting too civilian, just as in the East, other Christians were being charged with acting too Greek.[23] Why did Victorinus adopt the word that he did? (He is the first person we know of, in all of Roman history, ever to have used the word "civilian" to refer pejoratively to other Christians.) To begin with, for any Latin speaker to accuse a Roman of acting too Greek was to bestow on him one of the highest compliments around. Cicero had sent his son to study abroad in Athens specifically so that the boy would come back with a good, well-rounded Greek education. The way that Greek-speaking Christians were arguing with each other in the East—inside their group—made no conceptual sense in the Latin-speaking West—outside their group.

Second, Latin-speaking Christians already had access to a powerful metaphor of their own. Tertullian, we remember, had written about a world of Christian soldiers and Christians civilians in the third century A.D. Back then, martyrdom had brought all of these Christians together. Only the ones who had chosen to exclaim their beliefs proudly, who had chosen to take a visible stand, who had made their Christian identity publicly known were the real "Christians," Tertullian had argued. One lone Christian soldier had done just that; Tertullian had praised him for being "God's soldier." All the other Christians had been (shamelessly, in Tertullian's opinion) trying to "serve two masters."

One hundred and fifty years later, it must have seemed like the perfect description for what was happening in Victorinus's day. In an age where every Christian could now comfortably look like a member of mainstream Roman society, the need to wear a separate Christian identity was a pressing necessity—for those who still saw the world around them in fiercely dualistic terms. A culture war had been born between "Christian soldiers" and "Christian civilians." A new, polarizing era in Roman politics was set to begin. It would play out in both the Greek-speaking and Latin-speaking realms of the empire.

From A.D. 361 to 363, Constantine's nephew Julian governed the Roman Empire. In many books, Julian's brief time in the palace colors our vision of the entire fourth century. It's not hard to see why. Raised a Christian, Julian was adamant about restoring the Temple in Jerusalem for the empire's Jewish community; and he was equally passionate about defending traditional Greek and Roman gods. In short, to many anxious fourth century Christians—a Eusebius of Caesarea or a Victorinus in Rome—the emperor was overstepping his bounds on the two most urgent fronts in the new Christian culture war. He was guilty of acting too Greek and seeming too Jewish, simultaneously.

Perhaps for this reason, one bishop—Gregory of Nazianzus, in Cappadocia—tarred the Christian emperor as an "apostate," someone who had "defected from" or "rebelled against" his faith. It was a tendentious term.[24] The Jewish writer of 1 Maccabees had used it to slander

Jews who had sacrificed to the Hellenistic king. Mattathias, the father of the Maccabees, had railed at their participation ("Alas, why was I born to see this, the ruin of my people . . . ?"). Two hundred years later, by the end of the first century A.D., Jesus's followers had also taken the concept of "apostasy," or rebellion, and added their own dimension to it. The anonymous author of the letter known as 2 Thessalonians, forged and circulated under Paul's name, would claim that apostasy would be a sign of the second coming of the Messiah: "Let no one deceive you in any way [about the coming end time]," the writer explained. "For it will not come until the rebellion [*apostasía*] comes first and the lawless one is revealed, the son of destruction."[25] For Jesus's followers, rebellion against God, or apostasy, would be an important clue that the end-time was near—and that they should be ready. (It's worth noting that almost all apocalyptic language has this chronological and psychological dimension. It can persuade people to believe that the end-time really is imminent, but it can also compel people to modify their behavior even if they believe the end-time is going to be delayed. As a result, it's often difficult to know whether writers such as Gregory believed the end was near or whether they were using the specter of catastrophe to sway people's politics.)[26]

For Emperor Julian to be accused of "apostasy"—by a Christian priest from Cappadocia—must have stoked nervous fears among a certain group of Jesus's followers, but Gregory was unrelenting in his assault and unabashed in his word choices. He would later call the emperor "the dragon . . . the common, hateful enemy of all," and in a speech written to praise the memory of the Jewish Maccabees, he would question the legitimacy of the emperor's laws by smearing him as "another Antiochus IV [Epiphanes]." The ruler of Rome who had been raised in a Christian house was being transformed into the Hellenistic king who had defiled the Jewish Temple six hundred years earlier.[27]

What had caused Gregory's rancor?

In A.D. 362, the emperor decided that teachers, in Umbria, Italy, needed a certificate to confirm their moral character if they wanted to keep their jobs. In a letter dated the same year, Julian elaborated on the motivations behind his policy. Followers of Jesus, he explained, shouldn't be employed as teachers if they refused to educate children about the Greek and Roman gods—which is to say, the broader heritage of the Roman world they lived in. The text of this law no longer survives, but a year after Julian's death, it was repealed.[28]

In A.D. 362, Gregory's opposition was fierce. "I don't fear the war being waged against us from outside," he said. "Nor that wild beast or the fullness of evil which is now rising against the churches—even if he threatens fire, even if he threatens us with swords and wild beasts and impending cliffs and chasms."[29] So what kind of war did Gregory fear? He was equating the Roman emperor to Antiochus IV Epiphanes, the villain at the heart of the Daniel story; and he was transforming Julian into an evil beast, reminiscent of the supernatural visions in Revelation. A debate over educational policy had turned into spiritual battle, waged from Cappadocia. Two decades after Julian's death, the battlefront in these "Christian culture wars" would shift west.

The news began with a harmless piece of furniture, an altar that had stood in the Senate chamber since Augustus's day. By the mid fourth century, this tiny altar, dedicated to Victory, had watched the rise of an empire. It had eavesdropped on military deliberations during the year of Rome's four emperors, A.D. 69. In the early second century, it had blushed at tales of Trajan's accomplishments. During the third century, it had sweated through periods of governmental instability. And throughout Constantine's reign and the reign of Constantius II (r. A.D. 337–361), it had seen Roman senators come out as Christians. Senators continued to swear their oaths by it until one day, in A.D. 357, they entered to find that it was gone. Constantius II had made the executive decision to pack it up and remove it. The Altar of Victory affair had begun.

Regrettably, there are no governmental records, state archives, or imperial diaries that provide us with any hint of the emperor's motives. All we have is a scrap of news about what came next. The altar was put back. Senators burned incense on its by now discolored marble surface until imperial officials—in A.D. 382—showed up to cart it away again. The current resident of the palace had signed orders to remove it.[30] Two years later, in A.D. 384, the altar was still in storage.

That's finally when the Senate asked their esteemed colleague, Quintus Aurelius Symmachus, to petition the palace for its return. The political wrangling that followed—and Symmachus's role in it—throws an important light on social problems that were about to stymie Rome's leadership, Christian and non-Christian alike. These problems stemmed from the several unresolved identity issues that Jesus's followers had brought with them into the fourth century.

Symmachus was a voice of reason who crossed the theological aisle. Urban prefect in 384, mayor of a world capital, he had begun his career practicing oratory in Trier. His father had been a respected politician, too. The old man's statue was in the Forum of Trajan, where the family's legacy remained, perhaps inescapably, on display.[31] Tradition must have weighed on Symmachus heavily, in 384, as he struggled to find the right words for his petition. Colleagues—both Christians and non-Christians, as will become clear; this debate was not borne from any cultural clash— were depending on him to uphold centuries of Roman tradition.

"What is more fitting to the glory of our age than that we defend the practices of our ancestors and defend the laws and all those things that have been fated for our fatherland?" Symmachus began. It was quite an expansive, generous view of Rome, too. For three hundred years, non-Christians had seen the worship of Victory as vital to the state. More recently, two generations of Christian rulers, from emperor Constantine to the current officeholder, Valentinian II, had also supported the Senate's prerogative. In Symmachus's mind, then, "the practices of our ancestors" had broad support, and there was no substantial reason to deviate from them. A clear and overwhelming precedent had already been set "by the more 'diplomatic practices' [dissimulatio] of earlier times," that is, by the tolerance of other Christian emperors—emperors who did not see the world in black-and-white.[32]

This word (our word "dissimulation" derives from it) is not the sort of quality that would make a partisan proud. For one person's act of diplomacy is often another's act of ideological betrayal. The meaning of the Latin word skews towards this notion of concealment. Three centuries earlier, the Roman historian Tacitus had expressed his contempt for emperor Tiberius in just this term. To Tacitus, an inveterate defender of the Roman Republic, the emperor's knack "for concealing his true feelings by giving the outward appearance of something else" was a mark against the new constitutional framework.[33] Dissimulation, however (which is to say, diplomacy), is often the most effective way to appease two constituencies at once without offending either. Very likely, that's why Symmachus used it as his talking point. If five Christian emperors had let the altar stand, it was only natural that the current Christian emperor should allow it to return, Symmachus believed.

To others, the matter was not so simple. Aurelius Ambrose was not a resident of Rome, but the bishop likely remembered the time he'd spent there—once. Son of an administrator in Gaul, one of three siblings, Ambrose had trained in law in Rome before taking a government position of his own in northern Italy. There, he had been selected as bishop of Milan.[34]

Residents of Milan did not need to harbor any inferiority complex. Silver plates and exquisite glassware elevated daily life, for the rich. Finely carved statues of gods like Hercules could be seen throughout the city. All the regular Roman amenities—baths, a racetrack, temples, churches—were there. And by the late fourth century, the imperial palace had rolled in, too: not only the emperor and his family but their staff and everyone else who greased the wheels of the state were residing in Milan.[35] So it was that in A.D. 384, at the time Symmachus was petitioning the palace, any mail addressed to the palace arrived here.

Ambrose, in his role as a priest, was to offer his own advice for the emperor's benefit. Throughout his career, in fact, the bishop of Milan would become notorious for using his ink "to deliver a self-sufficient final word" wherever he saw that it was needed.[36] "To the most superlatively Christian emperor, Valentinian II," Ambrose began:

> Every person who is a "Christian" fights like a solider [*militat*] on behalf of the true God, and he who takes up the charge of worshipping God with the deepest desire does so not by looking the other way [*dissimulatio*] or shutting his eyes; he draws upon the zeal of faith and devotion.[37]

The bishop had decided to use the soldier metaphor as a tool. He was implying that Christians who practiced any form of diplomacy in their daily lives did not count as "real Christians." The emperor, Valentinian II, a boy of thirteen years in A.D. 384, was being served a stern warning. As the priest told his boss, the Roman emperor, "There is no childhood allowed in faith."[38]

Ambrose's audacity will probably seem shocking to us. We use constitutional walls to separate our "church" from our "state." In ancient Rome, no such wall existed because no such entities existed. There was only the matter of *religio*—and the never-ending power struggle over who got to define it. Rome's Department of Divine Affairs, that curious branch of government meant to oversee and ensure that every action had the blessing of the gods, or God, was still alive and well at the end of the fourth century. Ambrose wasn't standing outside this system. As a bishop, as a priest, he was embedded in it. He was exercising his constitutional right to imperial oversight.

During the old Republic, priests had always thrown down similar gauntlets. They blocked their senatorial colleagues from pursuing disagreeable legislation, or challenged the legitimacy of questionable policies. In the tense, fractured world of the late Republic—that progressive era of the Gracchi brothers and Catiline's coup, and Caesar's own legislation for those in economic need—this informal constitutional arrangement had become too quaint to be of any lasting value. Paralysis had seized Rome's government. Rarely could anything be agreed upon that didn't involve a senator and a priest who had "found" an omen to warn against it. It is a testament to the savvy of Augustus that after Caesar's death, he would wait until each living holder of these priesthoods died and then take their offices for himself. Rome's gridlock was suddenly gone. So, too, was the old Republic.

Four hundred years later, the bishop of Milan was prepared to offer a bold policy recommendation of his own: "For the sake of maintaining our proper relationship with the divine [*religio*], I come to you in my role as bishop," he told the emperor.[39] Why was he so eager to weigh in on current events? The conflict over the Altar of Victory was a proxy war in the escalating Christian conversation about how Jesus's followers should live in late fourth century Rome. Ambrose made his own opinion on this topic unimpeachably clear: "If there are any Christians-in-name-only who tell you that the altar should stay," he told the emperor, "then whoever is trying to persuade you—indeed, whoever decides in favor of letting the altar stay—is someone who sacrifices to the Roman gods!"[40] Christians who disagreed with the bishop's more militant Christianity were not to be counted among the Christian community at all.[41]

Later, Emperor Valentinian II, with the help of advisers or based on a gut feeling, would decide to keep the altar in storage. Symmachus's petition, which had been supported by a coalition of Christians and non-Christians alike, was denied. The ongoing battle to define what it meant to be a Christian in Rome had ended in a resounding defeat for the Christian civilians.

That's how Ambrose saw it, too. After the affair was over, he wrote an additional letter in which he gloated at the outcome of a political dispute that had tipped in his favor. In it, he warned his community (and any Christian who would listen) against the dangers of political compromise. Periods of "heavenly warfare" demanded resolve, Ambrose told them, and the battle ahead was undeniably grave. "We all may live down here," he explained, pretending to adopt the voice of Rome. "But we are fighting a battle taking place up there."[42] Ambrose was teaching his Christian community to see the Roman world as locked in a cosmic war. To him, the altar was no longer just a marble block. It was a sign, a symbol—a political surrogate—for something inherently, metaphysically evil. The rites that took place at it, he said, were an abomination to Christian "soldiers." Ambrose, bishop of Milan, was standing up and speaking for them.

Besides, he said, "I detest the rites of all the 'Neros.'"[43]

Nero—how one simple name snags the sequence of names and dates that we too often mistake for History. Chronologies move forward, yes, but behind them, even among the people of the past, there were memories. And memories interrupt the straightforward passage of time.

Last emperor of the Julio-Claudian dynasty, Nero died in A.D. 68, but his almost satanic ghost had haunted many people in the centuries since. Nero was cursed for having tried to kill his mother while she was boating on the bay of Naples, and the story did little for the emperor's image.[44] Nero had also appointed Vespasian to quell the revolt in Roman Judaea in A.D. 66. By the year 70, a Roman army had brought down the Jewish Temple, and Nero would forever after bear part of the blame for destroying the holiest Jewish site.[45] Not surprisingly, when a Jewish revolt enveloped Egypt forty years later, rumors began to spread that the beastly emperor was about to return. Rebels—we've encountered their manic views of history already—believed Nero's return was the sign that would precede the end of times. They waited. They lost. "Nero's return" was a common ingredient in apocalyptic writing.

Both Jews and Christians worked the theme. John of Patmos had done it, and in the mid third century A.D., another Christian had predicted the end-time would be fast approaching "when Nero is raised from hell." A century later, yet another Christian writer would stoke the same fears. The man who had killed the apostles—Nero—had done so "at the prompting of his father, the Devil."[46] Nero, as another fourth century Latin writer, Sulpicius Severus, implied, was worthy not only of being counted among the most despicable tyrants but among the most despicable of all mankind, even among monstrous beasts. For he was the one who began the first persecution, and he may be the last, too—that is, if what people are saying is true, that Nero will return right before the Antichrist.[47]

By the late fourth century, Christians in both halves of the Roman Empire were trafficking in this language. Delivering a homily to his congregation, John Chrysostom recalled how Nero had been, "as it were, a kind of Antichrist."[48] For all these Christians, the very name "Nero" was meant to lend the flavor of their writings a deep, spiritual fear. As recently as A.D. 362, even Gregory of Nazianzus had summoned his ghost to slander the policies of Emperor Julian.[49]

Among the mainstream, by contrast, Nero did not always evoke the prospect of worldwide, cataclysmic destruction. One story, written down in the sixth century A.D., lauded him. At dinner in the palace one evening, the emperor had been taking too long to finish his meal. It was an important game day in Rome, and people had already taken their seats in the circus. They were waiting for the emperor to inaugurate the race. Not prepared to rush through dinner, we're told, Nero ordered a napkin to be dropped from the palace window. People would see it and know that the games could start. Five hundred years later, in the sixth century A.D., this napkin, or *mappa*, was still a ceremonial feature of imperial chariot races. The bust of Nero himself was struck into several commemorative coins in the mid fourth and early fifth centuries. These tokens were distributed to celebrate the popularity of Roman games.[50]

When Ambrose denounced the Senate for indulging in "the rites of all the 'Neros,'" he was drawing upon a competing set of memories. He was drawing upon nervous, anxious memories, many of which associated "Nero" with the coming of the end-time. He was trying to convince his followers that living in the fourth century A.D. was no different from living in the first century A.D. The implication? It was as if the age of "persecution" had never really ended, not even under the most pious Christian ruler. (*Christianissimus*, Ambrose had called Valentinian II.) The malevolent spirit of the end-time beast, Nero, was being used to tarnish the Christian emperor's reputation because the emperor had made the political "mistake" of supporting long-established Roman custom. In Ambrose's eyes, for the sake of Rome's relationship with God, such accommodation could not stand.

And so the bishop had given his ultimatum: If you put the Altar of Victory back, Ambrose said, "you'll be permitted to come to church, but you're not going to find a priest there—or rather, I should say, you'll find a priest there who is going to stand against you."[51] There would be no communion for the Christian emperor, should he disobey the bishop's policy recommendation.[52] Other imperial office holders would soon be given similar ultimata.

For, as the bishop said to the Roman emperor, "You cannot serve two masters."[53]

What it meant to "serve two masters" in Ambrose's time had clearly changed from what it meant in Tertullian's time. It had morphed even more from what it had meant in the first century A.D. Back then, Jesus had been preaching about the relationship between God and wealth. Now, in A.D. 384, Ambrose was trying to win assurance from the Roman government that the Senate would no longer start its sessions with a prayer at the Altar of Victory. Christians were being forced to "come out" in public. Others were being mocked for being too civilian or acting too Greek. The most Christian emperor of Rome was no longer Christian enough, at least not for Ambrose. To Jesus's followers, it must have looked as if the rules for being Christian were being rewritten in the middle of the game—by one teammate against another.

It was a tumultuous time inside the group. Christians were grappling with unsettled questions about the relationship between Jesus's human and divine nature. Church leaders were quarreling over sacraments, particularly in North Africa, where many Christians had handed over their scriptures during the persecutions of A.D. 303–305; the urgent dilemma was, should these men and women be baptized a second time, to bring them back in the fold?[54] These internal disputes are crucial for understanding the history of Christianity, but they are only a part of the larger history of Rome.

How many Romans on the outside—from the ones who protected the grain against dampness to the slaves who inspected the city's aqueducts for leaks—had noticed the cracks and fissures that were now quite visibly dividing their Christian friends and neighbors from one another? The political rhetoric of late fourth century Rome was becoming less moderate, more polarized and increasingly alarmist.[55] Symmachus had recognized as much and tried to do something about it. "For all the reasons I outlined above," he wrote in his petition,

> we are seeking peace [*pacem*] for the gods of our fatherland and for our ancestors' gods. For regardless of the way in which each one of us worships these gods, it's right to think our worship is an expression of one and the same thing. For we all look up at the same stars, the heaven above is shared by all, and the world turns—for all of us. What difference does it make how each one of us, in good sense, searches for the truth? So great a mystery as this is not able to be attained by one route alone.[56]

Symmachus's letter of A.D. 384 is a paean to the Roman Empire as a place of toleration. His call for "peace" is even a faithful mirroring of language that Constantine and Licinius themselves had promoted. In A.D. 313, the two emperors had arrived at their decision for the very reason of ensuring "the peaceful well-being of our time [*quies*], so that each person may have a free opportunity to worship whatever god he has chosen."

By Symmachus's day, many other forceful advocates, men like Themistius and Libanius in the East—even Christian moderates like Emperor Valentinian I—would take up the task of maintaining Rome's diverse, pluralistic traditions.[57] Throughout the late fourth century, in particular, six senatorial embassies would travel back and forth between Rome and Milan to try to reach a political compromise about the fate of the tiny Altar of Victory. And many would argue from this august body, just as Symmachus had, that Rome remain as inclusive as possible.

Whether anyone "outside the beltway" knew what was at stake in these high-level deliberations is not clear, but the available evidence suggests that it was not an inconsequential moment in the history of Rome. At the palace, sustained, passionate pleas for moderation were increasingly being tossed aside, if they were read at all. This was no "debate" between non-Christians and Christians. To characterize it as such implies a false equivalency between the two sides, and the overwhelming source of the issue lay within the splintered and splintering Christian community. Fierce divisions that had been festering among Jesus's followers for centuries—symptoms of three hundred years of unresolved identity issues—had now brought Christian politicians to loggerheads with each other and with their non-Christian peers.[58] The long-running debate over what it meant to be a follower of Jesus had morphed into an empire-wide debate about the nature of being Roman. Many Christians and non-Christians were coalescing in ways that crossed the theological aisle.

And so, even as many traditional aspects of Roman life thrived— Rome's Temple of Saturn, for example, was newly scrubbed and bright white by the end of the fourth century A.D. (figure 15)—there must have been a noticeable change in the capital.[59] An aggressive campaign of Christian proxy wars had started to consume Roman politics. The public spat over the Altar of Victory would not be the last. The rhetoric at the highest level of the government was becoming poisonous. Some Christians were now talking as if they were locked in spiritual war, wrapping themselves in dualistic images, just as the writer of Revelation had done. Even emperor Constantine had spoken their language. Now, a half century later, Jesus's followers were busy dividing the world into two camps, good and evil, soldiers and civilians, just as Marius Victorinus had showed them how.

Many of Jesus's followers themselves were being given an ultimatum. It was no longer acceptable to act like a Greek or pass as a Roman civilian and still call oneself a Christian. Many others were being warned, in both Greek and Latin, not to act in ways that might confuse them with Jews. From the Greek-speaking East of Eusebius of Caesarea, Bishop Athanasius of Alexandria, and John Chrysostom of Antioch to the Latin-speaking West of Marius Victorinus, Ambrose of Milan, and Augustine of Hippo, Jesus's followers were now being bombarded with the idea that their Greek, Roman, and Jewish neighbors were people who had been cut off from God. This fiery conversation, which had been brewing inside the group throughout the fourth century, was about to spill over into the Roman world—with horrific side effects for everyone else.

CHAPTER 8

The Moment of the Eruption

Callinicum in Roman Syria, A.D. 388

Located a hundred miles from modern Aleppo, the town of Callinicum, like other towns along the Roman border with Persia, must have been a thriving, vibrant hub in the middle of Mesopotamia. A prominent Jewish community had worshiped there for centuries, peacefully as far as we know, until the late fourth century, when the social fabric unraveled. Christians, many of whom had grown up to hear about the dangers of seeming too Jewish, were about to take that message straight to their neighbors. In A.D. 388, zealous Christians, "at the instigation of the bishop," according to our source, torched a local synagogue. Word of the atrocity in Callinicum soon made its way to the emperor.

Born in Spain, Flavius Theodosius was Christian Roman emperor of the East (r. A.D. 379–392). From 392 to his death three years later, he would govern the entire Roman world. How did Theodosius's government craft its response to this disturbing attack? As with many matters that came before the palace in ancient Rome, the state archives are silent on it. We know what happened because of a response to the emperor's response.[1] Theodosius ordered the bishop and the Christian community of Callinicum to rebuild the synagogue and to do so, in particular, out of their own funds. When the bishop of Milan, Ambrose, found out about Theodosius' decision, he gave the emperor his own opinion.

Why was Ambrose of Milan so interested in Syria? One answer lies in a bit of information that had been leaked to him from inside the palace. Ambrose had learned that Theodosius—a Christian—was preparing to force the Christians at Callinicum to pay for the new synagogue. To Ambrose, it was unconscionable.[2] "Will you award this 'triumph' over the Church of God to the Jews?" he asked Theodosius. "Will you give them this 'victory monument' to erect over the people of Christ?" In Ambrose's mind, if Christians in Callinicum were punished, Jews would take this public "victory" over Christianity and make it a cause for celebration. "They will add this [new] 'celebration' to their list of festivals and will count it among the days on which they triumphed over the Amorites or the Canaanites or freed themselves from the Pharaoh, the king of Egypt, or from the hand of Nebuchadnezzar, the king of Babylon."[3]

Besides, Ambrose said, Christians did not deserve to be punished. The Jews' synagogue had been justly set on fire. The Jews of Callinicum were gathering in a "space dedicated to impiety," the bishop explained. "A place of perfidy," he called it, "a refuge of madness, which God himself has condemned." Reparations would look like an admission of Christian guilt when in fact the Christians in Callinicum had actually done no wrong—as far as Ambrose was concerned. As the bishop himself reminded the emperor, it was the Jews who had "killed Christ [the Messiah]."[4]

Ambrose also raised the prospect of civil disobedience. What would happen, the bishop mused, if his counterpart, the bishop of Callinicum, refused to comply with the emperor's orders? Very likely, there would be a highly public confrontation between the local bishop and the Christian authorities. This public spotlight might not be a good thing for Theodosius, Ambrose warned. People might start to think the Christian emperor was guilty of "persecuting" other Christians.[5] Seventy-five years after the Edict of Milan, three generations after Constantine had legalized Christianity, Ambrose was still living with the words and images of a bygone age. Ambrose's peroration, his final plea, was also questionably appropriate: "Why was I born to see the ruin of my people?" he lamented.

Today, we know that Ambrose added this line to his letter after he had edited his correspondence for publication. These were not the bishop's own thoughts or words, however. They were the voice of a Jewish man, Mattathias, father of the Maccabees.[6] Six centuries earlier, in Jerusalem,

Mattathias had lamented the king's "desolating sacrilege." He had bristled at the sacrifices that Jews were offering at their own temple. "Why was I born to see the ruin of my [Jewish] people?" Mattathias calls out, in 1 Maccabees. Six hundred years later, the bishop of Milan was quoting a Jew to try to explain why Christians had just burned a Jewish synagogue. At its most basic level, however, Mattathias's own plaintive cry had very little, if anything, to do with "Ambrose's people." The bishop of Milan was twisting Mattathias's words into an argument for his own gain.

In the end, whether for personal reasons, political ones, or some combination of the two, the Christian emperor Theodosius reversed course. At first, he decided that the arsonists would be punished, but the bishop of Callinicum would not have to pay replacement costs out of pocket. Later, after even more pleading—and a confrontation between Ambrose and Theodosius in the middle of a church service—the emperor backed down even more.[7] Officially, in A.D. 388, there would be no Roman response to the burning of a synagogue.

"The Jews," and, more important, the role they were thought to have in God's plan for salvation, would now preoccupy many Christian intellects. Men such as Augustine would treat this theological topic with great fervor.[8] Meanwhile, the ideas that Christians like Eusebius, Marius Victorinus, John Chrysostom, and others had been cultivating in their own writings—that Jesus's followers must not seem too Jewish—had given birth to something very real and very damaging.

Alexandria at Egypt, A.D. 392

The conversation about what it meant to be a Christian was about to take another horrible turn. Christians who had been taught to scorn Roman life were about to lash out in a spectacular act of violence. Their target was Alexandria's historic sanctuary, the Temple of Serapis. Soon, the pride of this Hellenistic seaside port—a building that was part worship space, library, lecture hall, civic memorial, and museum—would come toppling down in one of ancient history's most cataclysmic acts of destruction, an act wrought by Romans against other Romans and by Christians in the name of Christianity.[9]

Alexandria was a remarkable port city: salubrious breezes, the air tranquil and calm, "hardly ever a day when its residents weren't gifted to live under the beams of a radiant sun," one Roman wrote. History and myth lurked around every corner. A formidable queen, Cleopatra, had built the city's lighthouse. An island off the coast was thought to be the site where Homer had set part of his *Odyssey*. Over the years, grammarians, scientists, and professors of literature had called the city home. And if anyone in Athens or in Rome ever needed to call for a doctor, what better recommendation did a man need than to say he'd trained at Alexandria?[10]

The city's Temple of Serapis was equal to that of the most hallowed temple in Rome. Perched prominently atop a hill overlooking the harbor, it was the jewel in Alexandria's crown. That was quite a distinction, since Alexandria itself was "the crown of all cities," said Ammianus Marcellinus. Located in the southwestern part of the city, on a hill in the city's Rhakotis neighborhood,

> the Temple and Sanctuary of Serapis stand out above all. Although a poor choice of words can diminish it, it is decked out in such splendor—with spacious colonnaded courtyards, lifelike statues, and a great number of other art works—that there's really nothing like it in the whole world (besides Rome's Temple of Jupiter on the Capitoline, that is.)[11]

Inside was the colossal image of Serapis. His statue barely fit inside. The god's right hand touched one wall; his left hand touched the opposite—such was his awesome size. The inner hall itself was fitted with special windows so that those who visited at a fortuitous time would see the sun kiss Serapis's lips, a theatrical effect intended to highlight the god's power. Outside, the entire precinct towered over the cityscape, visible from land and sea.[12] The loss of Alexandria's architectural and cultural gem must have scarred the psyche of everyone who had looked up at it and felt the pride of living in this resplendent Hellenistic city.

Remarkably, the perpetrators of this tragedy have not been easy to identify. The earliest writer to describe it, a Christian, reports that the leader of the attack was "one of the soldiers." Commentators have traditionally understood his phrase to mean that the man was a Christian enlisted in the Roman army. The evidence is not so straightforward. The leader is characterized as a man who was "armed more with his faith than with weapons." This same language is used to describe other Christians who were said to be fighting in "the Lord's army," not Rome's.

The Roman magistrate who executed Jesus, Pontius Pilate, dedicated a temple to the Roman emperor Tiberius, as recorded here in this cast of a Latin inscription found at Caesarea Maritima, Israel.

The Roman emperor, his family, and the people of Lepcis Magna, Libya, participate in a public sacrifice. This sculptural relief was originally displayed on a Roman arch for the emperor Septimius Severus at Lepcis Magna, A.D. 203. Now in Tripoli, Libya.

A mosaic from the floor of a house in Thugga, Tunisia, shows the Homeric hero Odysseus enjoying the singing of the sirens while safely tied to the mast of his ship. From the third century A.D.

This scratched wall drawing, or graffito, mocks Alexamenos for praying to a donkey-headed crucified criminal. Found during excavations on the Palatine Hill, Rome, the image was no doubt meant to slander someone for being too open about his Christianity. Currently in the Palatine Antiquarium, it has been dated to the third century A.D.

A magical amulet, perhaps from the province of Roman Syria, depicting one of the earliest scenes of Jesus's crucifixion. The gem is made of bloodstone and has been dated to the early third century A.D.

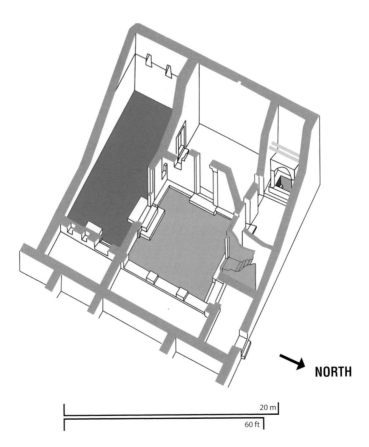

NORTH

20 m

60 ft

Around A.D. 241, owners of a house in Dura Europos, Syria, remodeled their first floor. Two rooms were combined to create an assembly hall (depicted in dark brown), and a basin was installed for baptism (highlighted in blue). The property likely continued to function as a house. Archaeologists discovered stairs leading from the central courtyard to a second floor (seen here in light brown).

The Christian baptistry at Dura Europos, Syria, contained an image of Jesus the "Good Shepherd," shown caring for a ram, holding it on his shoulders. (Below Jesus is a representation of Adam and Eve in Eden.) In the Roman world, the "Good Shepherd" personified the idea of "good will toward all." Dated prior to A.D. 256.

This model of Jerusalem, currently on display at the Israel Museum in Jerusalem, shows a reconstruction of the Second Temple complex during the late first century B.C., the age of Herod.

The stones of the Second Temple precinct walls, which fell in A.D. 70 during the war with Rome, still lie today at the base of the Temple Mount in Jerusalem. The site is also called the Noble Sanctuary, in Muslim tradition.

Amid a plush Egyptian stage setting, initiates and priests celebrate the rituals of Isis on this wall painting from the Bay of Naples, Italy. Excavated at Herculaneum, it is currently in the Museo Archeologico Nazionale, Naples.

This Roman coin, issued in the middle of the second century A.D., shows Isis holding her rattle and the rudder of a ship. Protector of sailors and shipping, she is shown in front of a tall lighthouse. Currently in the National Maritime Museum, Haifa, Israel.

A mosaic from a house in El Djem, Tunisia (ancient Thysdrus), represents well-established moments from the Roman year. Here, in a scene symbolizing the month of November, Isis worshippers are seen in the garb associated with their rituals, including linen gowns and the dog-headed mask of Anubis. From the third century A.D., currently in the museum at Sousse, Tunisia.

Today, only fragments of this colossal statue of the emperor Constantine remain, housed in Rome's Capitoline Museums. The statue itself was originally on display in the New Basilica, Rome, where it depicted Rome's first Christian emperor in the guise of the divine Jupiter, king of the Olympian gods.

From a series of coins issued at Constantinople (modern Istanbul) in A.D. 326–330, comes this bronze coin depicting the emperor Constantine. On its reverse is the logo of the Messiah, "Christ" (the first two letters of that word, *chi* and *rho*, in Greek), who is seen piercing a writhing and conquered serpent.

The Forum, ancient Rome's downtown business district. In the foreground rise the columns of the Temple of Saturn, a temple restored at the end of the fourth century A.D. To the left, behind the arch, is the Senate House, where a debate once raged about the fate of a tiny altar. In the distance the Colosseum still peeks above the landscape, at the back right.

One of five women prophets from Michelangelo Buonarroti's Sistine Chapel ceiling, in the Vatican (1508–1512). The Sibyls were the world-renowned seers of ancient Greece and Rome, located in cities across the Mediterranean. Whether any of these women would have been thrilled to be included in the story on the ceiling is doubtful.

As a result, there is a strong possibility that Christian militants, not members of the Roman military, were responsible for toppling one of the ancient world's most iconic buildings.[13] These "soldiers" were armed with their own ideological vision for a Christian Roman world.

What did the people of Alexandria—among them many Christian "civilians," non-Christians, and Jews—make of their own beliefs in the wake of the attack? For many, the fact that the temple's destruction was followed by exuberant cries of Christian triumph must have left a bitter aftertaste. One scrap of papyrus dated to this time, the late fourth or early fifth century A.D., gives us a vivid picture of the militant gloating they encountered.

In the margins of this scrap is depicted Alexandria's bishop, Theophilus. He is shown solemnly holding a book with a cross on its cover, standing triumphantly atop the Temple of Serapis. To those who saw the drawing, it must have seemed as if Holy Scripture itself, the word of the Christian God, had sanctioned this stunning act of violence.[14]

Throughout the empire, other Christians, who may have also fancied themselves as "God's soldiers," could not contain their enthusiasm for the catastrophe. The church historian Rufinus of Aquileia in northern Italy gives us their perspective. Writing at the turn of the fifth century A.D., Rufinus boasts:

> After Serapis' downfall, a god who never really existed, what temples of any other demon could possibly remain standing? To say that all the buildings in Alexandria, dedicated to whatever demon, came down would be an understatement. They all came down, almost column by column.[15]

Archaeology, as it has so often throughout our story, tells us Rufinus was speaking in hyperbole. Many temples, including one dedicated to Isis on the Nile island of Philae, would remain active sites of worship into the sixth century A.D.[16] The people of Alexandria picked up the pieces as best they could, even as a steady march of Christian legislation, directed against temples, increasingly disrupted people's lives.

To Romans of the late fourth century, especially those with only a bare minimum of familiarity with Christianity, the destruction of Alexandria's largest temple must have suddenly seemed like nothing less than a wholesale indictment of Christianity: warlike, intolerant, and incompatible with the well-established cultural traditions of the Roman world. But what was it that had granted Christians such perverse license to topple this temple? Was it something hidden in Christian scripture, as the papyrus drawing of the bishop, holding a cross-covered book, implies?

If we scour the crime scene in Alexandria, looking closely for clues that can help us reconstruct what happened, we find very little in our sources to explain it—except perhaps the frenzied words of a seer we've encountered before:

> And you, Serapis, who are set upon so many glistening-white
>   stones,
> you will lie in ruin in thrice-unhappy Egypt;
> and all those who were led to you by a longing for Egypt,
> they will lament ever having wrongly considered you an
>   imperishable god.
> But the ones who sing of God, they will know that you are
>   nothing.

The "prophet's" words, penned to sound like a Sibylline oracle, had traveled far in time. The bishop of Alexandria, Clement, had known them two centuries ago—and had taught them to his Christian community. At the time, he attributed them to a "Sibyl."[17] Did Christians in fourth century Alexandria also know about this prophecy? The mid fourth century bishop of Alexandria, Athanasius, was known for his skill in deciphering "prophetic lots" (although we don't know exactly what kinds of texts these were).[18] Alexandria itself had a long history of riots and violence, many of which had come about because of people's reliance on "oracles."[19] Could Christian "soldiers" in the late fourth century have acted on the "Sibyl's predictions" because they thought "her" words were goading them on?

The only tantalizing evidence we have comes from Rufinus, the Christian writer who described the temple's destruction in the fullest detail. Not only does he refer to Serapis with that curious echo of the "Sibyl's" poem, a god who never really existed ("They will know that you are nothing!"), after he mentions the temple's fall, Rufinus says that the Nile was ravaged by a flood.[20] The "Sibyl," too, had claimed that the land would be "in evil hands that day when the Nile would flood all of Egypt."[21] To readers of Rufinus's *Church History*, did the events of recent memory—the downfall of Serapis, the Nile flood—look like the eerie fulfillment of "God's prophecy"?

It is doubtful we will ever be able to determine whether this hypothesis is correct.

Are these two moments—the destruction of a synagogue in Callinicum in A.D. 388, and the destruction of the Temple of Serapis in Alexandria in A.D. 392—isolated events? A distant observer might see them as unfortunate by-products of peculiar local circumstances. Separated geographically, they are two random, albeit regrettable acts of violence, hardly worth mentioning in the story of later Rome, perhaps, apart from a noble desire to mourn the lives of Romans who suffered during them. Yet I think we can detect a crucial commonality to them (and to other instances of destruction that are littered throughout the later Roman world). What happened at Callinicum and at Alexandria are two manifestations of the same social problem.

In each instance, Jesus's followers were aggressively lashing out at the culture around them because they had been taught to regard that culture as morally depraved or spiritually corrupt. In Callinicum, some Christians were so anxious about seeming Jewish that they started a fire at a local synagogue. In Alexandria, others were so anxious about seeming Greek, or intent on passing for an ordinary Roman, that they toppled a historic Greco-Roman sanctuary. In both cases, violence was certainly the result of local circumstances. But it was also driven by the same pressing but ultimately unresolved issues that have popped up again and again in Eusebius, Marius Victorinus, Ambrose, John Chrysostom, and other Christian writers throughout the fourth century A.D. In academic parlance, we might say that these ancient concerns were transregional in the way that other scholars have talked about today's ideologies as "transnational."[22] Christians who had never resolved how to live as Jesus's followers in the Roman world were not only disrupting the social fabric of their individual cities. They were now violently altering the lives of Jews, non-Christians, and other Christians throughout the empire. By A.D. 394, less than a decade after Callinicum and Alexandria, there would be war.

The Roman Empire was changing. Both from the ground up and from the top down, life was being radically altered. Many who thought of themselves as fighting "God's battle" may have worked their way to the center of Roman power.

In A.D. 380, the people of Constantinople were required, by law, to identify with the Christian creed at Nicaea, drafted early in the fourth century.[23] Stringent and severe laws that banned aspects of Rome's own religious traditions also now entered the books in greater numbers and at quicker speed than in the decades prior. Three laws, dated between A.D. 391 and 392, wrought significant changes for Rome's non-Christian population.

On February 24, A.D. 391, the following edict was announced at Milan: "No person shall pollute himself with sacrificial animals. No person shall slaughter an innocent victim." It was an audacious piece of legislation. "No person," it continued, "shall go near the shrines or shall wander through sacred spaces of the city and revere the images within them that have been fashioned by mortal hands." The punishment for any citizen who transgressed this law is not specified, but government officials who were caught doing so would now be fined.

Later that same year, on June 16, a nearly identical decree was sent to the Roman imperial staff in charge of Egypt.[24] What was happening during these political deliberations in the palace? We are entirely shut out of the legislative process. Then, in November 392, a third piece of legislation was announced at Constantinople:

> No person at all from any class or order whatsoever of men or rank—whether he has been placed in a position of power or has completed these duties with honor; whether he is powerful because of the circumstances of his birth or is from a more humble background because of birth, legal status, or fortune— none shall slaughter an innocent victim to senseless images [that is, statues of the Greek and Roman gods] in any place at all or in any city. Nor shall he, by more secret act of wickedness, venerate with fire the gods of his family home, the Lares; nor venerate with wine his family's ancestral protector, the Genius of the house; nor venerate with fragrant incense the gods of his cupboards and hearth, the Penates. He shall not burn any lamps for them. He shall not place any incense before them. He shall not hang wreaths of flowers for them.[25]

Archaeologists have found these shrines in apartments and homes from the third and fourth centuries A.D.[26] At Pompeii, visitors can still walk into a Roman home and see, sometimes just near the door, how important these shrines could be to a family's health and security. In A.D. 79, however, one blast of a volcano had not wiped out the Roman people's traditions in Pompeii. On November 8, A.D. 392, words were posing a much more imminent threat. The "Rome" that Augustus had labored hard to shore up with new foundations was being dismantled, brick by brick.

In the aftermath of these laws, local enforcement and compliance would vary. Did they apply everywhere? What happened if a citizen missed the announcement or if a storm ripped the notice down or threw it to the wind? Eusebius tells us that Christians who were fed up with anti-Christian legislation at the beginning of the fourth century A.D. would tear the placards down and make a show of ripping them up. At the end of the fourth century, what if a local official didn't morally agree with this new legislation? Was he compelled to enforce it? If he didn't, who would enforce the enforcers?[27] The people of the Roman Empire must have been lost in a bureaucratic haze as many of their cherished customs were steadily being eliminated by the force of legislation.

Our vision should not be clouded. Christians who were eager to see their own political policies put into action—banning sacrifice, outlawing visits to the temples, penalizing and stigmatizing acts of worship in front of statues and altars—were using the power of the state to achieve their ideological vision. As a result, tables were turning on non-Christians, many of whom now awoke to find themselves in a world where they were now plagued by the same stigmas Christians once had endured. Within two years, in A.D. 394, there would be a civil war to control the direction of the empire.

Flavius Eugenius, a Christian, had taken command of the western empire in A.D. 392.[28] Among his first priorities, Eugenius had reversed one of the more extreme policies of his predecessors. The emperor Gratian, in A.D. 382, had canceled state subsidies for the priestly college of the Vestal Virgins. A group of six women of varying age, the Vestals had been tending Rome's eternal flame since the Republic. Their flame was the pulse of the empire, and it was enshrined in the Forum at the Temple of Vesta.

A decade and a half into his rule, Gratian (r. A.D. 367–83) decided that the Vestals' work would no longer be subsidized by the state.[29] Gratian did not snuff out the flame—priestesses had long been drafted from some of Rome's wealthiest families; they could afford to pick up the tab—but his symbolic decision to cut, or privatize, its funding may have struck many, Christian and non-Christian alike, as political overreach.

Sometime between A.D. 392 and 394, Eugenius restored the Vestals' subsidies. As with most acts of moderation, very few people at the time commented on Eugenius's action. To other Christians who found it abhorrent, though, ink and papyrus came out. "To the most merciful Roman Emperor," the bishop of Milan wrote. The year was A.D. 394, but Eugenius would have had a hard time recognizing it from Ambrose's letter. "Do you remember when the four-year festival was being held in the city of Tyre [in modern Lebanon] and the king of the Hellenistic settlement known as Antioch-in-Jerusalem had come to take part in it?" Eugenius's answer was probably no. The "festival" Ambrose was about to describe had taken place six hundred years ago, during the Maccabean period—the second century B.C.—and the Hellenistic king to whom he was referring, Antiochus IV Epiphanes, had been dead for just as long. Why was Ambrose digging up the Maccabees?

"That was the time," Ambrose explained, "when a most wicked man named Jason [the Jewish high priest] decided that certain Jewish men who held citizenship in his city would bring 300 silver drachmas from Jerusalem to the festival. Jason was sending them to be used for a sacrifice to Hercules." Maybe now the episode had jogged Eugenius's memory? Jason was the Jewish man whom the writer of 2 Maccabees had charged with acting too Greek.[30] But what was Jason's "crime"? Jason had asked fellow Jews to attend the king's sacrifice. When they refused, Jason relented. According to Ambrose, Jason had been guilty of "persecuting" other Jews.[31]

But what had Eugenius done wrong? To Ambrose, Eugenius's "crime" was obvious. No Christian Roman emperor should ever tolerate, let alone provide any financial underwriting for, the Vestal Virgins or their sacred fire. The Jewish example of Jason, yanked out of the second century B.C., was being suggested as a model for the fourth century Christian emperor. Ambrose was implying, in Latin, that Eugenius was acting too much like a Christian civilian—simply because he had chosen to be tolerant of Roman tradition. If he restored the subsidies, Eugenius risked doing as Jason had done when Jason, a Jew, had "persecuted" his fellow Jews. Eugenius would be guilty of persecuting other Christians. (Never mind that for the entire fourth century, Christian emperors, Constantine included, had never before threatened to revoke the Vestal's subsidies.)

Eugenius's political decision as a Christian, to live peacefully and amicably alongside non-Christians, was being characterized as Christian "persecution." Later that year, in September A.D. 394, he and his supporters, Christian and non-Christian alike, would find themselves dodging more than political invective. At the Frigidus River, between Italy and Slovenia, there would be weapons. There, one Christian would face another Christian for control of the Roman Empire: Theodosius vs. Eugenius.

Over the course of two days in September, Theodosius gained the upper hand. The commander of Eugenius's troops would commit suicide. Eugenius would be captured and put to death. Within a decade, Rufinus, the man who had so sensationally described the destruction of the Temple of Serapis, would use the battle at the Frigidus to bring his story of the history of the Church to a pious end. Its coda, in Rufinus's account, was the miraculous appearance of a "wind" that swept down the valley and turned the enemies' spears against themselves, as if God himself had smitten His enemies.[32] Was this yet one more of Rufinus's attempts at playing the "Sibyl"? ("And a wintry gust of wind will then blow across the land!" one of the counterfeit poems says.)[33]

To hear Rufinus tell it, the battle at the Frigidus River was the last in a series of divinely ordained events that had led to the rise of Christianity in Rome. Theodosius had fought on behalf of the "true set of worship practices" (*religio*), and for that reason, said Rufinus, he had won. Rufinus's shameless gloating has led historians to suspect that the causes for such a traumatic conflict might not lie in what we call "religious matters" but rather in social or economic ones. One approach to this war would see a "constellation" of motives luring Theodosius and Eugenius into that mountain valley against each other.[34] In our eagerness to identify the complexities that preceded the battle of the Frigidus River, however, I wonder whether we should not miss the obvious results of it. Whether Christians numbered fifty or fifty million at the end of the fourth century A.D., no Christian emperor would ever again make the same political mistake that the Christian emperor Eugenius had. No Roman emperor would ever again try to subsidize Rome's traditional worship practices.

Theodosius' victory at the Frigidus River did send a message, and it was a chilling one. All the temples of the empire, every brick-built shrine, every altar, every statue—all of the traditional practices associated with them would now be seared with a social stigma. There would be no going back. In the decades after Eugenius's defeat, more laws against sacrifice, against visiting shrines, against worshipping at statues would be added to the books, and many old laws would be now repeated, as if in exasperation (or desperation). Then, three final noteworthy moments, for us.

In A.D. 408 or just before, Rome's Sibylline Oracles, the official ones, were burned—destroyed by the general in charge of Rome, Stilicho.[35] Did Stilicho, a Christian, think that by destroying these ancient books he would quash the power they held over people? If he did, he may have miscalculated. People had been composing their own "Sibylline Oracles" for centuries. One bonfire was not going to rid the Roman world of these accursed prophecies, nor was it going to dissuade anyone from believing what they wanted to believe.

Less than two years later, another important piece of legislation appeared: In A.D. 409, the word *paganus* would be defined to mean "gentile." It is the first time in Roman history that there is any solid evidence to confirm that the word "pagan" meant what we think it means: non-Christian. The age of the Christian "civilians" had come to a forceful close. Whatever social distinctions may have divided Jesus's followers from each other throughout the polarizing fourth century were now being wished away—by law. Christian "civilians" could not legally call themselves "Christians" anymore. They were cut off from Christian community, tossed into the pool of "non-believers," or gentiles—a word that Jews used to describe non-Jews.[36]

Finally, in A.D. 438, these laws would be collected, published, and handed to the Roman emperor Theodosius II as a birthday gift. The Theodosian Code, as we have come to call it, provides an eye-opening look at the cultural battlefield of the late fourth and early fifth century. It is a law book, yes. But it is also a fable, filled with chimerical tales of all the Christians who had ever set out on an urgent, quixotic journey to protect their fellow Christians from the "dangers" of the Roman world.

Even in the fifth century A.D., none of the messiness behind these words ever really went away. Neither a political, military, or legislative accomplishment could ever cleanse the diversity of people's beliefs from everyone else's lives. Memories—of burning incense, or visiting a shrine on a feast day, or celebrating a festival—would now guide residents of Rome, Ostia, Athens, Carthage, and elsewhere through this disorienting period of social change.

We haven't been particularly good at letting non-Christians speak for themselves during this time, although one classicist, Ramsay MacMullen, has recently taken up the charge. In 2009, MacMullen calculated that Christians comprised only 3 percent of the empire at the turn of A.D. 400. "For the historian," he says, "it is a problem."[37] Indeed, it would be— if the numbers are correct. Had Jesus's followers really lost demographic ground from where they stood a hundred years earlier, at the time of Constantine? There is much we will never know about life in ancient Rome; hard census data from the early fifth century A.D. is always going to be among the missing pieces. If we listen closely, though, I think MacMullen is on to something.

There are plenty more stories yet to be told about life at the "end" of Rome's empire, and they sound much different from the ones we have traditionally heard about the dawn of a new age of Christian "spirituality" in late antiquity. That story might be a memory, too (a selected one).

In the end, did "the death of 'paganism'" transform the empire? Or was it Christianity's "intrinsic appeal"? Or was it the Christians' "intolerant zeal"? I don't believe it was any of these.[38] Power, policy, and politics changed the Roman Empire, but at the center of it was neither a clash of civilizations nor a successful campaign of Christian evangelism. What had ignited so much change was the inability of Jesus's followers to agree upon what it meant to be a "Christian" in Rome.

Life in Rome was clearly changing in the centuries that we now call late antiquity. Some change was environmental, an occasional earthquake or flood. Some of it was economic. Archaeologists have found that ceramic imports in parts of Spain, Britain, and Italy decline during the late fifth, sixth, and seventh centuries A.D. Many people had to make do with plates and cookware they already owned. It was not a sign of the end of civilization, but it wasn't the vibrant, interconnected world of the earlier empire.[39]

Some change was psychologically jarring. In A.D. 378, the Roman emperor was killed battling Gothic tribes. It was an event that Ammianus Marcellinus described as the biggest massacre in Roman military history since Hannibal had ravaged Italy in the second century B.C.[40] Sixty millions Romans had lost their leader—taken from them by "barbarians"—and, most troubling of all, they didn't know where he'd gone. Valens's body was never found. Thirty years later, in A.D. 410, Goths would attack Rome, striking at a city that hadn't been touched for centuries. Rome would rebuild (restoring statues in the Forum, for example).[41]

Last, some change was constitutional. In A.D. 476, the emperor, in Italy, would be replaced by a king. We tell ourselves that that year marks the "Fall of Rome." Eight years later, in A.D. 484, one resident—the consul, a government office that had been held by Cicero and Caesar— paid to repair the Colosseum.[42] Hadn't he heard the breaking news? Rome was supposed to have fallen! Maybe he had.

After the attack in 410, a Christian in the Eastern Roman Empire had penned a letter expressing his shock at what the citizens in the capital had suffered. Jerome, the saint who is famous for standardizing the Latin translation of scripture, had also heard the news, from Jerusalem. "The city that captured the whole world was captured!" Jerome wailed. It was a dramatic reversal for a once-glorious empire. Five hundred years before, the poet Horace had marveled at how Rome had captured Greece and in the process been captured by its sophistication and charm. For Jerome, writing in A.D. 410, Rome's glory had turned. In a nearly contemporaneous work, a commentary on the book of Ezekiel, he voiced his pessimism in a different way: "When I heard the brightest light in the whole world had been snuffed out—or rather, when the head of the Roman Empire was lopped off and the whole world died in that one city—I was dumbstruck and I was humbled," he said.[43]

Jerome was talking about the recent attack on Rome in terms that would have sounded familiar to many of his readers. John had described the Roman Empire as a beast "with seven heads" coming out of the sea (Revelation 13:1). Another poet who had penned a fake "Sibylline prophecy" had referred to Rome as a "many-headed" terror.[44] The great biblical translator had been exploring these themes for several years. In A.D. 407, he had been reading Daniel. Daniel mentions four beasts, or imperial powers, coming out of the sea (Daniel 7:3), the last of which Jerome interpreted as the Roman Empire. This fourth beast would fall, Jerome wrote in his commentary, "at the end of the world." Its destruction was necessary for fulfilling God's divine plans.[45] For Jerome, then, composing a theological treatise in A.D. 407, the Roman Empire had to fall. Three years later, he would draw upon this same rhetorical language to imply that it had.[46] Everything we know reassures us that it did not.

Life in Rome never came to a cataclysmic stop. Nor did residents of a fragmenting empire suddenly give up their fascination with looking and acting like Romans. Even after Vandals took control of Carthage, in A.D. 439, the people of North Africa continued to go to Roman horse races, amphitheaters, and baths. Schools continued to flourish there through the fifth and sixth centuries A.D., teaching the next generation the "classics." Their education lasted a lifetime. One man "drowned in bitter death" sometime during the sixth or seventh century A.D., according to his tomb. It was a poetic phrase adapted from Virgil's great poem, the *Aeneid*.[47] Populations may have shifted. Cities may have shrunk. Greek and Roman columns came down, too—violently in Alexandria, while elsewhere, other cities recycled them. But an older way of life was never fully extinguished, not even in Rome.

Why are Jerome's rhetorical musings about the "Fall of Rome" so important, then? Put simply, they suggest that our own fevered efforts to understand the "Fall of Rome" won't be resolved through additional archaeological excavation or more careful pottery analysis. In the hands of writers like Daniel, John, and the so-called Sibyls, the "Fall of the Great Empire" had long given audiences hope for the future in uncertain times. Sometimes, it evoked fear of an "even worse" reality yet to come. That's why it shows up in the Jewish book of Daniel, in the Christian book of Revelation, and even in those strange poems, the so-called Sibylline Oracles. Across generations, before and after Jesus, the "Fall of the Great Empire" was a long-standing trope of political rhetoric. Deployed by those who felt passionately about their own vision for the world, it drew upon notions that a divine hand was guiding each stage of history to its necessary end and final judgment. Jerome was expressing his belief in that process, too. That's why the "Fall of Rome" still remains so beguiling.[48] It's not a historical event; it's more akin to a theological idea.

Many people sitting in the Colosseum and cheering on a wild animal hunt in A.D. 484 no doubt thought about the world in more measured terms—for them, a change in government didn't portend the end of the world—but even after so many intervening centuries, it's been hard to hear their voices over the roar of lions.

Keeping an Open Mind

March 12, 2013, Vatican City and Rome

One hundred and fifteen cardinals from across the world, draped in crimson, locked themselves inside the Sistine Chapel. Their mission was to choose the new head of the Catholic Church. Five votes and one day later, the tiny chimney pipe in the roof of the chapel began to puff white smoke. To the crowds of pious and curious onlookers that had gathered in St. Peter's Square, it was a welcome sign. The selection process—of secret paper ballots and incinerated results, all of which had taken place under the watchful eye of Michelangelo Buonarroti's ceiling and his exuberant vision of the Last Judgment, behind the altar—had drawn to a close. A new pope had been chosen. Four months later, during his famous in-flight press conference in July, Francis would make news again, this time by wading into the issue of gay clergy. "Who am I to judge?" he said, to the gasps of many. Weren't Christians supposed to be intolerant?

The great Renaissance artist Michelangelo can guide us here. His ceiling and *Last Judgment* have witnessed countless papal elections—eleven in a row since 1878 and many more in the centuries that preceded Italy's birth, in 1870. Today, in the sweltering Roman summer, nearly twenty thousand people a day still line up to see his images of God creating

Adam and of Adam and Eve in the Garden of Eden. Between forbidden camera flashes, they might see the Jewish prophets, too (Ezekiel, Daniel, Isaiah, and others), enthroned like royalty because their words are thought to have predicted Jesus's birth. Is it any wonder that so many people are still arrested by that ceiling? Michelangelo was telling a story about God's plan for the world, but even he knew to add what we omit—usually out of embarrassment—when we retell that story to ourselves.

There, at the margins of the ceiling, are the women. Each of them is setting her words on paper. Some leaf through their books, others read or hold a scroll. Michelangelo has labeled them—from Erythraea, Delphi, Cumae, Libya, and Persia—borrowing from a list of ten names that dates back to a Roman antiquarian of the first century B.C., Varro.[1] These are the Roman Sibyls (figure 16). Michelangelo is telling us that they "predicted" the rise of Christianity. How many of us have stood in the Sistine Chapel and pushed these women to the side? Michelangelo knew better. He has them holding history in their hands. He's right, too. From Clement to Constantine to Lactantius, even Rufinus, many of Jesus's followers had been entranced by them.

In the fourth century A.D., how many of Jesus's followers feared they lived on the eve of Nero's return? How many believed that Mediterranean "Sibyls" had foreordained Christianity's triumph, overlooking the inconvenient truth that many of these poems had been written by Christians? Was anyone aware that still other texts had been intended for a Jewish audience during the fiercest moments of their own military conflict with Rome? The fact of the matter is that by the fourth century A.D., many of Jesus's followers who subscribed to these views must have sounded no different to their Roman neighbors and government officials than Lentulus had sounded to Cicero in 63 B.C.—which is to say, they probably sounded like raving lunatics.[2]

Many early Christians themselves raised a puzzled eyebrow at the kinds of things other Christians were thinking and saying. To Lactantius, the wild notion about Nero's return wasn't rooted in reality. The ghastly emperor's miraculous reappearance wasn't going to herald "the arrival of the Antichrist," he assured his Christian audiences. Nero was not "the precursor of the devil." Fantastic ideas like these, including nervousness about the end of the world, were being tossed about by "crazies" (deliri), Lactantius said. (He, too, uses the adjective as a noun.) Where people had gotten them, he couldn't really guess. It was likely they'd picked them up from some sketchy source—from some "Sibyl," Lactantius sneered.[3]

If Lactantius was praying for relief from these embarrassingly unful-filled Christian predictions of impending doom, very little had changed by the start of the fifth century A.D. Some of Jesus's followers were still babbling on about an approaching cataclysm, and they were doing so with such "a stubborn assurance," Augustine of Hippo said, that he marveled at their obstinacy.[4] From Lactantius to Augustine, an entire century had passed, but two of the most prolific Christians of late antiq-uity were trying to push back against deranged ideas that had been festering among Jesus's followers for generations. Even the bishop of Milan hadn't hesitated to draw upon this rhetoric—"I detest the rites of all the 'Neros,'" he said—because he must have thought the specter of "Nero" was a useful one to conjure. Yet Nero never did come back, the Antichrist never did arrive, and most important, the world never came to an end. We owe it to all the people of the Roman Empire to put this type of thinking under our microscope and study it.

Many of these people—Christians—fought against it, as silently, steadfastly, and passionately as they knew how. They went to popular Roman festivals with their friends and neighbors. They served alongside other Romans in the army. They enjoyed the theater, cheered on their favorite horses, delighted in a day at the baths, even signed up for membership in their local Roman social club. Cyprian and others may have marveled at their peculiar ability to do two things at once—"These things were predicted to happen at the end of times!" the bishop had shouted, in the third century A.D.—but after his death, the clock kept ticking, the world kept turning, and many of Jesus's followers kept on living their hyphenated lives.

Many must have looked upon Cyprian's prediction of an imminent end, with its accompanying terrifying idea of a Last Judgment, and found it wholly distasteful. Put simply, a large number of Jesus's followers—I wish we did have hard data—had learned to see the Roman world in shades of gray, not in black-and-white. Of course, their peers could and did see matters differently. "I prefer to be a partner with you in Good rather than Evil [bonum and malum]," Ambrose confessed to Theodosius at the beginning of the Callinicum affair.[5] Here was a man who did see the world as starkly divided. Just as Tertullian believed that angels were fighting demons, for Ambrose, there could never be any ethical or moral in-between.[6]

This world view will probably sound "Manichean," to some.[7] Mani was a visionary who lived in the third century Sasanian Empire, and he did profess a similar outlook. His teachings would eventually spread to Rome, where a series of fourth century laws tried to eradicate them. They also traveled east. By the mid eighth century, the Uighur kingdom, today an autonomous region in China, had adopted Manicheanism as its official worship practices, the first and only time in history a state has done so.[8]

Motifs of spiritual conflict predate Mani, however. They are not exclusively a Christian phenomenon, either.[9] They appear in literature as early as the third millennium B.C. Much later, they inspired Daniel in the second century B.C., and after him, Revelation. In Egypt, they gave a Jewish poet the tools to spur on Jewish rebels in the second century A.D. Even the emperor Constantine incorporated them into his speech, depicted them on his palace door, and stamped them on the empire's coinage. During times of crisis, real or perceived, many people drew upon these ideas: Jews, Christians, even disaffected Romans. Some did so in moderation. Others may have had no stomach for them.

That's why Michelangelo's Sibyl is such a powerful symbol. She embodies so many of the curious ideas we've encountered throughout this book. She is the writer who dwelled on the looming end-time, like Cyprian. She is the one who talked of spiritual war, like Ambrose. She is the voice of the person who saw history unfolding in discrete sequences, like the Jewish rebel in Egypt. She is the visionary who beheld a world of angels and demons, like Tertullian. She is someone who thought the present was in need of salvation and that a leader would come to protect it, like Constantine and Lentulus. And she is the one who believed that glory would come, soon, like the literal readers of Revelation. The Sibyl is the sign of all these people's world views. She speaks to the role that their beliefs played in shaping Roman history.[10] We cannot ignore them.

History, after all, is not just what we choose to see about the past. It also includes things we might wish were never there.

Our story spans six hundred years, from the Maccabees to Theodosius. During that time we've strolled streets in Carthage, Rome, and Constantinople. We've analyzed the splintered and fracturing politics of people in Jerusalem, Alexandria, and Milan. We've listened to the stories of men and women who lived vastly different lives, sometimes right next door to each other: bald initiates of Isis, Jews who campaigned for safe space in Ephesos, Jesus's followers who found camaraderie in a house on the banks of the Euphrates River. Above all, we've eavesdropped as the people of this great ancient empire argued passionately with each other about their different visions for "Rome." What was it? What had it been? What could it be?

After such a long time on the road and at sea, it's about time that we took account of where we are. By the time Eugenius died, in the last decade of the fourth century A.D., the Roman world had reached a crucial turning point. How had it gotten there? Perhaps we can find guidance by looking down the road. The historian Richard Landes, who has studied the anxious beliefs that accompanied the arrival of the year A.D. 1000 in an essay drafted to reflect upon fears of A.D. 2000, has offered this helpful note:

> Until historians become familiar with the nature of millennial hopes and the dynamics of apocalyptic excitation and disap-pointment, until their radar screens have been adjusted to pick up certain kinds of data and to follow its effects past the period when it is most visible, they may most resemble some hypotheti-cal nuclear scientists who deny the existence of subatomic parti-cles by dismissing the shady traces of their trails as smudges on paper.[11]

For me, that's another way of capturing what I said at the beginning of this book and what I have tried to explore on each of its pages: what people believe—and what people are taught to believe—can and does inform the way they engage the world. It is essential that we find ways to talk about these people with nuance and complexity. The study of "reli-gion," then, as we call it, is indispensable for our understanding of the conflict that so profoundly shaped people's lives during this divisive (and decisive) time in Roman history.[12]

Indeed, throughout Roman history, many looked the other way at this ugly, strange phenomenon on which we have tried to shine a light here. Those who chose to face it, Christians, Jews, and non-Christians, confronted it as best they could. I have tried to tell as many of their stories as I was able. I only hope I have done so empathetically and with justice to all sides—and that, in some small way, I have freed these people from a stigma imposed on them centuries ago, when many were charged with the crime of "intolerant zeal." If I have erred, at least let it be said that I have stayed true to my discipline. For "if there's an acceptable bias in the writing and teaching of history," the historian John Lewis Gaddis has written, "let it tilt towards liberation."[13] And to my mind, the Christians have always deserved better than they got from Edward Gibbon.

I thought of all these ideas again on the evening in March 2012 when Francis left the Sistine Chapel and made his way to the loggia of St. Peter's. Some people looking up that night at the spiritual successor of St. Peter saw, in the crimson-clad men gathered around him, the blood of all the martyrs of early Christian history. Others just saw red.

What do I see now when I look back at four hundred years of Jesus's followers in Rome?

I don't just see the red of the martyrs. I see a group waving a flag of many colors.

Acknowledgments

In writing this book, I followed sage advice: "Select with authority, then move on." There will be many readers, no doubt, who were hoping for a few more pit stops in places where I kept driving, and many of the questions, topics, and approaches I have raised here will need to be explored in more depth later. My hope, though, is that by arriving at a new destination, we can retrace our steps together.

My thanks to friends across disciplines who offered me feedback while I wrote: Felicity Harley-McGown, Brent Nongbri, Maíjastina Kahlos, Joshua Burns, Candida Moss, and L. Michael White. Although they might not agree with everything in the final version here, I would never have embarked on a journey with any other group. I am also fortunate to count among them mentors such as Karl Galinsky, as well as Michele Salzman, Rita Lizzi Testa, and Marianne Sághy, the latter of whom witnessed the birth of my research on the word "pagan" while we were together in Rome. The Institute for the Study of Antiquity and Christian Origins at the University of Texas at Austin has also been a constant source of intellectual support.

During my time writing this book, I had the honor of moving from my undergraduate alma mater to my mom's undergraduate alma mater, from the oldest Jesuit university in America, Georgetown University, to the second oldest Jesuit university in America, Saint Louis University. In the process, I also happened to move from a department of classics to a department of history. Any move can be jarring and disruptive, but in my case, where I started out has dovetailed so naturally with where I have arrived that both groups of friends, colleagues, and students deserve recognition.

First, thank you to the chair of the History Department, Phil Gavitt, and the dean of the College of Arts and Sciences, Michael Barber, S.J., at Saint Louis University for their invitation to join such an outstanding department, as well as for the leave they granted me in the fall of 2013 to finish this manuscript. At Georgetown, I thank my former colleagues and my students. The roundtable discussions that we had in our seminars nurtured many of my ideas. My thanks as well to my undergraduate research assistants, Ranjani Atur and Drew Cunningham, for helping get my words and images to press on time. Fitting so many pieces together would also never have happened without the support of countless libraries and museum collections. I am grateful to the American Academy in Rome; the Soprintendenza speciale per i beni archeologici di Roma (including Ostia); the Israel Antiquities Authority, with a special note of thanks to Ari Rabinovitch in Jerusalem; the German Archaeological Institute in Rome; Georgetown University; and Washington University in St. Louis for their assistance, as well as to Marta Zlotnick for her help at Dumbarton Oaks in Washington, D.C. My thanks to Jamie Emery at Saint Louis University, in particular, for smoothing my transition to a new set of stacks.

I leave some of my greatest appreciation for Ayesha Pande and Peter Ginna. I was and remain humbled by their votes of confidence and their support for this project long ago. I also give my thanks to George Gibson, Rob Galloway, Patti Ratchford, and the entire Bloomsbury team for their enthusiasm and guidance.

Latin and Greek Texts and Selected Archaeological Sources

Below are the Latin and Greek texts that I have cited. Although I have used my own translations, most of these sources are available in English, and many appear in the bilingual series of ancient texts published by the Loeb Classical Library (Cambridge, MA: Harvard University Press). Readers will also find here reference material for the study of ancient inscriptions and coins. Archaeological sources—such as the gem depicting the crucifixion, the synagogue at Sardis, or the Temple of Saturn in Rome—are historical sources, too. But at the risk of cataloging these objects in a list, I have provided the bibliography for them in my notes.

For quotations from Hebrew texts, such as 1 Maccabees and texts of the Hebrew Bible, I have used the New Revised Standard Version in the HarperCollins Study Bible, edited by H. Attridge (San Francisco, 2006). The dates for each author below are based on entries in the Oxford Classical Dictionary, fourth edition, edited by S. Hornblower, A. Spawforth, and E. Eidinow (Oxford: Oxford University Press, 2012). The one exception is the entry for Ignatius of Antioch. The man who coined the word we often translate as "Christianity," the Greek noun which I have translated as "being openly Christian" (*Christianismos*), was not given a space of his own in the Oxford Classical Dictionary. I've culled our best-guess range for his life span from *The Concise Oxford Dictionary of the Christian Church*, revised edition, edited by E. Livingston (Oxford: Oxford University Press, 2006).

Ambrose (A.D. c. 340–397). *Letters*. An English translation is available in W. Liebeschuetz, *Ambrose of Milan: Political Letters and Speeches* (Chicago: University of Chicago Press, 2005). I have used the Latin text edited by M. Zelzer in the series *Corpus Scriptorum Ecclesiasticorum Latinorum* 82.3 (Vienna: Tempsky, 1982).

Ammianus Marcellinus (A.D. c. 330–395). I used the Latin text from the three-volume Loeb edition, edited by J. Rolfe (1935–1940). A good English translation is by W. Hamilton (New York: Penguin, 1986).

Apuleius (A.D. c. 125–c. 180). *The Golden Ass [Metamorphoses]*. A witty translation is available from Jack Lindsay, *The Golden Ass* (Bloomington: Indiana University Press, 1962). The Latin text was edited by R. Helm (Stuttgart: Teubner, 1992).

Augustine (A.D. 354–430). *Confessions*. I prefer the English translation by Maria Boulding (New York: Viking, 1998). Thanks to editor J. O'Donnell, the Latin text of Augustine's *Confessions* lives online; it was originally published in three volumes (Oxford: Clarendon Press, 1992).

——. *Letters*. "Letter to Publicola." English translations of Publicola's letter and Augustine's reply (*Ep.* 46–47) are available in the series *Nicene and Post-Nicene Fathers*, first series, volume 1, edited by P. Schaff (Buffalo: Christian Literature Publishing, 1887). For the Latin text of the letter, I have used the series *Corpus Scriptorum Ecclesiasticorum Latinorum* 34.2, edited by A. Goldbacher (Vienna: Tempsky, 1898).

——. *City of God*. An English translation is available from H. Bettenson (London: Penguin, 1972). I have taken the Latin from the series *Corpus Christianorum*, Series Latina, volumes 47–48, edited by B. Dombart and A. Kalb (Turnhout: Brepols, 1955).

Cassius Dio (A.D. c. 164–c. 229). *History*. Greek and English editions are available in the Loeb Classical Library, nine volumes, translated by E. Cary (1914–27).

Christian Scripture. For writers associated with "the Bible," I have used the Greek text edited by E. Nestle and K. Aland (Stuttgart, 1979). Readers looking for a good English translation should consider the HarperCollins Study Bible, New Revised Standard Version, edited by H. Attridge (San Francisco, 2006). It also includes 2 Maccabees, which is part of the Catholic, but not the Protestant, canon.

Cicero (106–43 B.C.). *Catilinarian Orations.* Latin and English texts are available in the Loeb Classical Library, translated by C. MacDonald (1976).

Clement of Alexandria (A.D. c. 150–c. 215). *Exhortation [Protrepticus].* Greek and English editions are available in the Loeb Classical Library, translated by G. Butterworth (1919).

——. *The Teacher [Paedagogus].* The Greek text is from the series *Sources chrétiennes* 108, edited by M. Harl, H.-I. Marrou, C. Matray, and C. Mondésert (Paris: Éditions du Cerf, 1965).

[CIJ] *Collection of Jewish Inscriptions.* The inscriptions have been edited by J.-B. Frey, in two volumes (Rome: Pontificio istituto di archeologia cristiana, 1936–1952).

[CIL] *Collection of Latin Inscriptions.* Published in seventeen volumes with approximately seventy contributions, under various editors (Berlin: BBAW, 1863–present).

[CPJ] *Collection of Jewish Papyrus Fragments.* The fragments are available in three volumes, edited by V. Tcherikover with A. Fuks (Cambridge, MA: Harvard University Press, 1957–1964).

Commodian (c. third century A.D.). *Instructions.* The English text is available in the series *Ante-Nicene Fathers,* volume 4, edited by A. Roberts and J. Donaldson, revised by A. Coxe (Peabody, MA: Hendrickson, 1994). For the Latin I have used the *Corpus Christianorum,* Series Latina 128, edited by J. Martin (Turnhout: Brepols, 1960).

Constantine (A.D. c. 272–337). *Speech to the Assembly of the Saints.* An English translation is available in *Constantine and Christendom,* edited and translated by M. Edwards (Liverpool: Liverpool University Press, 2003). I have used the Greek edition of the text edited by I. Heikel, *Eusebius Werke* 1, in the series *Die griechischen christlichen Schriftsteller* (Berlin: Akademie Verlag, 1902, reprinted 1991).

Cyprian (A.D. c. 200–258). *On the Lapsed* and *Letters.* English translations are available in the series *Ante-Nicene Fathers,* volume 5, edited by A. Roberts and J. Donaldson, revised by A. Coxe (Peabody, MA: Hendrickson, 1994). I have used the Latin text in the series *Corpus Christianorum,* Series Latina 3, edited by M. Bévenot (Turnhout: Brepols, 1972).

Dionysius of Halicarnassus (first century B.C.–first century A.D.). *Roman Antiquities.* The English and Greek texts are available in the Loeb Classical Library edition, in seven volumes, edited by E. Cary (1937–1950).

Eusebius (A.D. c. 260–339). *History of the Church.* An English translation is available from P. Maier (Grand Rapids: Kregel, 2007). I have used the

Greek edition of the text edited by E. Schwartz and T. Mommsen, *Eusebius Werke* 2, in the series *Die griechischen christlichen Schriftsteller* (Berlin: Akademie Verlag, 1903).

——. *Life of Constantine*. An English translation is available under the same title, edited and translated by A. Cameron and S. Hall (Oxford: Clarendon, 1999). The Greek edition was edited by F. Winkelmann, *Eusebius Werke* 1.1, in the series *Die griechischen christlichen Schriftsteller* (Berlin: Akademie Verlag, 1975).

——. *The Proof of the Gospel* [*Demonstratio Evangelica*]. An English translation is available from W. J. Ferrar (New York: Macmillan, 1920). The Greek text appears in the series *Die griechischen christlichen Schriftsteller* 23, edited by I. A. Heikel (Leipzig: Hinrichs, 1913).

Gregory of Nazianzus (A.D. 329–389). *Orations*. An English translation of selected orations is available from M. Vinson, *The Fathers of the Church: St. Gregory of Nazianzus*. I have used the Greek text as it appears in *Patrologia Graeca*, volume 35, edited by J.-P. Migne (Paris: Migne, 1857–1866).

Hippolytus of Rome (A.D. c. 170–c. 236). *Refutation of All Heresies*. An English translation is available in the series *Ante-Nicene Fathers*, volume 5, edited by A. Roberts and J. Donaldson, revised by A. Coxe (Peabody, MA: Hendrickson, 1994). For the Greek text, I used *Patristische Texte und Studien*, volume 25, edited by M. Marcovich (Berlin: De Gruyter, 1986).

Hymn to Demeter (c. seventh century B.C.). The Greek and English texts appear in the Loeb Classical Library, edited by H. Evelyn-White (1936). A helpful commentary appears in *The Homeric Hymns* by Susan Shelmerdine (Newburyport, MA: Focus Publishing, 1995).

[IG] *Collection of Greek Inscriptions*. Published in fifteen volumes, some with multiple contributions, under various editors (Berlin: BBAW, 1873–present).

Ignatius of Antioch (A.D. c. 35–c. 107). *Letters*. An English and a Greek text are printed in the Loeb Classical Library series, edited by B. Ehrman (2003).

Jerome (A.D. c. 347–420). *Commentary on Daniel, Commentary on Ezekiel, and Letters*. An English translation of the Daniel commentary is available from G. L. Archer (Grand Rapids: Baker Book House, 1958). *Ezekiel* and the *Letters* appear in the *Nicene and Post-Nicene Fathers*, second series, volume 6, translated by W. H. Fremantle (New York, 1893). The Latin texts appear in the series *Corpus Christianorum*, Series Latina 56 (*Letters*), edited by I. Hilberg, 1910–1918); volume 75A (*Daniel*) and 75 (*Ezekiel*), edited by F. Glorie (Turnhout: Brepols, 1964).

John Chrysostom (A.D. c. 354–407). *Catechesis.* An English version, titled *Baptismal Instructions,* is available from P. Harkins (Westminster: Newman Press, 1963). The Greek text is from the series *Sources chrétiennes* 50, edited by A. Wenger (Paris: Éditions du Cerf, 1970).

——. *Homilies on 2 Thessalonians.* An English translation of the homilies, by multiple authors, appears in *Library of Fathers of the Holy Catholic Church,* volume 14 (Oxford: James Parker & Co., 1879). The Greek text is taken from *Patrologia Graeca* 62, edited by J.-P. Migne (Paris: Migne, 1857–1866).

Josephus (A.D. c. 37–c. 100). *Jewish Antiquities.* Greek and English texts are available in the Loeb Classical Library, thirteen volumes, translated by H. Thackeray, R. Marcus, A. Wikgren, and L. Feldman (Cambridge, MA: Harvard University Press, 1930–1965).

Lactantius (A.D. c. 240–c. 320). *On the Death of the Persecutors.* An English translation is available in the series *Ante-Nicene Fathers,* volume 7, edited by A. Roberts and J. Donaldson, revised by A. Coxe (Peabody, MA: Hendrickson, 1994). I have used the Latin edition of the text edited by J. L. Creed, *De mortibus persecutorum* (Oxford: Clarendon Press, 1984).

"Letter to Diognetus" (c. second century A.D.). I used the Greek text edited by H.-I. Marrou, "À Diognète" in the series *Sources chrétiennes* 33 (Paris: Éditions du Cerf, 1965). An English translation is available in *Early Christian Fathers,* edited by C. Richardson, translated by E. Fairweather (New York: Touchstone, 1996).

2 Maccabees (c. late second century B.C.). Readers of this text, a ghostly presence in the life of late antique Jews but a palpable one in the world of late antique Christians, will find an English translation in the HarperCollins Study Bible, New Revised Standard Version, as above. For the Greek, I have used *Septuaginta,* edited by A. Rahlfs (Stuttgart, 1935).

Marius Victorinus (mid fourth century A.D.). *Commentary on Paul's Letter to the Galatians.* Marius is one of the most important but least understood Christians of the fourth century. Marius's commentary on Paul is printed in the *Corpus Scriptorum Ecclesiasticorum Latinorum* 83.2, edited by F. Gori (Vienna, 1986). I have also consulted S. Cooper's *Marius Victorinus' Commentary on Galatians: Introduction, Translation, and Notes* (Oxford: Oxford University Press, 2005).

Philo of Alexandria (c. end of first century B.C.–c. middle of first century A.D.). *Against Flaccus* and *On the Embassy to Gaius.* Greek and English texts available in the Loeb Classical Library, volumes 9 and 10, translated by F. Colson (1941–1962).

Pliny the Younger (A.D. c. 61–c. 112). *Letters*. Latin and English text available in the Loeb Classical Library, volume 2, edited by B. Radice (1969).

Plutarch (before A.D. 50–c. 120). "On Isis and Serapis," in the *Moralia*, volume 5. Greek and English text available from the Loeb Classical Library, edited by F. C. Babbitt (1936).

Pseudo-Ambrose (mid to late fourth century A.D.), often called Ambrosiaster. *Commentary on 2 Thessalonians*. Although I know of no available English translation, the work of K. Hughes, *Constructing Antichrist: Paul, Biblical Commentary, and the Development of Doctrine in the Early Middle Ages* (Washington, D.C.: Catholic University Press, 2005) offers a good introduction to the apocalyptic theme that is central to my thesis. The Latin text is printed in the *Corpus Scriptorum Ecclesiasticorum Latinorum* 81.3, edited by H. Vogels (Vienna: Tempsky, 1969).

[RIC]. *Collection of Roman Imperial Coins*. Thirteen volumes, with various editors, covering material from 31 B.C. to 491 A.D. (London: Spink & Sons, 1926–1994).

Rufinus of Aquileia (A.D. c. 345–411). *History of the Church*. The commentary with translation by P. Amidon, S.J., *The Church History of Rufinus of Aquileia: Books 10 and 11*, is helpful for the destruction of the Temple of Serapis in Alexandria (New York: Oxford University Press, 1997). The Latin text is from the series *Clavis Patrum Latinorum*, edited by J. Dekkers, third edition (Turnhout: Brepols, 1995).

Servius (fourth century A.D.). *Commentary on Virgil*. I have used the Latin text edited by G. Thilo and H. Hagen (Hildesheim: Georg Olms Verlag, 1986). Readers looking to learn more might consult D. Fowler, "The Virgil Commentary of Servius," in *The Cambridge Companion to Virgil*, edited by C. Martindale (Cambridge: Cambridge University Press, 1997), 73–78.

So-Called Fifth Oracle of the Sibyls (A.D. 115–117). This enchanting gem is available in English, translation by J. Collins in *The Old Testament Pseudepigrapha*, edited by J. Charlesworth (Garden City: Doubleday, 1983), 390–405. For my translations, I used the Greek text *Die Oracula Sibyllina* in the series *Die griechischen christlichen Schriftsteller*, edited by J. Geffcken (Leipzig: Hinrichs, 1902).

Suetonius (A.D. c. 70–c. 130). *Lives of the Caesars*. Latin and English text available in the Loeb Classical Library, translated by J. C. Rolfe (1914).

Sulpicius Severus (A.D. c. 360–c. 420). *Chronicle* [*Chronica*]. An English text is available in the *Nicene and Post-Nicene Fathers*, second series, volume 11, edited by P. Schaff, A. Roberts, J. Donaldson, and H. Wace

(Peabody, MA: Hendrickson, 1996). The Latin text appears in the series *Corpus Scriptorum Ecclesiasticorum Latinorum* 1, edited by K. Halm (Vienna: Tempsky, 1866).

Symmachus (A.D. c. 340–402). *State Papers [Relationes]*. An English text is available in *Nicene and Post-Nicene Fathers*, second series, volume 10, edited by P. Schaff, A. Roberts, J. Donaldson, and H. Wace (Peabody, MA: Hendrickson, 1996). I have used the Latin text of *Relatio* 3 as it appears in the volume edited by J.-P. Callu (Paris: Les Belles Lettres, 2009).

Tacitus (between A.D. 56 and 58–c. 120). *Annals*. Latin and English text available in the Loeb Classical Library, translated by C. Moore and J. Jackson (1931–1937).

Tertullian (A.D. c. 160–c. 240). *Apology [Apologeticus]*. The Latin and English texts are available in the Loeb Classical Library, edited by T. R. Glover and G. Rendall (1931).

——. *On the Crown*. The English text is available in the series *Ante-Nicene Fathers*, volume 3, edited by A. Roberts and J. Donaldson, revised by A. Coxe (Peabody, MA: Hendrickson, 1994). I have used the Latin text in *Corpus Christianorum*, Series Latina, volume 2, ed. by A. Gerlo (Turnhout: Brepols, 1954).

The Theodosian Code (compiled A.D. 429–438). For an English translation, see *The Theodosian Code and Novels and Sirmondian Constitutions*, edited and translated by C. Pharr (Princeton: Princeton University Press, 1952). For the Latin text of the religious laws, I have used the edition of book 16 edited by J. Rougé and translated into French by R. Delmaire and F. Richard, *Les lois religieuses des empereurs romains de Constantin à Théodose II (312–438)* (Paris: Éditions du Cerf, 2005).

Trajan (A.D. c. 53–117, Roman emperor A.D. 98–117). "Reply to Pliny." Latin and English text available in the Loeb Classical Library, volume 2, edited by B. Radice (1969).

Valerius Maximus (early first century A.D.). *Memorable Deeds and Sayings*. The Latin and English text are available in the Loeb Classical Library, edited by D. Shackleton Bailey (2000).

Valerius Publicola (c. late fourth and early fifth century A.D.). "Letter to Augustine." I have used the Latin text of the letter in the collection of Augustine (= *Ep.* 46), as above.

Notes

Preface: "Who Am I to Judge?"

1 Pope Francis's comments about gay clergy inspired me here; see "Video of the Pope's 'Gay Lobby' Remarks," by R. Mackey (July 29, 2013).

2 K. Hopkins, "Christian Number and Its Implications," *Journal of Early Christian Studies* 6 (1998) 185–226, presents a good overview of Christian demographics, with the discussion of 10 percent at the turn of the fourth century at p. 192.

3 Edward Gibbon published the first volume of *Decline and Fall of the Roman Empire*, from which I lifted this quotation, in 1776 (New York: Modern Library, 2003), 383. On Gibbon's ideas about the rise of Christianity, see H. Drake, "Models of Christian Expansion," in *The Spread of Christianity in the First Four Centuries: Essays in Explanation* (Leiden: Brill, 2005), edited by W. Harris, 1–13.

4 R. Krautheimer, *Three Christian Capitals: Topography and Politics* (Berkeley: University of California Press, 1983), 32; L. Vaage, "Why Christianity Succeeded (in) the Roman Empire," *Religious Rivalries in the Roman Empire and the Rise of Christianity*, edited by L. Vaage (Waterloo: Wilfred Laurier Press, 2006) 253–78, at p. 253.

5 C. Hedrick also pushes the argument in this direction in *History and Silence: Purge and Rehabilitation of Memory in Late Antiquity* (Austin: University of Texas Press, 2000).

6 Theodosian Code 16.10.2, dated A.D. 341; see also 16.10.35, dated A.D. 435. For the criminals, madmen, and insane, see M. Salzman, "The Evidence for the Conversion of the Roman Empire to Christianity in Book 16 of the 'Theodosian Code,'" *Historia* 42 (1993) 362–78, particularly pp. 367–68.

7 Those looking to explore this Rome will find an easy entry through the 2006 novel by A. Lakhous, *Scontro di civiltà per un ascensore a Piazza Vittorio*. An English translation is available from A. Goldstein, *Clash of Civilizations over an Elevator in Piazza Vittorio* (New York: Europa Editions, 2008).

8 I also have kept the insightful work of Harold Drake nearby; see H. Drake, "Intolerance, Religious Violence, and Political Legitimacy in Late Antiquity," *Journal of the American Academy of Religion* 79 (2011) 193–235; and "Lambs into Lions: Explaining Early Christian Intolerance," *Past and Present* 153 (1996) 3–36.

9 I have drawn the measurements from D. Davis, "Commercial Navigation in the Greek and Roman World," Ph.D. dissertation (University of Texas at Austin, 2009), 17.

10 The population estimates, with bibliography, are taken from S. Friesen and W. Scheidel, "The Distribution of Income in the Roman Empire," *Journal of Roman Studies* 99 (2009) 61–91, at p. 68, and estimates on income distribution at pp. 84–85.

11 E. Mayer, *The Ancient Middle Classes* (Cambridge, MA: Harvard University Press, 2012), 100–65.

12 Four recent works on identity will suffice to introduce the theme: *Being Christian in Late Antiquity: A Festschrift for Gillian Clark*, edited by C. Harrison, C. Humfress, and I. Sandwell (Oxford: Oxford University Press, 2014); É. Rebillard, *Christians and Their Many Identities in North Africa, 200–450* (Ithaca: Cornell University Press, 2012); M. Kahlos, *Debate and Dialogue: Christian and Pagan Cultures, c. 360–450* (Burlington, VT: Ashgate, 2007); and J. Perkins, *Roman Imperial Identities in the Early Christian Era* (London: Routledge, 2009).

13 R. Stark, *The Rise of Christianity: How the Obscure, Marginal Jesus Movement Became the Dominant Religious Force in the Western World in a Few Centuries* (New York: HarperCollins, 1997), 209–16. In *Pagans and Christians* (New York: Alfred A. Knopf, 1989), R. Lane Fox explains it this way: "Christianity's subsequent progress [in the fourth century] owed less to legal prohibition than to a subtler compound, composed of legal privilege, the faith's intrinsic appeal and a continued use of force," p. 667.

Chapter 1: A Bewitching Sibyl

1 E. Gruen, *The Last Generation of the Roman Republic* (Berkeley: University of California Press, 1974), 416–33.

2 Cicero, *Against Catiline* 3.9; see also Sallust, *Catiline's War* 47.2, Appian, *Civil War* 2.4, Plutarch, *Life of Cicero* 17.4.

3 For the history of the Sibyls, see S. Takács, *Vestal Virgins, Sibyls, and Matrons: Women in Roman Religion* (Austin: University of Texas Press, 2008), 62–70; and also E. Orlin, *Temples, Religion, and Politics in the Roman Republic* (Leiden: Brill, 1997), 76–115. Additional works will be discussed below.

4 This version of the story is reported in Dionysius of Halicarnassus in his *Roman Antiquities* 4.62.

5 Livy reports the prodigies, or signs, at *History* 22.1.8–20. Bibulus' story is reported by Suetonius, *Julius Caesar* 20. I follow the interpretation of the events in M. Beard, J. North, and S. Price, *Religions of Rome* (New York: Cambridge University Press, 1998), 1.126–29.

6 Dionysius of Halicarnassus, *Roman Antiquities* 4.62.5.

7 Cicero, *Against Catiline* 3.9.

8 F. Santangelo, *Divination, Prediction and the End of the Roman Republic* (New York: Cambridge University Press, 2013), 185–86.

9 B. Ward-Perkins, *The Fall of Rome and the End of Civilization* (Oxford: Oxford University Press, 2005), 180.

10 R. G. Collingwood, *The Idea of History* (Oxford: Oxford University Press, 1946), 317.

11 For Rome, in particular, see C. King, "The Organization of Roman Religious Belief," *Classical Antiquity* 22 (2003) 275–312.

12 J. L. Gaddis, *The Landscape of History: How Historians Map the Past* (Oxford: Oxford University Press, 2002), 140.

13 P. Weiss, "The Vision of Constantine," *Journal of Roman Archaeology* 16 (2003) 237–59. I will discuss the bishop, Cyprian, below.

14 C. Geertz, *The Interpretation of Culture* (New York: Basic Books, 1973), 90, is not the only one to attempt a definition. The sociologist Robert Bellah provided a working definition in his last book, *Religion in Human Evolution*: "Religion is a system of beliefs and practices relative to the sacred that unite those who adhere to them in a moral community" (Cambridge, MA: Harvard University Press, 2011), 1. Bellah refers to something akin to Geertz's "religious symbol systems" in his preface, 2011, xvii–xix. I will say more about the relevance of "religion" as a concept in a later chapter. Essential now is B. Nongbi, *Before Religion: A History of*

a Modern Concept (New Haven: Yale University Press, 2013), 46–64, 154–59, also discussed below.

Chapter 2: The Quieter Ones

1 These data are from the December 19, 2011, Pew Research: Religion and Public Life Project report, "Global Christianity–A Report on the Size and Distribution of the World's Christian Population," published online at pewforum.org.

2 For a methodological discussion about these ideas, see B. Ehrman, *Jesus: Apocalyptic Prophet of a New Millennium* (Oxford: Oxford University Press, 2001) 125–39; see also L. M. White, *Scripting Jesus: The Gospels in Rewrite* (San Francisco: HarperCollins, 2010).

3 White, *Scripting Jesus*, 2010, 277–78.

4 C. M. Lehmann and K. Holum, *The Greek and Latin Inscriptions of Caesarea Maritima* (Boston: American Schools of Oriental Research, 2000), 67–70, no. 43, dated to the first two centuries A.D., commemorating a temple dedicated A.D. c. 26–36.

5 White, *Scripting Jesus*, 2010, 138–41; see also L. M. White, *From Jesus to Christianity* (San Francisco: HarperCollins, 2004), 32–34.

6 White, *Scripting Jesus*, 2010, 108–14.

7 Tertullian, *Apologeticus* 50.12.

8 See, for example, J. D. Crossan's *God and Empire: Jesus Against Rome, Then and Now* (San Francisco: HarperCollins, 2007), which frames the story of Christian origins as a struggle against the imperialism of Rome.

9 Eight times, as a pair, in the *Apologeticus* (22.25, 22.34, 23.1, 23.8, 23.11, 23.43, 27.9, and 29.1). Elsewhere, as a pair, throughout his corpus: *De spectaculis* 8.7; *Against Marcion* 4.484, line 23; *Against Valentinian* 200, line 2; *De anima* 57.50; *De resurrectione mortuorum* 58.14; *De idolatria* 33.13; and *De fuga in persecutione* 10.12.

10 The most accessible treatment of this topic is J. Rives, *Religion and Authority in Roman Carthage: From Augustus to Constantine* (Oxford: Oxford University Press, 1995), 100–72, which draws on archaeological evidence from nearby Thugga to illuminate life in Carthage.

11 The inscription, with text and translation, appears in *The Inscriptions of Roman Tripolitania*, edited by J. Reynolds and J. B. Ward Perkins (1952), 98, no. 321. For its relevance to the Augustan Age, see K. Galinsky, *Augustus: Introduction to the Life of an Emperor* (New York: Cambridge University Press, 2012), text box 7.3.

12 A foundational study is G. Woolf, *Becoming Roman* (Cambridge: Cambridge University Press, 1998), 206–37. The bibliography on what scholars have referred to as "Romanization" abounds. I prefer to avoid the term "Romanization" by framing discussions in terms of cultural power and exchange. For that approach, see D. Mattingly, *Imperialism, Power, and Identity: Experiencing the Roman World* (Princeton: Princeton University Press, 2011). I have found that T. Friedman, *The Lexus and the Olive Tree* (New York: Anchor, 2000), also helps put these questions in some perspective.

13 L. Revell, *Roman Imperialism and Local Identities* (New York: Cambridge University Press, 2009), 179–90.

14 The quotation about Tertullian is from R. Wilken, *The Christians as the Romans Saw Them* (New Haven: Yale University Press, 1984), 45.

15 Tertullian, *To Scapula* 2.1.

16 Compare with V. Arena, "Tolerance, Intolerance, and Religious Liberty at Rome: An Investigation in the History of Ideas," in *Politiche religiose nel modno antico e tardo antico*, edited by G. Cecconi and C. Gabrielli (Bari: Edipuglia, 2011), 147–64.

17 Tertullian, *Apologeticus* 24.2.

18 See A. Clark, *Divine Qualities: Cult and Community in Republican Rome* (Oxford: Oxford University Press, 2007); and also C. Noreña, *Imperial Ideals in the Roman West: Representation, Circulation, Power* (New York: Cambridge University Press, 2011).

19 Tertullian, *Apologeticus* 24.2.

20 For discussion, see M. Beard, J. North, and S. Price, *Religions of Rome*, volume 1 (New York: Cambridge University Press, 1998), 225–27. For Tacitus' use of *superstitio*, see *Annals* 15.44.5. For Pliny, see *Letters* 10.96.8.

21 Readers who are familiar with the book by Candida Moss titled *The Myth of Persecution: How Early Christians Invented a Story of Martyrdom* (New York: HarperCollins, 2013) will detect some resemblance in what follows. I mention the parallel because at least one reviewer of Moss's book has questioned the validity of her conclusions; see N. Clayton Croy, "Review of *The Myth of Persecution*," *Review of Biblical Literature* (October 3, 2013). I offer my chapter as a forceful rebuttal to that review. On the power of martyr stories in the formation of Christian community, see E. Castelli, *Martyrdom and Memory: Early Christian Culture Making* (New York: Columbia University Press, 2004). For the first 250 years, see now J. Rives, "The Decree of Decius and the Religion of Empire," *Journal of Roman Studies* 89 (1999) 135–54.

22 For "Christians," see Luke–Acts 11:26 (written between A.D. 90 and 100, possibly as late as 110), but also 1 Peter 4:16 (written c. A.D. 80–90) and Josephus, *Jewish Antiquities* 18.64 (A.D. 93–94).

23 P. Trebilco, *Self-Designation and Group Identity in the New Testament* (New York: Cambridge University Press, 2012), 272–97; see also D. Horrell, "The Label 'Christianos': 1 Peter 4:16 and the Formation of Christian Identity," *Journal of Biblical Literature* 126 (2007) 361–81, with discussion of appropriating a harmful label at pp. 376–80. P. Holloway, *Coping with Prejudice: 1 Peter in Social-Psychological Perspective* (Tübingen: Mohr Siebeck, 2009) also explores the theme.

24 For a bibliography, see the discussion of Paul in the next chapter.

25 Ignatius of Antioch, "Letter to the Magnesians" 10.1. For further discussion of the word *Christianismos* and the difficulties of translating it, see chapter 7, below.

26 Trebilco, *Self-Designation and Group Identity*, 2012, argues that the slur "Christian" was in use during Nero's time but rightly asserts that that the group would have seemed no different from Jews to anyone looking in from the outside, p. 274; see also Moss, *Myth of Persecution*, 2012, 138–39.

27 Colossians is dated A.D. 70–80, or 85–95. Ephesians is dated A.D. 85–95. 1 Peter is dated A.D. 80–95. Scholars refer to these passages as the "household duty code." For discussion, see D. Balch and C. Osiek, *Families in the New Testament World: Households and House Churches* (Louisville: Westminster John Knox Press, 1997), 118–21, 182–85.

28 Aristotle, *Politics* 1.3 (= 1253b).

29 "An informer": Pliny, *Ep.* 10.96.6.

30 Repeatedly identifying as a "Christian," Pliny, *Ep.* 10.96.3; "swearing oaths" and "paying debts," 10.96.7; citizens showing signs of *amentia*, 10.96.4; the cult as a *superstitio*, 10.96.8.

31 CIL 6.960.

32 Eutropius, *Breviarum* 8.5.3.

33 Trajan's correspondence to Pliny is included in the same collection (*Ep.* 10.97). Trajan's reply, which I quote, is at 10.97.2; see also Moss, *Myth of Persecution*, 2012, 139–45.

34 Important works on Roman religion include J. Rüpke, *Religion of the Romans* (Malden, MA: Polity Press, 2009, translated by Richard Gordon), as well as J. Scheid, *An Introduction to Roman Religion* (Bloomington: Indiana University Press, 2003, translated by Janet Lloyd). I have been selective here.

35 See R. Bellah, "Civil Religion in America," *Daedalus* 96 (1967) 1–21.

36 The text of the martyrs of Lyon appears in Eusebius, *History of the Church* 5.1–4. Both it and the "Passion of Perpetua and Felicitas" are available in H. Musurillo, *The Acts of the Christian Martyrs*, introduction, texts, and

translation (Oxford: Clarendon Press, 1972). For discussion, see Moss, *Myth of Persecution*, 2012, 69–72, 112–14 (Blandina, whose profile is crafted after the mother of the Maccabees); and 73–74, 117–124 (Perpetua). For the relevance of the Maccabees, see chapter 4, below. Perpetua's story has also been told recently by K. Cooper, *Band of Angels: The Forgotten World of Early Christian Women* (London: Atlantic Books, 2013). For the calendar from Rome, see M. Salzman, *On Roman Time: The Codex-Calendar of 354 and the Rhythms of Urban Life in Late Antiquity* (Berkeley: University of California Press, 1990), 45.

37 For an overview, see M. Kulikowski, *Late Roman Spain and Its Cities* (Baltimore: Johns Hopkins University Press, 2004), 216–18.

38 For a bibliography on sacrifice, see Beard, North, and Price, *Religions of Rome*, 1998, 2.148–50. For representations of the *victimarii*, the bare-chested slaves assigned to slaughter the animals, see I. S. Ryberg, "Rites of the State Religion in Roman Art," *Memoirs of the American Academy in Rome* 22 (1955) 1–227. For the rise of Neoplatonist, or philosophical, interpretations of sacrifice, see G. Stroumas, *The End of Sacrifice: Religious Transformations in Late Antiquity*, translated by S. Emanuel (Chicago: University of Chicago Press, 2009), 56–109. The best new book on the topic is D. Ullucci, *The Christian Rejection of Animal Sacrifice* (New York: Oxford University Press, 2011).

39 The details of this story, as related here and in the following paragraphs, are preserved only in Cyprian, *Ep.* 67: "the certificate and sacrifice," "the burial society," 67.6.1; "bishop Martial," 67.1.1.

40 Cyprian, *Ep.* 67.7.

41 Cyprian, *On the Lapsed* 16.

42 Cyprian's judgment was hardly motivated by ideological purity. He had abandoned his flock in Carthage and spent the festival in an undisclosed location to avoid taking part; see A. Brent, *Cyprian and Roman Carthage* (Cambridge: Cambridge University Press, 2010), 117–249. A. Brent, *A Political History of Early Christianity* (London: T&T International, 2009), who talks about the "apocalypticism of [the Roman emperor] Decius," 277, and the "metaphysical collapse of nature and of society that were at the transcendental root of the woes of the third century," 262, has third century Rome entirely upside down. Cyprian is the apocalypticist, and the fact that the bishop used the same language to lament Christians who sacrificed as he did to describe the purported effects of a third century plague (*On Mortality*) raises doubts about whether we can rely upon his rhetoric to explain the "rise of Christianity"; see Stark, *Rise of Christianity*, 1997, 77–78.

43 See D. Potter, *The Roman Empire at Bay, A.D. 180–395* (London: Routledge, 2004), 255–56, 337–77; and also Moss, *Myth of Persecution*, 2012, 154–59.

44 For the details under Valerian, see the *Acta Proconsularia* 1.1 in Musurillo, *Acts of the Christian Martyrs*, 1972, 168–75. For the details of Diocletian's persecution, see Eusebius, *History* 8.2.3–4, and Lactantius, *On the Death of the Persecutors* 13.1. Eusebius gives us the reports of those who chose martyrdom over accommodation at *History* 8.1.4–5, 8.6.1, 7.32.2–4 (death of Gorgonius and Dorotheus), 8.6.2–4 (death of a Christian named Peter); see also Moss, *Myth of Persecution*, 2012, 151–53.

45 Lactantius, *Death of the Persecutors* 15.1–2.

46 Lactantius, *Death of the Persecutors* 2.4 (eleven apostles), 2.8 (Nero).

Chapter 3: The New Neighbors Who Moved In Next Door

1 G. Snyder, *Ante Pacem: Archaeological Evidence of Church Life before Constantine*, revised edition (Macon: Mercer University Press, 2003) 113–14; see also Vatican Museum inv. 31542.

2 See P. Finney, *The Invisible God: The Earliest Christians on Art* (New York: Oxford University Press, 1994); and his "Early Christian Architecture: The Beginnings (A Review Article)," *Harvard Theological Review* 81 (1988) 319–39.

3 L. Hurtado, *The Earliest Christian Artifacts: Manuscripts and Christian Origins* (Grand Rapids: W. B. Eerdmans Publishing, 2006), 31.

4 For Paul's conversion as understood within the Jewish matrix, see W. Meeks, "Judaism, Hellenism and the Birth of Christianity," in *Paul beyond the Judaism/Hellenism Divide*, edited by T. Engberg-Petersen (Louisville: Westminster John Knox Press, 2001), 17–27; and also P. Fredriksen, "Judaizing the Nations: The Ritual Demands of Paul's Gospel," *New Testament Studies* 56 (2010) 232–52, on Paul's letter to the Romans in particular.

5 White, *From Jesus to Christianity*, 2004, 150–51.

6 Jeremiah 1.5 (prophet to the Nations); Isaiah 49.6 (light to the Nations). For my translation of *Ioudaismos* in Galatians, see the bibliography in chapter 7, below.

7 White, *From Jesus to Christianity*, 2004, 143–45.

8 1 Corinthians 8:1–12.

9 1 Corinthians 10:14, 22.

10 1 Corinthians 8:10.

11 See also Exodus 24:16–18, 24:12–13.

12 J. Magness, *The Archaeology of the Holy Land: From the Destruction of Solomon's Temple to the Muslim Conquest* (New York: Cambridge University Press, 2012), 75–82.

13 E. Meyers and M. Chancey, *Alexander to Constantine: Archaeology of the Land of the Bible*, volume 3 (New Haven: Yale University Press, 2012), 13–42.

14 S. Fine, *Art and Judaism in the Greco-Roman World: Toward a New Jewish Archaeology* second edition (Cambridge: Cambridge University Press, 2010), 69–73.

15 M. C. Murray, *Rebirth and Afterlife: A Study of the Transmutation of Some Pagan Imagery in Early Christian Funerary Art* (Oxford: BAR International Series, 1981); and M. Charles-Murray, "The Emergence of Christian Art," in *Picturing the Bible: The Earliest Christian Art*, edited by J. Spier (Fort Worth: Kimbell Art Museum, 2007), 51–64.

16 1 Corinthians 11:20–22, translation adapted from the New Revised Standard Version.

17 1 Corinthians 1:11 (Chloe), Romans 16:1–2 (Phoebe), 1 Cor 1:15–16 (Stephanas).

18 S. Friesen, "Injustice or God's Will: Explanations of Poverty in Proto-Christian Communities," in *A People's History of Early Christianity*, edited by R. Horsely (Minneapolis: Fortress Press, 2005), 240–60.

19 For one attempt to break down these socioeconomic levels, see S. Friesen, "Injustice or God's Will," ibid.

20 Holloway, *Coping with Prejudice*, 2009, 40–75, 76–136.

21 Revelation 12.9 (great dragon), 12.3 (threatening the woman and child); see now S. Friesen, *Imperial Cults and the Apocalypse of John: Reading Revelation in the Ruins* (Oxford: Oxford University Press, 2001), 135–51.

22 J. Collins, *The Apocalyptic Imagination: An Introduction to Jewish Apocalyptic Literature*, second edition (Grand Rapids: W. B. Eerdmans Publishing, 1998), 1–42, with the reference to a "supernatural backdrop" at p. 110; see also now the *Oxford Handbook of Apocalyptic Literature*, edited by J. Collins (New York: Oxford University Press, 2014).

23 W. Meeks, "Apocalyptic Discourse and Strategies of Goodness," *Journal of Religion* 3 (2000) 461–75; see also A. Yarbro Collins, *Crisis and Catharsis: The Power of the Apocalypse* (Philadelphia: Westminster Press, 1984), 141–63.

24 Collins, *Apocalyptic Imagination*, 1998, 12–14.

25 For the idea of apocalyptic literature as part of political discourse, see B. McGinn, *Visions of the End: Apocalyptic Traditions in the Middle Ages*, new and expanded edition (New York: Columbia University Press, 1998), 40–41.

26 Letter to Diognetus 5.1–2 (*oute bion parasēmon askousin*).
27 K. Yoshino, *Covering: The Hidden Assault on Our Civil Rights* (New York: Random House, 2006), 111–41, with quotation at p. 118. The language of passing and covering was pioneered by E. Goffman, *Stigma: Notes on the Management of Spoiled Identity* (Englewood Cliffs, NJ: Prentice Hall, 1963). I showed how these tools complicate our interpretation of archaeological material in my *Ostia in Late Antiquity* (New York: Cambridge University Press, 2013), 39–43.
28 Tertullian, *On the Crown* 7.2.
29 Tertullian, *On the Crown* 11.4–5. I have used some editorial interpolations to give this passage the coherence that a literal translation would lack. Researchers looking for a fuller discussion of it should consult the introductory note to chapter 7, below.
30 Clement of Alexandria, *The Teacher* 3.11.
31 The reference to a lyre on Polycrates's ring is otherwise unmentioned in the famous account narrated by Herodotus (*Histories* 4.40–43). A newly published fragment of the poet Posidippus of Pella (c. early third century B.C.) shows that Clement did not invent the detail; see *The New Posidippus*, edited by K. Gutzwiller (Oxford: Oxford University Press, 2005) with an English translation of the fragment (no. 9) by F. Nisetich at p. 19.
32 See also P. Finney, "Images on Finger Rings and Early Christian Art," *Dumbarton Oaks Papers* 41 (1987) 181–86.
33 Clement, *Teacher* 2.1 (*agapē, knisa*, "the smell that comes from sacrificial meat"), 2.3 (gold and silver plates).
34 Justin Martyr, *First Apology* 55. Artemidorus, a non-Christian, also saw the mast as a sign of capital punishment in his second century *The Interpretation of Dreams* 2.53; for discussion, see D. MacDonald, *Christianizing Homer: The Odyssey, Plato, and the Acts of Andrew* (New York: Oxford University Press, 1994), 259–60.
35 Davis, "Commercial Navigation," 2009, 65–77, and discussion of papyrus evidence at pp. 69–70.
36 Mayer, *Ancient Middle Classes*, 2012, 1–21.
37 The mosaic is discussed by L. L. Sebaï, "Belief, Gods, and Myths," in *Stories in Stone: Conserving Mosaics of Roman Africa; Masterpieces from the National Museums of Tunisia*, edited by A. Ben Abed (Los Angeles: J. Paul Getty Museum, 2006), 47–62, with photographs at pp. 53–54.
38 Hurtado, *Earliest Christian Artifacts*, 2006, 135–54, discusses the staurogram as an early sign of the crucifixion in Christian manuscripts. The dating of these early manuscripts is an ongoing issue.

39 For publication, see V. Väänänen, H. Solin, and M. Itkonen-Kaila, *Graffiti del Palatino* 1 (Helsinki: Acta Instituti Romani Finlandiae, 1966), no. 246.

40 Minucius Felix, *Octavius* 9.3.

41 Josephus, *Against Apion* 2.80. The charge was in circulation about two hundred years before Josephus; see *Flavius Josephus: Translation and Commentary* (volume 10: *Against Apion*), edited by S. Mason and J. Barclay (Leiden: Brill, 2007), 350–53.

42 This facet of Jewish-Christian relations has received new attention: See now P. Fredriksen, "What 'Parting of the Ways'? Jews, Gentiles, and the Ancient Mediterranean City," in *The Ways That Never Parted: Jews and Christians in Late Antiquity and the Early Middle Ages*, edited by A. Becker and A. Yoshiko Reed (Tübingen: Mohr Siebeck, 2003; Minneapolis: Fortress Press, 2007), 35–64.

43 See F. Harley and J. Spier, "Magical Amulet with Crucifixion," in *Picturing the Bible: The Earliest Christian Art* (New Haven: Yale University Press, 2007), 228–29, no. 55. The larger topic is the subject of a forthcoming study by F. Harley-McGowen. She presented an overview, "Roman Graffiti and the Evidence for the Depiction of the Crucifixion in the Ancient World," at the annual meeting of the Society of Biblical Literature (Chicago, November 19, 2012).

44 CIL 6.33899. I adapted my translation of lines 2–11, 14, from J. Rüpke, *Religion of the Romans*, translated by R. Gordon (Cambridge: Polity Press, 2007), 169.

45 Augustine, *City of God* 18.18.

46 H. S. Versnel, "Some Reflections on the Relationship Magic–Religion," *Numen* 38 (1991) 177–97.

47 See now *Dura Europos: Crossroads of Antiquity*, edited by L. Brody and G. Hoffman (Chestnut Hill, MA: McMullen Museum of Art, Boston College, 2011).

48 The final report was published by C. Kraeling with C. B. Wells, *The Christian Building: Excavations at Dura-Europos; Final Report 8, Part 2* (New Haven: Dura-Europos Publications, 1967), with measurements of the house at p. 9.

49 J. Baird, "Re-excavating the Houses of Dura-Europos," *Journal of Roman Archaeology* 25 (2012) 146–70.

50 The standard interpretation (of women processing toward a tomb) was advanced by the excavator, Carl Kraeling. M. Peppard, "New Testament Imagery in the Earliest Christian Baptistry," in *Dura Europos: Crossroads of Antiquity*, 2011, 169–87, sees the image as a marriage scene. His new study of the house is forthcoming.

51 Dio Chrysostom, *Discourse* 3 ("On Good Kingship") 39–41, with the quotation at p. 39.

52 L. M. White, *The Social Origins of Christian Architecture*, volume 1, (Valley Forge: Trinity Press International, 1996), 102–23.

Chapter 4: A Safe Space—for Being Jewish

1 The diploma is CIL 10.867. The evidence is discussed in L. Keppie, "Colonization and Veteran Settlement in Italy in the First Century A.D.," *Papers of the British School at Rome* 52 (1984) 77–114, with discussion at pp. 98–102.

2 "Losing both it and his life" is a paraphrase from Keppie (1984, 102). The site where the diploma was found is the object of a new study by Steven Ellis and Gary Devore. Steven has been instrumental in bringing the diploma to wider attention, and I thank him for bringing it to mine while he was visiting Washington, D.C., in 2012. His public talk "Pompeii from the Bottom-up: Excavations into the History of Pompeii's Working-Class Families," from which I've drawn, was delivered at George Washington University on January 12, 2012.

3 For an introduction to the archaeology of Jerusalem, two new books offer a good start: Magness, *Archaeology*, 2012, and Meyers and Chancey, *Alexander to Constantine*, 2012, both discussed in the last chapter. The volume by J. Murphy-O'Connor, *The Holy Land: An Oxford Archaeological Guide* (Oxford: Oxford University Press, 1998), is also still useful.

4 For the idea of Jerusalem as a global theme park, see A. Wharton, *Selling Jerusalem: Relics, Replicas, Theme Parks* (Chicago: University of Chicago Press, 2006), 189–232.

5 D. Demetriou, *Negotiating Identity in the Ancient Mediterranean: The Archaic and Classical Greek Multiethnic Emporia* (New York: Cambridge University Press, 2012).

6 S. Rotroff, "Material Culture," in *The Cambridge Companion to the Hellenistic World*, edited by G. Bugh (New York: Cambridge University Press, 2006), 136–57, with discussion of ceramics at pp. 141–43, 147–48.

7 The city seems to have been abandoned by the middle of the second century B.C.; see F. Holt, *Into the Land of Bones: Alexander the Great in Afghanistan* (Berkeley: University of California Press, 2005), 156–64.

8 See *From Pella to Gandhara: Hybridisation and Identity in the Art and Architecture*, edited by A. Kouremenos, S. Chandrasekaran, and R. Rossi (Oxford: Archaeopress, 2011).

9 E. Gruen, *Heritage and Hellenism: The Reinvention of Jewish Tradition* (Berkeley: University of California Press, 1998), 1–40.

10 1 Maccabees 1:48 (circumcision); 1 Macc 1:41, 1:47 (sacrifice unclean animals such as pigs); 1 Macc 1:54–59 (sacrifice on the king's birthday). For Jewish ritual identity and Antiochus's possible involvement at the Temple, see P. Schäfer, *Judeophobia: Attitudes toward the Jews in the Ancient World* (Cambridge, MA: Harvard University Press, 1997), 66–69.

11 1 Maccabees 2:7–8, translation from the New Revised Standard Version.

12 1 Maccabees 4:36–40 (new altar dedicated at Temple), 1 Macc 4:55–56 (festival lasting eight days), 1 Macc 2:44 (Jews who sided with the king). For discussion, see J. Collins, "Cult and Culture: The Limits of Hellenization in Judea," in *Hellenism in the Land of Israel*, edited by J. Collins and G. Sterling (South Bend: University of Notre Dame Press, 2001), 38–61, particularly 42–47, 51.

13 D. Schwartz, *Commentaries on Early Jewish Literature* (Berlin: De Gruyter, 2008), 43–44, with discussion of the thematic differences between 1 and 2 Maccabees. Scholars agree that the events in 2 Maccabees are highly caricatured, a point developed by M. Himmelfarb, "Judaism and Hellenism in 2 Maccabees," *Poetics Today* 19 (1998) 19–40. For further discussion, see my "Hellenistic 'Judaism' and the Social Origins of the 'Pagan-Christian' Debate," *Journal of Early Christian Studies* 22 (2014) 167–96, also cited in the introductory note at chapter 7.

14 1 Maccabees 1:15.

15 2 Maccabees 4:9–19 (gymnasium, *ephebate*, hat, discus throwing, games at Tyre), 6:7–9 (birthday celebrations).

16 2 Maccabees 4:13 (usually translated as "the height of 'Hellenism'"). For issues of Jewish identity, see L. Levine, *Judaism and Hellenism in Antiquity* (Peabody, MA: Hendrickson, 1998). For Herodotus, see his *Histories* 8.144.2 and elsewhere; Boin, "Hellenistic 'Judaism,'" 2014, with discussion. The idea of Jews "acting Greek" is mentioned by S. Schwartz, *Imperialism and Jewish Society, 200 B.C.E. to 640 C.E.* (Princeton: Princeton University Press, 2001), 22–36.

17 CIJ 2.1440 (dated 246–222 B.C.); see also CIJ 2.1432 (c. late first century B.C.) and additional evidence at CIJ 2.1441–42.

18 CPJ vol. 1, no. 9a (dated September 17, 253 B.C.).

19 CPJ vol. 1, no. 24 (Jewish servicemen in the Ptolemaic army, 174 B.C.), no. 25 (policeman, 173 B.C.) and Josephus, *Jewish Antiquities* 13.284–5 (c. 107 B.C., generals in the Ptolemaic army). More evidence has been collected and presented by M. Williams, ed., *The Jews among the Greeks and Romans: A Diasporan Sourcebook* (Baltimore: Johns Hopkins University Press, 1998), 88–91.

20 2 Maccabees 2:21, 8:1. "Judaism" is also used twice at 14.38 and also appears in the text 4 Maccabees (4 Macc 4:26), which is based on 2 Maccabees.

21 Nongbri, *Before Religion*, 2013, 46–50.

22 For Elezer, see 2 Macc 6:18–31. For Razis, see 14:37–38. The story of the mother with her seven sons at 2 Macc 7 (= 4 Macc 8–17) may be a later interpolation; see Himmelfarb, "Judaism and Hellenism," 1998, 31–32.

23 2 Maccabees 2:19–21. For the history of the word, see S. Mason, "Jews, Judaeans, Judaizing, Judaism: Problems of Categorization in Ancient History," *Journal for the Study of Judaism* 38 (2007) 457–512.

24 For this reading of the text, I follow B. Nongbri, "The Motivations of the Maccabees and Judean Rhetoric of Ancestral Traditions," in *Ancient Judaism in Its Hellenistic Context*, edited by C. Bakhos (Leiden: Brill, 2005), 85–111.

25 For a narrative, see M. Goodman, *Rome and Jerusalem* (New York: Alfred A. Knopf, 2007).

26 The inscriptions appear in J. Reynolds, "Inscriptions," in *Excavations at Sidi Khrebish, Benghazi (Berenice)*, volume 1, *Buildings, Coins, Inscriptions, Architectural Decoration*, edited by J. Lloyd (Tripoli: Department of Antiquities, 1977), 233–54, nos. 16–18. For a recent discussion, see also P. Harland, *Associations, Synagogues, Congregations: Claiming a Place in Ancient Mediterranean Society* (Minneapolis: Augsburg Fortress, 2003), 224–27.

27 Josephus, *Jewish Antiquities* 14.235.

28 Excavators have dated the building's transformation to the mid fourth century A.D.; see A. Seager and A. Kraabel, "The Synagogue and the Jewish Community," in *Sardis from Prehistoric to Roman Times: Results of the Archaeological Exploration of Sardis, 1958–1975*, edited by G. Hanfmann (Cambridge, MA: Harvard University Press, 1983), 168–90. J. Magness, "The Date of the Sardis Synagogue in Light of the Numismatic Evidence," *American Journal of Archaeology* 109 (2005) 443–75, dates the transformation to the sixth century.

29 T. Rajak, "Was There a Roman Charter for the Jews?" (1984) in *The Jewish Dialogue with Greece and Rome: Studies in Cultural and Social Interaction* (Leiden: Brill, 2001), 301–33.

30 Boin, *Ostia*, 2013, 119–22.

31 For context, see Z. Várhelyi, *The Religion of Senators in the Roman Empire* (Cambridge: Cambridge University Press, 2012), 201–08. The same language also appears in a Jewish inscription from Croatia (CIJ 1.678a, dated A.D. 195–209).

32 Philo, *Against Flaccus* 55.

33 S. Gambetti, *The Alexandrian Riots of 38 C.E. and the Persecution of the Jews* (Leiden: Brill, 2009), 167–94, 195–212.

34 Philo's *Against Flaccus* almost single-handedly preserves everything we think we know about the events, which took place under Caligula, known as Gaius. Flaccus was the Roman administrator responsible for instigating the events. Philo composed his text, an attack on Flaccus, during the reign of Caligula's successor, Claudius, and also composed a paper addressed to Caligula, called the "Embassy to Gaius." Scraps of information relevant to anti-Jewish sentiment can also be adduced from the Acts of the Alexandrians, preserved in fragments (CPJ vol. 2, 154–59).

35 Interpreting the Alexandrian events is not easy. A balanced starting point is J. Collins, "Anti-Semitism in Antiquity? The Case of Alexandria," in *Jewish Cult and Hellenistic Culture: Essays on the Jewish Encounter with Hellenism and Roman Rule* (Leiden: Brill, 2005), 181–201. E. Gruen, *Diaspora: Jews amidst Greeks and Romans* (Cambridge, MA: Harvard University Press, 2002), 54–83, makes a case for seeing the episode in a positive light over the longer term.

36 Here, I follow Schäfer, *Judeophobia*, 1997, 151–52, who sees the two Jewish embassies to Claudius (CPJ vol. 2, no. 153, lines 90–91) as a manifestation of social divisions within the Jewish community at Alexandria.

37 J. Osgood, *Claudius Caesar* (New York: Cambridge University Press, 2011), 65–67, 77–79.

38 The letter is CPJ vol. 1, no. 141, lines 8–9. For discussion, see J. Modrzejewski, *The Jews of Egypt: From Ramses II to Emperor Hadrian*, translated by R. Cornman (Philadelphia: Jewish Publication Society, 1995), 153–57. For the *misanthrōpia* trope, including the inversions of Exodus, see Schäfer, *Judeophobia*, 1997, 15–33.

39 For methodology, see K. Stern, "Limitations of 'Jewish' as a Label in Roman North Africa," *Journal for the Study of Judaism* 39 (2008), 1–31.

40 For a brief discussion, see Friesen, *Imperial Cults*, 2001, 135–51.

41 So-called Fifth Sibylline Oracle line 15 (Augustus), lines 16–23 ("Memphis and Babylon").

42 So-called Fifth Sibylline Oracle lines 28–29.

43 So-called Fifth Sibylline Oralce lines 47–48 (rise of Hadrian, predicted to be a beneficent ruler). I have limited my analysis to lines 1–51 of the so-called Fifth Sibylline Oracle because this portion of the text can be securely dated to the early second century A.D. whereas the complete text, as we have it, may be a later compilation. I will say more about this aspect of the text in my treatment of Constantine, below. For further discussion, see J. Collins, "Sibylline Oracles," in *The Old Testament Pseudepigrapha*, volume 1, *Apocalyptic Literature and Its Testaments*, edited by J. Charlesworth (Garden City: Doubleday, 1983), 391; S. Felder, "What Is

'The Fifth Sibylline Oracle'?" *Journal for the Study of Judaism* 33 (2002) 363–85; and J. Collins, *Sibylline Oracles of Egyptian Judaism* (Missoula, MT: Scholars' Press, 1974), 73–95. D. Potter, *Prophecy and History in the Roman Empire: A Historical Commentary on the Thirteenth Sibylline Oracle* (Oxford: Clarendon Press, 1990), 96, is skeptical of dating any of the so-called Sibylline poems before the sixth century A.D., but in my approach, I have followed Collins and Felder.

44 McGinn, *Visions of the End*, 1998, xvii.

45 Cassius Dio, *History* 49.12–14; Eusebius, *History of the Church* 4.6.3. See also A. Wharton, *Refiguring the Post-Classical City: Dura Europos, Jerash, Jerusalem and Ravenna* (New York: Cambridge University Press, 1995), 98–100.

46 Schwartz, *Imperialism and Jewish Society*, 2001, 101–76.

47 For the fragments, see Fine, *Art and Judaism*, 2005, 174–85. For the graffiti, see K. Stern, "Tagging Sacred Space in the Dura Europos Synagogue," *Journal of Roman Archaeology* 25 (2012) 171–94.

48 The original publication is by C. Kraeling, *The Synagogue: Excavations at Dura-Europos; Final Report 8, Part 1*, edited by A. Bellinger, F. Brown, A. Perkins, and C. Bradford Welles (New Haven: Yale University Press, 1956).

49 On patronage and adaptation at the synagogue, see White, *Social Origins*, 1996, 1.74–97.

Chapter 5: What Goes On Behind Closed Doors

1 On the owl and the statue from 53 B.C., see Cassius Dio, *History* 40.47.1–2; for the bees, the earthquake, and the blood, as well as the second owl in 48–47 B.C., see Cassius Dio, *History* 42.26.1–2, 4.

2 The evidence is collected in V. Tran Tam Tinh and Y. Lacrecque, *Isis Lactans: Corpus des monuments gréco-romains d'Isis allaitant Harpocrate* (Leiden: Brill, 1973). For the emergence of Mary's iconography, see the catalog by M. Vassilaki, *Mother of God: Representations of the Virgin in Byzantine Art* (Milan: Skira, 2000).

3 Plutarch recounts the developments of the cult under Ptolemy I ("On Isis and Serapis" 362a–b).

4 "The Chinese-Takeout Container Is Uniquely American," by H. Greenbaum and D. Rubinstein, *New York Times* (January 15, 2012, Sunday magazine, p. 20). On Isis and acculturation, see G. Naerebout, "How Do You Want Your Goddess? From the Galjub Hoard to a General Vision on Religious Choice in Hellenistic and Roman Egypt," in *Isis on the Nile: Egyptian Gods in Hellenistic and Roman Egypt*, edited by L. Bricault and M. J. Versluys (Leiden: Brill, 2007), 55–73.

5 Explanations for the spread of Isis worship, which do not need to be contingent upon Ptolemaic politics, are treated by V. Tran Tam Tinh, "Serapis and Isis," in *Jewish and Christian Self-Definition*, edited by B. Meyers and E. Sanders (Philadelphia: Fortress Press, 1982), 101–17.

6 Tertullian, *To the Nations* 1.10.17–18, purporting to quote Varro on the events of 59–58 B.C.

7 The story of the magistrate, Lucius Aemilius Paulus (consul in 50 B.C.), is preserved in one ninth century manuscript of the early imperial text *Memorable Deeds and Sayings* by Valerius Maximus at 1.3.4.

8 Valerius Maximus, *Deeds and Sayings* 1.3.4.

9 Cassius Dio, *History* 53.2.4.

10 This decree was implemented by Agrippa while Octavian was not in Rome (Cassius Dio, *History* 54.6.6).

11 Cassius Dio, *History* 56.30.3 speaks of the "strength of empire," and Suetonius, *Life of Augustus* 28.3 about Rome's "foundations" (*fundamenta*).

12 For an overview in English, see the entry "Iuppiter Optimus Maximus (Capitolinus), Aedes," in *A New Topographical Dictionary of Ancient Rome* by L. Richardson, Jr. (Baltimore: Johns Hopkins University Press, 1992), 221–24.

13 "*ut is locus orbi imperitaret, in quo illud caput esset inventum,*" Servius, *Commentary on the Aeneid* 8.345; see also Isidore of Seville 15.

14 Ovid, *Fasti* 4.725–28, 731–34.

15 See M. Beard, "A Complex of Times: No More Sheep on Romulus' Birthday," in *Proceedings of the Cambridge Philological Society* 33 (1987) 1–15, upon which I have drawn for this paragraph.

16 Athenaeus 8.361e-f.

17 Compare with the following: "After the fall of the republic," Franz Cumont once wrote, "indifference spread, the temples were abandoned and threatened to tumble into ruins, the clergy found it difficult to recruit members, [and] the festivities, once so popular, fell into desuetude," *The Oriental Religions in Roman Paganism* (Chicago: Open Court Publishing, 1911), 37.

18 K. Clifton, "The Eleusinian Mysteries: Roman Initiates and Benefactors, Second Century B.C. to A.D. 267," in *Aufstieg und Niedergang der römischen Welt* 2.18.2 (1989) 1499–1539.

19 A helpful commentary appears in S. Shelmerdine, *The Homeric Hymns* (Newburyport, MA: Focus Publishing, 1995), 29–58.

20 Hymn to Demeter lines 256–62, 270–74.

21 Hymn to Demeter lines 380–83, 473–78, 480–82.

22 See H. Bowden, *Mystery Cults of the Ancient World* (Princeton: Princeton University Press, 2010), 26–48; see also A. Lawrence, *Greek Architecture*, with revisions by R. Tomlinson, fifth edition (New Haven: Yale University Press, 1983), 191–93.

23 Hymn to Demeter lines 478–79.

24 The quotation is from the third century writer Hippolytus of Rome, *Refutation of All Heresies*, 5.8.40.

25 Clement of Alexandra, *Exhortation* 2.22; see also *The Ancient Mysteries: A Sourcebook of Sacred Texts*, edited by Marvin Meyer (Philadelphia: University of Pennsylvania Press, 1987), 15–46.

26 Eumolpus appears in the hymn at lines 154 and 457. The family is discussed in J. Mikalson, *Ancient Greek Religion*, second edition (Malden, MA: Wiley-Blackwell, 2010), 83 and 127.

27 V. Turner, *The Ritual Process: Structure and Anti-Structure* (Ithaca: Cornell University Press, 1969), 95–129. The classic study of initiation rites is A. van Gennep, *The Rites of Passage*, translated by M. Vizedom and G. L. Caffe, with an introduction by Solon T. Kimball (Chicago: University of Chicago Press, 1961).

28 For a discussion of the stigma assigned to marginal social groups, see M. Douglas, *Purity and Danger* (London: Routledge, 1966), 94–97, 138–39.

29 Apuleius, *Metamorphoses* 1.3 (*"magico susurramine"*), the man who became a beaver (1.9), Lucius hears the rumor about his innkeeper (2.6).

30 See M. Swetnam-Burland, "'Egyptian' Priests in Roman Italy," in *Cultural Identity in the Ancient Mediterranean*, edited by E. Gruen (Los Angeles: Getty Research Institute, 2010), 336–53. Her monograph on the reception of Egyptian motifs in Italy is forthcoming.

31 L. H. Petersen, *The Freedman in Roman Art and Art History* (New York: Cambridge University Press, 2006), 22–52.

32 CIL 10.846.

33 The new name of the city is attested on an inscription from shortly before 2 B.C. (CIL 10.787).

34 Apuleius, *Metamorphoses* 11.17, with the ceremony and procession at 11.5–12. For the coins, see RIC vol. 3, no. 1726 (late second century A.D.). For the late second century or early third century list, see Salzman, *On Roman Time*, 1990, 74–78.

35 The painting is discussed in Boin, *Ostia*, 2013, 204–12. The mosaic was published by L. Foucher, *Découvertes archéologiques à Thysdrus en 1961* (Tunis: Institut National d'Archéologie et d'Art de Tunis, 1961), 30–50, plates 32–34.

36 Boin, *Ostia*, 2013, 208–9 (quoting from the Isis inscription).

Chapter 6: At the Threshold of the Palace

1 See my "A Hall for Hercules at Ostia and a Farewell to the Late Antique 'Pagan Revival,'" *American Journal of Archaeology* 114 (2010) 253–66, with discussions of the town's oldest temple and baths. Other examples are discussed below. A bibliography on this topic also appears in Boin, *Ostia*, 2013, 124–64. Generally, see also *The Archaeology of Late Antique Paganism*, edited by L. Lavan and M. Mulryan (Leiden: Brill, 2012); and F. Trombley, *Hellenic Religion and Christianization, c. 370–529*, volume 1 (Leiden: Brill, 1995) 1–97.

2 R. Stark, *Rise of Christianity*, 1996, p. 147 ("immense popular appeal"), 149 ("social dislocation"), 161 ("revitalization movement").

3 M. Clauss, *The Roman Cult of Mithras*, translated by R. Gordon (New York: Routledge, 2001), 3–6. For the fourth and early fifth centuries A.D., see now J. Bjørnebye, "'Hic locus est felix, sanctus, piusque benignus': The Cult of Mithras in Fourth-Century Rome," Ph.D. dissertation (2007), University of Bergen, Norway. Mithras's followers lived with a social stigma, too; their group never received state funding. Perhaps for that reason, we find them meeting in out-of-the-way rooms, in buildings originally designed for other purposes, such as houses—yet one more minority group in Rome finding a safe space of their own through the kindness of patrons.

4 C. Witschel, "Re-evaluating the Roman West in the 3rd. c. A.D.," *Journal of Roman Archaeology* 17 (2004) 251–81.

5 For a discussion of the period leading up to the battle, see D. Potter, *The Roman Empire at Bay, A.D. 180–395* (London: Routledge, 2004), 280–90, 340–56.

6 Lactantius, *Death of the Persecutors* 44.5. For discussion, see J. Bardill, *Constantine, Divine Emperor of the Christian Golden Age* (New York: Cambridge University Press, 2012), 160–68.

7 The detail is recorded in Lactantius, *Death of the Persecutors* 44.8.

8 Lactantius, *Death of the Persecutors* 34–35 (with the date and place of issue); see also E. DePalma Digeser, *The Making of a Christian Empire: Lactantius and Rome* (Ithaca: Cornell University Press, 2000), with discussions of Galerius at pp. 12–13, 55–56, and Milan at pp. 122–23, 138–39.

9 Lactantius, *Death of the Persecutors* 48.1–12. Eusebius, *Church History* 10.5.2–14, preserves a Greek copy of the decree.

10 Lactantius, *Death of the Persecutors* 48.6.

11 R. Van Dam, *Remembering Constantine at the Milvian Bridge* (New York: Cambridge University Press, 2007), 1–18.

12 On the defeat of Licinius in A.D. 324, see D. Potter, *Constantine the Emperor* (Oxford: Oxford University Press, 2013), 207–14.

13 Van Dam, *Remembering Constantine*, 2007, 56–100.

14 Eusebius, *Life* 1.28 ("about noon"), 29–30 ("protection"), 1.30–31 (description of the *chi-rho*) 1.32, ("no other god").

15 Eusebius, *Life of Constantine* 3.2–3 (with the Greek participle from *enabrunomai*). For the verb used to describe men in effeminate dress, see Lucian, *The Dance* 2.6 and Cassius Dio, *History* 43.43.2 (the latter on Caesar, specifically).

16 For an introduction to debates and themes in Constantinian studies, see N. Lenski, "The Reign of Constantine," in *The Cambridge Companion to the Age of Constantine*, edited by N. Lenski, second edition (New York: Cambridge University Press, 2012), 59–90; see also H. Drake, *Constantine and the Bishops: The Politics of Intolerance* (Baltimore: Johns Hopkins University Press, 2000). Other works will be cited below. Proponents of immediate, widespread change in Constantine's time cite Eusebius (*Life* 2.45, 3.54.3–7, and 4.25, for example) and now, Palladas. T. Barnes, *Constantine: Dynasty, Religion and Power in the Later Roman Empire* (Malden, MA: Wiley-Blackwell, 2011) champions this view, as does C. Odahl, *Constantine and the Christian Empire*, second edition (London: Routledge, 2010), which I also discuss below.

17 For Christian legal developments, see J. Harries, *Law and Empire in Late Antiquity* (New York: Cambridge University Press, 1998); and N. Lenski, "Evidence for the *Audientia episcopalis* in the New Letters of Augustine," in *Law, Society, and Authority in Late Antiquity*, edited by R. Mathisen (Oxford: Oxford University Press, 2001), 83–97. For Jewish requests to have jurisdiction over their internal matters, a precedent not often mentioned in these discussions, see Rajak, *Jewish Dialogue*, 2001, 321–22. For the longevity of gladiatorial combat, see D. Potter, "Constantine and the Gladiators," *Classical Quarterly* 60 (2010) 596–606.

18 Constantine's vision of Apollo is mentioned in the Latin *Panegyric* 6(7).21.4–5 from A.D. 310. For a text and translation, see *In Praise of Later Roman Emperors: The Panegyrici Latini* (Introduction, Translation and Historical Commentary = Pan. Lat.), edited by C. Nixon and B. Rodgers. The statue of Apollo on the column in Istanbul is discussed in Bardill, *Constantine*, 2012, 28–57, 88–104. The cameo of Constantine is from the collection at Dumbarton Oaks, Washington, D.C. (acquisition number BZ.1958.23). I have reprised the chess metaphor from Boin, *Ostia* 2013, 10–11, 34.

19 The famous statue of Constantine was reexamined by C. Parisi Presicce, "Costantino come Giove: Proposta di ricostruzione grafica del colosso acrolitico dalla Basilica Costantiniana," *Bullettino della Commissione Archeologica Comunale di Roma* 107 (2006) 127–62.

20 CIL 6.1139. N. Lenski, "Evoking the Pagan Past: Instinctu divinitatis and Constantine's Capture of Rome," *Journal of Late Antiquity* 1 (2008) 204–57, suggests that the Senate may have been sending the emperor a nervous message to reconsider his profession of Christianity, p. 257; see also N. Lenski, "Constantine," 2012, 70–71. Other examples of vague language appear in speeches praising the emperor in A.D. 313, Pan. Lat. 12(9).2.4–3.4, 4.1, 5, 26.1; and in A.D. 321, Pan. Lat. 4(10).17.1; see also Bardill, *Constantine*, 2012, 92–104.

21 See K. Wilkinson, "Palladas and the Age of Constantine," *Journal of Roman Studies* 99 (2009) 36–60.

22 C. Freeman claims that an "assault on paganism" was "perhaps inevitable" by the end of the fourth century, in *A New History of Early Christianity* (New Haven: Yale University Press, 2009), 260.

23 The charge of "Hellenism," at Eusebius, *Demonstratio Evangelica* 1.2.1; and *Praeparatio Evangelica* 1.5.12, as I interpreted it in Boin, "Hellenistic 'Judaism,'" 2014. For another perspective, see A. Johnson, "Hellenism and Its Discontents," in *The Oxford Handbook of Late Antiquity*, edited by S. Johnson (Oxford: Oxford University Press, 2012), 437–66; and G. Bowersock, *Hellenism in Late Antiquity* (Ann Arbor: University of Michigan Press, 1990).

24 John Chrysostom, *Catechesis* 6.15–16. For further discussion, see I. Sandwell, *Religious Identity in Late Antiquity: Greeks, Jews, and Christians in Antioch* (Cambridge: Cambridge University Press, 2007), 66–75 although I interpret the word "Hellene" differently.

25 For an overview of "Jewish Christians" in the fourth century, see now A. Jacobs, *Christ Circumcised: A Study in Early Christian History and Difference* (Philadelphia: University of Pennsylvania Press, 2012), 100–18. See also discussions in S. Drake, *Slandering the Jew: Sexuality and Difference in Early Christianity* (Philadelphia: University of Pennsylvania Press, 2013); and A. Jacobs, *Holy Land and Christian Empire in Late Antiquity* (Stanford: Stanford University Press, 2012), 139–99.

26 The charge of "Judaism" in Eusebius, *Demonstratio Evangelica* 1.2.1, and *Praeparatio Evangelica* 1.5.12, as I interpreted it in Boin, "Hellenistic 'Judaism,'" 2014; Mason, "Jews, Judaeans, Judaizing, Judaism," 2007, is vital.

27 In fourth century Antioch: John Chrysostom *Against the Jews* 1.5.7, with discussion at Sandwell, *Religious Identity*, 2007, 82–90.

28 Theodosian Code 16.8.7 (A.D. 357), 3.7.2 (A.D. 388). For discussion, see H. Sivan, "Why Not Marry a Jew? Jewish–Christian Marital Frontiers in Late Antiquity," in Mathisen, *Law, Society, and Authority*, 2001, 208–19.

29 S. Bassett, *The Urban Image of Late Antique Constantinople* (New York: Cambridge University Press, 2004), 22–36. For buildings, see also J. Matthews, "The *Notitia Urbis Constantinopolitanae*," in *Two Romes: Rome and Constantinople in Late Antiquity*, edited by L. Grig and G. Kelly (Oxford: Oxford University Press, 2012) 81–115. For temples, see L. Ramskold and N. Lenski, "Constantinople's Dedication Medallions and the Maintenance of Civic Traditions," *Numismatische Zeitschrift* 119 (2012) 31–58.

30 Eusebius, *Life* 3.3 and also 2.46, which preserves Constantine's letter.

31 Bardill, *Constantine*, 2012, 143, dates the coins to A.D. 326–330.

32 H. Drake, *Constantine and the Bishops: The Politics of Intolerance* (Baltimore: Johns Hopkins University Press, 2000), 292–98, with the phrase "stump speech" at p. 295.

33 Constantine, *Speech* 1.1. On the interpretation of angels and "holy ones" in Daniel 7:18–22, 8:24, and in Revelation 18:20–24, for example, see Trebilco, *Self-Designations and Group Identity*, 2012, 123–163, specifically discussions at pp. 122–24, 140–47 (Daniel) and pp. 154–58 (Revelation).

34 Constantine, *Speech* 6.5 (sky and stars), 26.2 (battles).

35 Constantine, *Speech* 21, an interpretation of Virgil's *Eclogue* 4. The best analysis of Constantine's misreading of Virgil is Robin Lane Fox, *Pagans and Christians*, 1989, 649–53.

36 Porphyry as quoted in Jerome's *Commentary on Daniel*, preface. For discussion and reconstruction of Porphyry's times and writings, see E. DePalma Digeser, *A Threat to Public Piety: Christian, Platonists, and the Great Persecution* (Ithaca: Cornell University Press, 2012), 171.

37 Collins, *Apocalyptic Imagination*, 1998, 85–115.

38 Constantine, *Speech* 17.3 ("true God"), 17.6 ("Jesus the Messiah"). Eusebius, *Life* 3.49, mentions the fountains in Constantinople.

39 Constantine, *Speech* 17.1. "Cut off their souls" follows the translation by M. Edwards, *Constantine and Christendom* (Liverpool: Liverpool University Press, 2003), 38.

40 Eusebius, *Life* 3.18 (*kyrioktonia*).

41 Compare with Potter, *Constantine*, 2013, 279–80.

42 Constantine, *Speech* 18–19, quoting from the so-called Eighth Sibylline Oracle, lines 217–50. Augustine discusses a similar acrostic in his *City of God* 18.23.

43 Cicero, *On Divination* 2.54.

44 See now B. Ehrman, *Forgery and Counterforgery: The Use of Literary Deceit in Early Christian Polemics* (Oxford: Oxford University Press, 2012) with discussion of the so-called Sibylline Oracles at pp. 508–19; compare with Potter, *Prophecy and History*, 1990, 95–140.

45 Clement of Alexandria, *Protrepticus* 4.50.3 and then 6.71.4 ("prophetess of the Hebrews").

46 Constantine's uses and abuses of other so-called Sibylline texts are the object of a new study by M. Hooker, "The Use of Sibyls and Sibylline Oracles in Early Christian Writers," Ph.D. dissertation, University of Cincinnati, 2007, with discussion at pp. 239–64. Lactantius in *Divine Institutes* quotes from the so-called Fifth Sibylline Oracle, line 249, at 4.20.11; at 7.15.18, he paraphrases lines 158–61; at 7.18.6, quotes lines 107–10; at 7.24.6, quotes lines 420–21; and at 7.24.14, quotes lines 281–83. For discussion of these examples, see Hooker, "Use of Sibyls," 2007, 446–52. J. Schott, *Christianity, Empire, and the Making of Religion in Late Antiquity* (Philadelphia: University of Pennsylvania Press, 2008), 81–95, discusses Lactantius's use of the "Sibyls," as does J. Walter, *Pagane Texte und Wertvorstellungen bei Lactanz* (Göttingen: Vandenhoeck & Ruprecht, 2006), 172–91, who discusses Lactantius's complex relationship to them.

47 Constantine, *Speech* 16.2. What I have translated as "seen with my own eyes" (*epoptēs* in Greek) is also the same word used to describe those who have been initiated into the mysteries at Eleusis.

48 For a brief discussion, see Friesen, *Imperial Cults*, 2001, 135–51.

49 For earlier interpretations, see Potter, *Constantine*, 2013, 63, and Lenski, "Constantine," 2012, 60, who interpret the place names as details of the emperor's biography.

50 I discussed Constantine's apocalyptic world view in my talk "Constantine and the Jewish 'Prophet' Who Predicted the Overthrow of Rome," delivered at the International Society of Biblical Literature meeting in Vienna, Austria (July 7, 2014). I am grateful to the organizer of this session on "Apocalypticism," Lorenzo DiTommaso, for his feedback and for the potential to explore these ideas in more depth elsewhere. Some believe that Constantine was using this language to pander for the support of the empire's most disaffected Christians, see C. Odahl, "The Use of Apocalyptic Imagery in Constantine's Christian Propaganda," *Centerpoint* (1981)

9–19. Compare that interpretation to the discussion of consensus building in Drake, *Constantine*, 2000, 192–272.

51 See now E. Pagels, *Revelations: Visions, Prophecy and Politics in the Book of Revelation* (New York: Penguin, 2012), 133–70.

52 Eusebius, *History of the Church* 7.24 (Bishop Nepos and the intervention of Bishop Dionysius of Alexandria), 7.25 (incomprehensible text).

53 See P. Brown's characterization of the fourth century as "bipolar" in *Through the Eye of a Needle: Wealth, the Fall of Rome, and the Making of Christianity in the West, 350–550* A.D. (Princeton: Princeton University Press, 2012), 34; the age of Constantine as giving rise to a "bipolar society," p. 51; "the bipolar world ushered in by Constantine," p. 63; "the bipolar world set in place by Constantine," p. 331. This theme was explored by R. MacMullen using different data in "What Difference Did Christianity Make?" *Historia* 35 (1986) 322–43.

Chapter 7: "Soldiers" in God's Heavenly Army

Readers interested in exploring more of the details behind the story of Marius Victorinus should consult my "Hellenistic 'Judaism' and the Social Origins of the 'Pagan-Christian' Debate," *Journal of Early Christian Studies* 22 (2014) 167–96.

1 Ammianus Marcellinus, *Roman History* 16.10.17 and 17.4.13 (obelisk).

2 Ammianus Marcellinus, *Roman History* 14.6.19 (famine and foreigners), 14.6.3 (the eternal city), 14.6.1 (riots over wine), 19.10.1 (food shortage).

3 Ammianus Marcellinus, *Roman History* 27.9.1.

4 Ammianus Marcellinus, *Roman History* 23.6.75–84 (Persians), 31.2.1–11 (Huns).

5 Ammianus Marcellinus, *Roman History* 14.6.6 (eternal city; mistress and queen), 16.10.13 (speaker's platform), 16.10.14 (Temple of Jupiter, Pantheon, Colosseum).

6 S. Greenblatt, *The Swerve: How the World Became Modern* (New York: W. W. Norton, 2011), 100.

7 H. Chadwick, "Augustine on Pagans and Christians: Reflections on Religious and Social Change," in *History, Society and the Churches*, edited by D. Beales and G. Best (New York: Cambridge University Press, 1985), 9–27, with the quotation at p. 9.

8 R. Chenault, in "Statues of Senators in the Forum of Trajan and the Roman Forum in Late Antiquity," *Journal of Roman Studies* 102 (2012) 103–32, sees Victorinus' rank as an honorary one, pp. 111–12, 130. On the statues in the Forum of Trajan, reconstructed from their inscriptions, see now H.

Niquet, *Monumenta virtutum titulique: Senatorische Selbstdarstellung im spätantiken Rom im Spiegel der epigraphischen Denkmäler* (Stuttgart: Steiner, 2000).

9 Augustine, *Confessions* 8.2.3.

10 Augustine, *Confessions* 8.2.4

11 The best reading of this episode is now T. Furher's essay, "'Denkräume': Konstellationem von Personen, Texten und Gebäuden im spätantiken Mailand," in *Rom und Mailand in der Spätantike: Repräsentationen städtischer Räume in Literatur, Architektur und Kunst*, edited by T. Fuhrer (Berlin: De Gruyter, 2012), 357–78.

12 Augustine, *Confessions* 8.2.5.

13 Augustine, *Confessions* 8.2.4. On Augustine's social connections, see now J. Ebbeler, *Disciplining Christians: Correction and Community in Augustine's Letters* (Oxford: Oxford University Press, 2012).

14 For Isis in the fourth century, see Salzman, *On Roman Time*, 1990, 169–76. For the Capitoline temple in Rome, see L. Grig, "Imagining the Capitolium in Late Antiquity," in *The Power of Religion in Late Antiquity*, edited by A. Cain and N. Lenski (Burlington: Ashgate, 2009), 279–92. On the persistence of sacrifice, see the discussion in chapter 2, above, and Trombley, *Hellenic Religion*, 1995, 1.1–97, in chapter 6, above.

15 Valerius's queries are preserved in a letter to Augustine (*Letter to Augustine* 46, dated A.D. 398). For the sacred grove, section 7; for the wine and oil, section 6; anxiety at the butcher, sections 8 and 10. D. Shanzer, in "Who Was Augustine's Publicola?" *Revue des Études Juives* 171 (2012) 27–60, suggests that Publicola was a Jewish convert.

16 Cyprian, *Lapsed* 8 (running to the forum), 15 (reeking of smoke).

17 R. Stark, *The Triumph of Christianity: How the Jesus Movement Became the World's Largest Religion* (New York: HarperCollins, 2011), 157.

18 For a basilica at Ephesos dedicated to Artemis, see D. Knibbe and M. Büyükkloanci, "Die Bauinschrift der Basilica auf dem sog. Staatsmarkt von Ephesos," in *Jahreshefte des Österreichischen archäologischen Instituts in Wien 59* (1989) 47–54, with discussion at p. 43. For discussion of the basilica at Corinth, see P. Scotton, "The Julian Basilica at Corinth: An Architectural Investigation," Ph.D. dissertation, University of Pennsylvania, 1997, 191, 245–55. For basilicas located within sanctuaries in France, see *L'Année épigraphique* 2001, 1383 (= L'Année épigraphique 1969/70, 405a). I will be returning to this topic in a forthcoming study.

19 For Christian architecture, see H. Brandenburg, *Ancient Churches of Rome from the Fourth to the Seventh Century: The Dawn of Christian Architecture in the West*, translated by A. Kropp (Turnhout: Brepols, 2005), 55–91. The

vexed question of Rome's circus-forum churches cannot be taken up here. "Who or what dictated the oddity, no one knows," R. MacMullen, *The Second Church: Popular Christianity*, A.D. *200–400* (Atlanta: Society of Biblical Literature Press, 2009), 69–89, with the quotation at p. 82. I wonder whether such an architecturally diverse set of churches should really surprise us, given that the Christian community was just as socially varied. See also M. Johnson, "Architecture of Empire," in *The Cambridge Companion to the Age of Constantine*, edited by N. Lenski, revised edition (New York: Cambridge University Press, 2012), 278–97, who calls them a "variation on the basilica," at p. 287.

20 M. Salzman, *The Making of a Christian Roman Aristocracy: Social and Religious Change in the Western Roman Empire* (Cambridge, MA: Harvard University Press, 2002), 5 and p. 186, suggests that the senatorial class was predominantly non-Christian until the late 360s. The bishop of Milan might be tantalizing us with rhetorical claims that the Senate was "majority Christian" at the end of the fourth century (*Ep.* 72.8–9); see discussion in W. Liebeschuetz, *Ambrose of Milan: Political Letters and Speeches* (Chicago: University of Chicago Press, 2005), 65–66.

21 K. Bowes, *Private Worship, Public Values, and Religious Change in Late Antiquity* (New York: Cambridge University Press, 2008).

22 The classic treatment of Christians as "soldiers of God" is A. von Harnack, *The Expansion of Christianity in the First Three Centuries*, volume 2, translated and edited by J. Moffat (New York: G. P. Putnam's Sons, 1904–1905), 19–22.

23 Marius Victorinus, *Commentary on Galatians* 2.3, 4.3; see also Boin, "Hellenistic 'Judaism,'" 2014.

24 Gregory of Nazianzus, *Orations* 4 (PG 35 col. 549) and *Orations* 5 (PG 35 col. 668). On Julian and Gregory, see now S. Elm, *Sons of Hellenism, Fathers of the Church: Emperor Julian, Gregory of Nazianzus, and the Vision of Rome* (Berkeley: University of California Press, 2012), discussed below.

25 1 Maccabees 2:15–19 (in the Greek text, *apostasía* at verse 15, the verb at verse 19); and 2 Thessalonians 2:3 (*apostasía*). For discussion of the text, see Ehrman, *Forgery and Counterforgery*, 2012, 155–71.

26 McGinn, *Visions of the End*, 1998, xvii–xviii.

27 Gregory of Nazianzus, *Orations* 4 (dragon and enemy, at PG 35 col. 532). For "another Antiochus," *Orations* 15 at PG 35 col. 920 and also at col. 932 ("a Antiochus present among us daily"); see now also R. Flower, *Emperors and Bishops in Late Roman Invective* (Cambridge: Cambridge University Press, 2013), 144, where Hilary of Poitiers summons Antiochus IV in a discussion with the Christian emperor Constantius II.

28 Julian's letter is *Ep.* 36 in the Loeb Classical Library edition of Julian's works, edited by W. Wright (Cambridge, MA: Harvard University Press, 1993). J. Matthews, *Laying Down the Law: A Study of the Theodosian Code* (New Haven: Yale University Press, 2000), 274–77, suggests that the law in the Theodosian Code at 13.3.5 has "no connection in substance or form," p. 276, with Julian's letter. The repeal was included in the Theodosian Code at 13.3.6 (January 11, A.D. 364); see now Elm, *Sons of Hellenism*, 2012, 139–43; and on Julian generally, K. Rosen, *Julian: Kaiser, Gott, und Christenhasser* (Stuttgart: Klett-Cotta, 2006).

29 Gregory of Nazianzus, *Orations* 2 ("the war being fought against us," at PG 35 col. 492); see also Elm, *Sons of Hellenism*, 2012, 147–53, 341–42.

30 A. Cameron, *The Last Pagans of Rome* (Oxford: Oxford University Press, 2010), 33–34; and now also P. Brown, *Eye of a Needle*, 2012, 93–119.

31 C. Sogno, *Q. Aurelius Symmachus: A Political Biography* (Ann Arbor: University of Michigan, 2006), 1–30 (early career, statue of his father), 44 (frontier defenses).

32 Symmachus, *Relatio* 3.2 ("the glory of our age"), 3.3 (*religio* and *dissimulatio*).

33 For Tactitus's view of Tiberius, see *Annals* 6.50. The quotation here is from C. Vout, "Representing the Emperor," in *The Cambridge Companion to the Roman Historians*, edited by A. Feldherr (New York: Cambridge University Press, 2009), 273.

34 Paulinus's *Life of Ambrose*, written in the early fifth century A.D., provides a biographical sketch; see also Brown, *Eye of a Needle*, 2012, 120–47.

35 D. Caporusso et al., *Sezione Milano Antico (Civico museo archeologico): V secolo A.C.–V secolo D.C.* (Milan: Comune di Milano, 2007), 85–87, 88–90, 118–20.

36 N. McLynn, *Ambrose of Milan: Church and Court in a Christian Capital* (Berkeley: University of California Press, 1994), xvii.

37 Ambrose, *Ep.* 72.2 (*militent; militatis*), with military language also at 72.1 and 72.7 (*militari*). Sogno, *Symmachus*, 2006, 50, argues that Ambrose wrote his letter "before he had a chance to read Symmachus's petition." Cameron, *Last Pagans*, 2012, 36, argues that the bishop "wrote a detailed refutation of it." I follow Cameron's reconstruction of the sequence.

38 Ambrose, *Ep.* 72.15. I have tried to expand upon the discussion of this rhetoric that was first put forward by T. Sizgorich in *Violence and Belief in Late Antiquity: Militant Devotion in Christianity and Islam* (Philadelphia: University of Pennsylvania Press, 2009), 77–78.

39 Ambrose, *Ep.* 72.13.

40 Ambrose, *Ep.* 72.8 (*aliqui nomine Christiani*). J. Matthews, *Western*

Aristocracies and Imperial Court, A.D. 364–425 (Oxford: Clarendon Press, 1975) 209, labels them "'liberal' Christians." Sogno, *Symmachus*, 2006, 50, pushes back against that interpretation.

41 Sizgorich, *Violence and Belief*, 2009, 46–80, discusses this theme but not the example.

42 Ambrose, *Ep.* 73.7 (*caelestem militiam; illic militamus*).

43 Ambrose, *Ep.* 73.7 (*odi ritus Neronum*). One other invocation of Nero in Ambrose's writing is in his eulogy for the emperor, *On the Death of Theodosius*, 50. We should add this example to McLynn's study of the bishop's political rhetoric, *Ambrose*, 1994, 166–167, even if this letter never physically came to the emperor's attention, as argued at p. 167 n35. Drake, *Constantine*, 2000, 439, notes that some Christians used Roman culture as a weapon when challenging the faith of other Christians. Flower, *Emperors and Bishops*, 2013, 93–94, 113, discusses the Nero theme but not the example.

44 Suetonius, *Nero* 58, Tacitus, *Histories* 2.8, and Cassius Dio, *History* 66.19.3 also speak to the Roman people's anxiety about having to endure the rule of another Nero.

45 The conflicting sources for the death of Agrippina are Tacitus, *Annals* 16.5–8; Suetonius, *Life of Nero* 34; and Cassius Dio, *History* 63.12–14. Josephus, *War* 3.1–7 reports the appointment of Vespasian in A.D. 66.

46 Mid third century Christian: Commodianus, *Instructions* 41.7. Fourth century Christian: the commentary by the writer known as Pseudo-Ambrose on the spurious Pauline text 2 Thessalonians at 2.7.

47 Sulpicius Severus, *Chronica* 2.28.1.

48 John Chrysostom's words appear in "Homily 4" on the same false Pauline letter, 2 Thessalonians (PG 62, col. 485).

49 Elm, *Sons of Hellenism*, 2012, 352 (discussion of Julian's "theatricality").

50 Cassiodorus relates the napkin story (*Variae* 3.51.9). Cameron, *Last Pagans*, 2010, 691–94, has discussed the commemorative coins. For discussion of the positive reception of Nero, see E. Champlain, *Nero* (Cambridge, MA: Harvard University Press, 2003), 31–33.

51 Ambrose, *Ep.* 72.13.

52 Drake, *Constantine*, 2000, 402–09, 441–48, discusses a similar dynamic between Theodosius and Ambrose after a riot at Thessaloniki in A.D. 390.

53 Ambrose, *Ep.* 72.14.

54 See B. Shaw, *Sacred Violence: African Christians and Sectarian Hatred in the Age of Augustine* (Cambridge: Cambridge University Press, 2011), 66–73, 96–101.

55 On the importance of a "moderate middle," see A. Gutmann, "The Lure and Dangers of Extremist Rhetoric," *Daedalus* 136 (2007) 72.

56 Symmachus, *Rel.* 3.10.

57 Sizgorich, *Violence and Belief,* 2009, 86–107.

58 For further treatment of the intra-Christian debate, see now R. Chenault, "Damasus, the Altar of Victory, and Intra-Christian Conflict at Rome," in *Pagans and Christians in Late Antique Rome,* edited by M. Salzman, R. Lizza Testa, and M. Sághy (New York: Cambridge University Press, forthcoming).

59 CIL 6.937. The capitals on the temple have been dated to the late fourth century A.D. by P. Pensabene, *Tempio di Saturno: Architettura e decorazione* (Rome: De Luca, 1984). For other studies of late fourth century religious vitality, see D. Trout, "*Lex* and *iussio*: The Feriale Campanum and Christianity in the Theodosian age," in Mathisen, *Law, Society, and Authority,* 2001, 162–78; and also chapter 6, above.

Chapter 8: The Moment of the Eruption

1 McLynn, *Ambrose,* 1994, 298–309; see also M. Gaddis, *There Is No Crime for Those Who Have Christ: Religious Violence in the Roman Empire* (Berkeley: University of California Press, 2005), 194–96.

2 Sizgorich, *Violence and Belief,* 2009, 81–84.

3 Ambrose, *Ep.* extra coll. 1A.20.

4 Ambrose, *Ep.* extra coll. 1A.10 (a space dedicated to impiety, "*templum impietatis*"); 14 ("place of perfidy, refuge of madness"); 26 (Christ, whom they killed, "*Christus quem occiderunt*").

5 Ambrose, *Ep.* extra coll. 1A.7 ("prevaricator," "persecution"); Gaddis, *There Is No Crime,* 2005, 7, 26–27.

6 Ambrose, *Ep.* 74.33, an addition to *Ep.* extra coll. 1A.32, citing 1 Macc 2:7. McLynn, *Ambrose,* 1994, 298–309, discusses the politics of "persecution" but does not address the Maccabean rhetoric.

7 We learn the outcome from Ambrose, *Ep.* extra coll. 1.28, in which the bishop relates the events in church to his sister.

8 See P. Fredriksen, *Augustine and the Jews: A Christian Defense of Jews and Judaism,* second edition (New Haven: Yale University Press, 2010).

9 The date has been difficult to pin down; I follow J. Hahn, "The Conversion of the Cult Statues: The Destruction of the Serapeion 392 A.D. and the Transformation of Alexandria into the 'Christ-Loving City,'" in *From Temple to Church: Destruction and Renewal of Local Cultic Topography in Late Antiquity,* edited by J. Hahn, S. Emmel, and U. Gotter (Leiden: Brill, 2008), 335–66.

10 Ammianus Marcellinus, *Roman History* 22.16.7–11 (crown, breezes, Cleopatra, Homer), 22.16.16–18 (professions).

11 Ammianus Marcellinus, *Roman History* 22.16.12–13.

12 Rufinus, *Church History* 11.23 (statue). For the testimony of Apthonius ("visible to land and sea"), as well as other evidence, see J. McKenzie, S. Gibson, and A. Keyes, "Reconstructing the Serapeum in Alexandria from Archaeological Evidence," *Journal of Roman Studies* 94 (2004) 73–121, specifically p. 105.

13 Rufinus, *Church History* 11.23 (*"unus ex militibus fide quam armis magis munitus"*); see also his description of Christians at 11.4 (*exercitum Domini, non mortalibus telis sed fide religionis armatum*). C. Haas, *Alexandria in Late Antiquity* (Baltimore: Johns Hopkins University Press, 1997), 89, 159–68, identifies the attackers as members of the Roman army although Rufinus mentions no other "soldiers" stationed in Alexandria before, during, or after this attack. For violence in Alexandria, see T. Myrup Kristensen, "Embodied Images: Christian Response and Destruction in Late Antique Egypt," *Journal of Late Antiquity* 2 (2009) 224–50, with extensive bibliography; as well as T. Myrup Kristensen, "Religious Conflict in Late Antique Alexandria: Christian Responses to 'Pagan' Statues in the Fourth and Fifth Centuries A.D.," in *Alexandria: A Cultural and Religious Melting Pot*, edited by G. Hinge and J. Krasilnikoff (Aarhus: Aarhus University Press, 2010), 158–75.

14 The papyrus is P. Goleniscev 6, verso. It was first published in 1906 by A. Bauer and J. Strygowski, "Eine alexandrinische Weltchronik," in *Denkschriften der Kaiserlichen Akademie der Wissenschaften* (Vienna) 51: 1–204.

15 Rufinus, *Church History* 11.28.

16 J. Dijkstra, "The Fate of the Temples in Late Antique Egypt," in *The Archaeology of Late Antique Paganism*, edited by L. Lavan and M. Mulryan (Leiden: Brill, 2012), 389–436, specifically pp. 408 and 421–30. For an archaeological overview of Alexandria, see J. Mackenzie, *The Architecture of Alexandria and Egypt: c. 300 B.C. to A.D. 700* (New Haven: Yale University Press, 2007).

17 Clement of Alexandria, *Protrepticus* 6.71.4 (he calls the Sibyl a "prophetess of the Hebrews"). For social context, see also D. Frankfurter, "The Legacy of Jewish Apocalypticism in Early Christianity: Regional Trajectories," in *The Jewish Apocalyptic Heritage in Early Christianity*, edited by J. VanderKam and W. Adler (Minneapolis: Fortress Press, 1996), 129–200.

18 Ammianus Marcellinus, *Roman History* 15.7.8.

19 Ammianus Marcellinus, *Roman History* 22.11.4. For context, see also E. Watts, *Riot in Alexandria: Tradition and Group Dynamics in Late Antique*

Pagan and Christian Communities (Berkeley: University of California Press, 2010).

20 Rufinus, *Church History* 11.29 (fall of Serapis statues and cult), 11.30 (Nile flood).

21 So-called Fifth Sibylline Oracle lines 55–57.

22 On transnationalism, see A. Appadurai, *Modernity at Large: Cultural Dimensions of Globalization* (Minneapolis: University of Minnesota Press, 1996), 64. For an analysis of the local and "global" in Rome, see K. Rieger, "Lokale Tradition versus überregionale Einheit: der Kult der Magna Mater," *Mediterranea* 4 (2007) 89–120. R. Aslan, *Beyond Fundamentalism: Confronting Religious Extremism in the Age of Globalization* (New York: Random House, 2010), 24, explores these ideas in a contemporary context.

23 Theodosian Code 16.1.2 (February 27, A.D. 380).

24 Theodosian Code 16.10.10 and 11. I have adapted my translation of 16.10.10 from *The Theodosian Code and Novels and Sirmondian Constitutions*, edited and translated by C. Pharr (Princeton: Princeton University Press, 1952), 473, with my reading of "sacred space" for *templum*.

25 Theodosian Code 16.10.12, preface. To make the meaning of the law clearer in English, I have elaborated upon the translation by Pharr, *Theodosian Code*, 1952, 473.

26 Boin, *Ostia*, 2013, 98–103 (household and workplace shrines).

27 Eusebius, *History of the Church* 8.5. For the complexities of the law code, see now J. Matthews, *Laying Down the Law*, 2000, 187–90.

28 Eugenius's Christianity is acknowledged by Sozomen, *History of the Church* 7.22.4, and can be deduced from Ambrose's letter, discussed here.

29 On this point, I follow R. Lizza Testa, "Christian Emperor, Vestal Virgins, and Priestly Colleges: Reconsidering the End of Roman Paganism," *Antiquité Tardive* 15 (2007) 251–62. By contrast, Cameron, *Last Pagans*, 2010, does not support the idea of "thriving paganism," 41, and reads the sources differently. Brown, *Eye of a Needle*, 2012, describes the act as a "mean-minded budget cut," p. 104.

30 Ambrose, *Ep.* extra coll. 10.9 (*patres, viris fidelibus, resistebant*). Ambrose counts inclusively, calling it a "five-year festival."

31 Ambrose, *Ep.* extra coll. 10.9 (*persecutio*); see also Gaddis, *There Is No Crime*, 2005, 5–10, on the lasting nature of the "persecution" theme in fourth century Christian rhetoric.

32 Rufinus, *History of the Church* 11.33, following a homily of Ambrose; see Cameron, *Last Pagans*, 2010, 93–131; and also now M. Salzman, discussing John Chrysostom, in "Ambrose and the Usurpation of Arbogastes

and Eugenius: Reflections on Pagan-Christian Conflict Narratives," *Journal of Early Christian Studies* 18 (2010) 191–223, specifically pp. 209–21.

33 So-called Fifth Sibylline Oracle line 375 (a wintry wind).

34 Salzman, "Usurpation of Arbogastes and Eugenius," 2010, quoting from p. 222.

35 Rutilius Namatianus, *On His Return* line 52; see also the discussion by Cameron, *Last Pagans*, 2010, 213–17. In general, see also Potter, *Prophets and Emperors*, 1994, 98–110.

36 Theodosian Code 16.5.46; discussed in Boin, "Social Origins," 2014.

37 MacMullen, *Second Church*, 2009, 95–114, with the quotation at p. 112.

38 "Roman paganism [*sic*] was not extinguished on the field of battle or even by imperial laws. It died a natural death, and was already mortally ill [at the end of the fourth century A.D.]," Cameron, *Last Pagans*, 2010, 131; for the faith's "intrinsic appeal" and Christianity's "intolerant zeal," see discussion in my preface, above. Another recent explanation should also be mentioned here: "It was the entry of new wealth and talent into the churches from around the year 370 onward, rather than the conversion of Constantine in 312, which marks the turning point in the Christianization [*sic*] of Europe. From then onwards, as members of a religion [*sic*] that had been joined by the rich and powerful, Christians could begin to think the unthinkable—to envision the possibility of a totally Christian society," Brown, *Eye of a Needle*, 2012, 528.

39 Ward-Perkins, *Fall of Rome*, 2005, 104–108. For a picture of Mediterranean exchange during this time, see C. Wickham, *Framing the Middle Ages: Europe and the Mediterranean, 400–800* (Oxford: Oxford University Press, 2005), 693–824.

40 Ammianus Marcellinus, *Roman History* 31.13.1–19. For discussion, see N. Lenski, *Failure of Empire: Valens and the Roman State in the Fourth Century A.D.* (Berkeley: University of California Press, 2002).

41 Ammianus Marcellinus, *Roman History* 31.14.8 (*oraculo tripodis*). For statues and recovery, see the collection of essays and the helpful introduction by J. Lipps, C. Machado, and P. von Rummel, "The Sack of Rome in 410: An Introduction," in *The Sack of Rome in 410 A.D.: The Event, Its Context and Its Impact*, edited by J. Lipps, C. Machado, and P. von Rummel (Wiesbaden: Ludwig Reichert Verlag, 2014), 11–16.

42 CIL 6.1716a–c, dedicated by Decius Marius Venantius Basilius in A.D. 484 or perhaps 508; J. R. Martindale (ed.), *The Prosopography of the Later Roman Empire*, volume 2, A.D. 395–527 (Cambridge: Cambridge University Press, 1980), "Basilius 13," p. 218.

43 Jerome, *Letter* 127.12 (city seized, echoing Horace, *Epistles* 2.1.156–57); *Commentary on Ezekiel*, preface to book 1 (*"immo romani imperii truncatum caput [est]"*).

44 So-called Third Sibylline Oracle line 176.

45 Jerome, *Commentary on the Book of Daniel* 2.7, written A.D. 407 (*"in consummatione mundi, quando regnum destruendum est romanorum"*); language also at *Ep.* 121. For other sources, E. Demougeot, "Saint Jérôme, les oracles sibyllins et Stilicon," *Revue des Études Anciennes* 54 (1952) 83–92; see also Cameron, *Last Pagans*, 2010, 213–17, and J. Doignon, "Oracles, prophéties, 'on-dit' sur la chute de Rome (395–410): Les réactions de Jérôme et d'Augustin," *Revue des Études Augustiniennes* 36 (1990) 120–46.

46 For other examples of Jerome's literary license, see L. Grig, "Deconstructing the Symbolic City: Jerome as Guide to Late Antique Rome," *Papers of the British School at Rome* 80 (2012) 125–43.

47 See A. Merrills and R. Miles, *The Vandals* (Malden, MA: Wiley-Blackwell, 2010). For a discussion of North African cities, see A. Leone, *Changing Townscapes in North Africa from Late Antiquity to the Arab Conquest* (Bari: Edipuglia, 2007), 140–62; and also the archaeological evidence discussed in A. Leone, *The End of the Pagan City: Religion, Economy, and Urbanism in Late Antique North Africa* (Oxford: Oxford University Press, 2013). For schools, see now J. Conant, *Staying Roman: Conquest and Identity in North Africa and the Mediterranean, 439–700* (New York: Cambridge University Press, 2013), 135, and the Latin tombstone at p. 341 n160 (quoting Virgil, *Aeneid* 6.429).

48 In the fifth and sixth centuries A.D., Greek and Syriac writers reflected on the Vandal attack on Rome, in A.D. 455, and the deposition of the last western emperor, in A.D. 476, using similar motifs; see E. Watts, "Interpreting Catastrophe: Disasters in the Works of Pseudo-Joshua the Stylite, Socrates Scholasticus, Philostorgius, and Timothy Aelurus," *Journal of Late Antiquity* 2 (2009) 79–98, particularly pp. 81–95.

Afterword: Keeping an Open Mind

1 Varro's list of ten Sibyls was passed down through Lactantius, *Divine Institutes* 1.6.

2 Thus, see Celsus's opinion, critiquing Christians for their reliance on Sibylline prophecy, at Origen's *Against Celsus* 7.53.

3 Lactantius, *Persecutors* 2.8 (*Sibylla dicente*).

4 Augustine, *City of God* 20.19 (*haec tanta praesumptio*).

5 Ambrose, *Ep.* extra coll. 1A.3.

6 For discussions of Good and Evil, see Ambrose, *Exameron* 5.7; *De parad-iso* 2.8, 6.30, 6.31, 6.32, 6.33, 7.36, 8.39, 11.52, 12.60, 13.61, 15.74; *De Cain et Abel* 1.3; *De Noe* 2.3, 2.5; *De Abraham* 2.2, 2.6; *De Isaac vel anima* 7.60; *De bono mortis* 1.1, 1.2; *De patriarchis* 6.30; *De fuga saeculi* 5.25, 7.37; *De interpellatione Iob et David* 4.6; *Explanatio psalmorum xii* 1.51, 35.12, 40.22, 43.44; *Expositio psalmi cxviii* 5.9, 18.47, 20.58; *Expositio evangelii secundum Lucam* 3, 4, 6; *De officiis* 1.25; *De virginibus* 2.5; *De viduis* 11.69; *Exhortatio virginitatis* 9.59; *De spiritu sancto* 1.5; *De excessu fratris Satyri* 2.39; *Epistulae* 1.3.13, 2.7.19, 4.11.16, 6.34.3. Some of these passages contain multiple references.

7 D. Cannadine, *The Undivided Past: History Beyond Our Differences* (New York: Alfred A. Knopf, 2013), 11–13, uses the term "Manichean" as short-hand for the concept of "spiritual dualism."

8 V. Hansen, *The Silk Road: A New History* (New York: Oxford University Press, 2012), 108.

9 J. Collins, "Apocalypticism: From Prophecy to Expectation of the End," in *The Continuum History of Apocalypticism*, edited by B. McGinn, J. Collins, and S. Stein (New York: Continuum, 2003), 64–88, with the idea expressed here at p. 85. For the earlier history, see the essay by R. Clifford, S.J., "The Roots of Apocalypticism in Near Eastern Myth," 3–29, in the same volume.

10 Here, I have recapitulated the characteristics of an apocalyptic world view presented in Collins, *Apocalyptic Imagination*, 1992, 12–14, which I discussed earlier.

11 R. Landes, "Introduction: The *Terribles espoirs* of 1000 and the Tacit Fears of 2000," in *The Apocalyptic Year 1000: Religious Expectation and Social Change, 950–1050*, edited by R. Landes, A. Gow, and D. Van Meter (Oxford: Oxford University Press, 2003), 3–15, with the quotation at p. 11.

12 M. Errington characterizes the battle at the Frigidus River, including the war that preceded it, as "an irrelevance" to "the religious history of the period" in *Roman Imperial Policy from Julian to Theodosius* (Chapel Hill: University of North Carolina Press, 2006), 258.

13 Gaddis, *Landscape of History*, 2002, 147.

Image Credits

Figure 1: Cast of a Latin inscription found at Caesarea Maritima, Israel. Author's photograph, used with the permission of the Israel Antiquities Authority.

Figure 2: The Roman emperor, his family, and the people of Lepcis Magna, Libya, participate in a public sacrifice. This sculptural relief was originally displayed on a Roman arch for the emperor Septimius Severus at Lepcis Magna, A.D. 203. Now in Tripoli, Libya. © Gilles Mermet, Art Resource, NY (ART 416222).

Figure 3: A mosaic from the floor of a house in Thugga, Tunisia. From the third century A.D., now in the Musée National du Bardo, Tunis. Vanni/Art Resource, NY (ART 115678).

Figure 4: Scratched wall drawing, or graffito. Currently in the Palatine Antiquarium, it has been dated to the third century A.D. Alinari/Art Resource, NY (ART 393157).

Figure 5: A magical amulet. 20 x 25 x 8.5 mm. London, British Museum (PE 1986,0501.1, from the collection of Roger Periere, Paris).

Figure 6: A house in Dura Europos, Syria. Author's drawing based on L. M. White, *The Social Origins of Christian Architecture*, volume 2 (Valley Forge: Trinity Press International, 1996), 127, fig. 3.

Figure 7: The Christian baptistry at Dura Europos, Syria. Dated prior to A.D. 256, the painting is currently in the Yale University Art Gallery (1932.1200), available for public use.

Figure 8: Model of Jerusalem. Currently on display at the Israel Museum in Jerusalem. Photo © Holyland Tourism 1992, Ltd., by Garo Nalbaldian, courtesy of the Israel Museum, Jerusalem.

Figure 9: The stones of the Second Temple precinct platform. Author's photograph, used with the permission of the Davidson Center, Jerusalem.

Figure 10: Wall painting from the Bay of Naples, Italy. Excavated at Herculaneum, it is currently in the Museo Archeologico Nazionale, Naples. Scala/Art Resource, NY (ART 47606).

Figure 11: Roman coin issued in the late second century A.D. Currently in the National Maritime Museum, Haifa, Israel. Erich Lessing/Art Resource, NY (ART 12720). For further discussion of this coin, consult J. Milne, *Catalogue of Alexandrian Coins* (Oxford: Oxford University Press, 1971), 47–48, no. 2001.

Figure 12: A mosaic from a house in El Djem, Tunisia. From the third century A.D., currently in the museum at Sousse, Tunisia. © Gilles Mermet/Art Resource, NY (ART 418978).

Figure 13: Fragments of the colossal statue of the emperor Constantine. © ArcTron 3-D.

Figure 14: Bronze coin depicting the emperor Constantine. London, British Museum (1890,0804.11).

Figure 15: The Forum, ancient Rome's downtown business district. Photograph by Darius Arya, used with permission.

Figure 16: From Michelangelo Buonarroti's Sistine Chapel ceiling in the Vatican (1508–1512). Erich Lessing/Art Resource, NY (ART 214640).

Index

A NOTE ON THE AUTHOR

Douglas Boin is an expert on the religious history of the Roman Empire. He is currently assistant professor of ancient and late antique Mediterranean history at Saint Louis University and has worked extensively as an archaeologist in Rome, studying the site of the synagogue at Ostia Antica. From 2010 to 2013, he taught in the Department of Classics at Georgetown University in Washington, D.C. This is his first trade book. He lives in St. Louis.